HOW TO HUNT EVERYTHING

OUTDOOR LIFE

HOW TO
HUNT
EVERYTHING

EDITED BY
ANDREW McKEAN

weldon owen

TROPICAL SPECIES

30° NORTH–15° SOUTH

186

SUBTROPICAL SPECIES

15° SOUTH–60° SOUTH

218

THE WORLD AT YOUR FEET

TO HUNT IS TO WANDER WITH PURPOSE. Meat-eaters have been doing this as long as we've had appetites and feet to take us to our next meal.

Though some may consider hunting to be elective, more for recreation than caloric necessity, the pursuit of food has long been the engine of human expansion across the globe. You can bet prehistoric Asians crossed the Bering land bridge in search of more and better vittles, just as the descendants of Cro-Magnon followed game from one African vale to the next.

That universal, essentially human, meat-inspired mobility is the spirit and the structure of this book. It explains why hunting remains a global pursuit. Along with our upright gait, the ability to create languages and tools, and our tendency to break into crazy dance moves, hunting remains a human imperative that transcends continents and cultures. Even though most of us get our food from markets and fields, hunting remains important as a wildlife management tool, a cultural expectation, and a way to collect organic, honest meat for our tables. And for some of us, hunting is an unexplained compulsion that can only be answered by doing more of it.

Still, will you ever hunt *everything*? Probably not, but to be a hunter is to be constantly on the lookout for the next experience and the next rump roast. I wanted this book to be a guide to all the places and animals you haven't hunted, as well as a reminder of all the experiences that you have had. Plus, the collection of information and perspectives between these covers is just cool. Who knew some deer have fangs instead of antlers, or that India has such diverse antelope species? Or that Aussies call feral horses "brumbies"?

A book of this scope is necessarily incomplete. While I wanted to include every major—and many minor—species, a global view of hunting is selective. I could have listed the dozens of subspecies and regional variations of African hartebeest, for instance, or detailed the two dozen subspecies of North America's common whitetail deer. But that would have made this book more of a dictionary than what I hope it is: an earthy reminder of why hunting matters, and a lyrical description of the remarkable animals and their habitats to be found around the world.

In conceiving this book, I struggled with its structure. Should this be an alphabetical list? No. Again, too encyclopedic. Should it be ordered by continent? That would make some chapters overly large (North America) while others (Australia) would be of necessity rather skimpy. In the end, I decided to order by latitude. By starting at the North Pole and working south, it's possible to talk about animals that share habitats, such as the coastal waterfowl of South America, as well as families whose distribution is circumpolar, such as the caribou and moose families that range all the way from Scandinavia through Russia and across Canada.

HOW TO NAVIGATE THIS BOOK This structure allowed me to focus on specific species in some instances and collections of families in others. These familial clusters, which are called out now and then throughout the book, enabled me to include dozens of animals without detailing specifically where they live and how to hunt

them. But it also created some redundancies. For instance, you'll see that the wild goat and sheep families are messy, with some goats defined as sheep, and some sheep species discussed in more than one place.

You may find some animals have been omitted, either intentionally or not. But this book is not a catalog; it's a reminder that the wild world is robust, diverse, and full of wonder. And meat.

I also hope this book is an encouragement—something to compel you to broaden your horizons. If you're a whitetail hunter, I urge you to consider hunting antelope in Africa. If you're a European stag hunter, consider pursuing its Colorado-based cousin, the North American wapiti. And if you're a Russian forest-grouse hunter, I hope this book encourages you to travel to South Dakota to hunt prairie grouse and partridges on the wide-open grasslands.

As I have traveled the world with a gun and a bow, I've encountered some remarkable animals and some gorgeous country. I'm often sad to leave these places, because I know I will probably never return. But here's the real secret of hunting, one that our carnivorous ancestors knew: By eating animals from these places—the tenderloin of a Yukon sheep or the drumstick of a Nile goose or the ribs of a Texas hog—we make the places we hunt a part of us. I think Cro-Magnon would smile through his shattered teeth to know that we remain a planet of hunters.

ANDREW MCKEAN
Editor-in-Chief
Outdoor Life magazine

NORTHERN SPECIES

90° NORTH – 40° NORTH

90° NORTH – 40° NORTH

I WAS SITTING IN WET SNOW, GLASSING A WIDE RIVER VALLEY in northern British Columbia, looking for a moose with antlers wider than my rifle was long. I had seen mostly cows with calves so far, but this was the heart of the rut on the Spatsizi Plateau, and, in mid October, where you find cows, you'll find bulls—if you look hard enough and wait long enough.

As I scanned the spruce trees my thoughts drifted far from this wildlife-rich wilderness, to a compact little German who, two centuries ago in the university town of Gottingen, helped amplify my experience here.

The man's name was Carl Bergmann, and we mainly know him today for putting forth a thesis that was revolutionary back in pre-confederation Germany. He concluded, after studying wild animals from the tropics to the poles, that the body size of mammals increases the farther they live from the equator.

That conclusion is known to zoologists as Bergmann's Rule, and it has become one of the foundations of evolutionary biology. The idea is that animals that live in warm climates need to dissipate heat. They do that by having sparse fur, long ears and legs, and smaller bodies. But the farther north an animal lives, the colder the climate, and these northern animals have the opposite problem. They need to conserve body heat, and they do that by growing thick fur and large, stocky bodies.

Generally speaking, the larger the body of an ungulate, such as a mule deer or a moose, the larger the antlers. Which brings me back to the Spatsizi in October. I was hunting Canadian moose, and the benchmark for a trophy bull in this northern latitude is an antler width of around 60 inches (152 cm). Back in Montana, we hunt Shiras moose, and if you see a 40-inch (102-cm) bull, you'd better be thinking of killing it.

Bergmann's Rule applies to white-tailed deer, too. The Keys deer of Florida might weigh 100 pounds (45 kg) soaking wet. The common Virginia deer of the Eastern seaboard will weigh twice that, and the whitetails of the northern prairies can tip the scales at close to 250 pounds (113 kg). In northern Alberta and Saskatchewan, the northern limit of the whitetail range, hefty bucks can weigh nearly 350 pounds (159 kg).

Bergmann's Rule helps explain why Canada, Russia, Scandinavia, and the northern United States have become destinations for trophy hunters. The game is bigger here, and the headgear more impressive than anywhere else on the globe.

The habitat at these latitudes is also conducive to hunting. The region is defined by mixed terrain, with plenty of edges and wide-open vistas that allow hunters to spot a trophy and then move into stalking range. And the terrific diversity of elevation—from coastal river valleys to mountain peaks draped with snow—means that you can hunt multiple species in the same spot.

I was thinking of that very dynamic as I scanned the nearby willows for moose. As I raised my binocular to the peaks, I watched china-white mountain goats balance on pinnacles. A band of Stone's sheep grazed a frost-touched meadow to my right, and a grizzly bear and her cubs gorged on blueberries just below me.

Big-game paradise, indeed, and a picture that would only be complete with the arrival of a big, swaggering bull moose.

POLAR SPECIES

CRASHING SEA ICE, crushing cold, and closing darkness are all part of the arctic hunting experience. Add apex predators that can materialize out of the frozen gloam like nightmares, and you'll understand hunting the polar regions is not for the timid. It is, however, the last frontier for the intrepid. Whether you hunt the hardy musk ox, the solitary polar bear, or the overlooked creatures of the arctic—ptarmigan, hares, and foxes—you will rarely encounter another person. Whether that fills you with thrill or dread says a lot about you and your likely experience.

Journeys to the last desolate threads of land that crumble into the frozen Arctic Ocean begin with a series of rides on ever-smaller airplanes that deliver you to lonely native outposts. They typically end with dog sleds, frostbite, and an abiding sense of accomplishment that you have experienced—and presumably survived—the most elemental hunt on earth.

Arctic hunting is defined by the starkness of the place and the singular purpose of the experience. No trees, little topographical variety, only horizontal lines defining the horizon, and variations of sterile white on glacial blue. This barrenness actually improves the hunting; if you can see an animal, there's a good chance you can kill it. That's especially true of the curious musk ox, a great long-maned holdover from the Pleistocene era, when woolly mammoths and saber-toothed tigers roamed much of the northern half of the globe.

While you might think that these frozen lands are unclaimed, most arctic hunting takes place on Inuit or First Nations territory. Be mindful that you are visiting a landscape and hunting culturally significant animals. Don't bring in alcohol or other controlled substances, be respectful of locals, and be prepared to participate in cultural and culinary traditions that may be far beyond your experience. Pudding made from the contents of a caribou's stomach, seal flippers, and all manner of dried fish and meat are staples of the local diet and may well sustain you during your arctic adventure. Almost all these hunts are arranged by outfitters. The price can be as daunting as the environment, but by leaving the logistics to someone else, you can concentrate on the elemental experience before you.

PLANNING A TRIP

The jumping-off place for most arctic trips is one of several native communities huddled on the frozen coast of Canada. The towns of Inuvik, in the Northwest Territories, and Resolute, Nunavut are popular destinations for polar bear and musk ox hunters, respectively. Both towns receive daily jet service from either Edmonton or Montreal. From the villages, you must either charter a bush plane or wait for one of the infrequent scheduled flights to the outback.

Depending on the season and the destination, you'll probably begin your penultimate leg of the hunt on a snowmobile or a dogsled, which will deliver you to a base camp.

POLAR BEARS The great trophy of the arctic is the white northern bear, and hunting polar bears can be even more elemental than hunting musk ox. Most hunts take place in late winter and early spring, as days get longer and the sea ice begins to break up, bringing the bears closer to land. Days are spent on polished pinnacles of sea ice, glassing for movement on great wastes of ice and snow.

MUSK OXEN Hunting musk ox employs the same strategies everywhere: cover ground—either on snow machine or dogsled—until you find a herd, then begin your approach. The animals tend to stand their ground, and bulls form protective circles around cows and calves, a behavior that allows hunters to make judicious decisions about trophy quality as well as shot selection.

The waning of the Ice Age pushed most musk ox to the northernmost edge of land. The barren-ground musk ox is widespread on the northernmost reaches of continental Canada and on many of the larger arctic islands, especially Banks and Victoria islands. The Greenland subspecies roams much of its namesake island and has been introduced to parts of arctic Alaska.

SMALLER GAME Rock ptarmigan cluster wherever dwarf birch thrusts for the sun. Arctic hares bound between tufts of tundra, and arctic wolves and foxes mince across the moor, ever hungry.

GEAR UP

ESSENTIAL ARCTIC GEAR

The arctic coast is possibly the most inhospitable place on earth, especially considering that you are at sea level and not way up a mountain. Your gear will determine whether you make it home intact or whether your heirs will divvy up the rest of your possessions. Here's what you should bring:

PARKA The most insulated, fur-lined parka you can buy. There's a reason native hunters dress in fur; it's light, warm, and insulates even when wet.

MITTENS Heavy mittens, sized to accept liners, and thick shooting gloves

PANTS Down-insulated, wind-blocking pants

BOOTS Insulated boots with heavy liners. Do not bring battery-heated models, even if you expect to find a generator in camp.

UNDERWEAR Wool long underwear—two pairs. You'll never take these off, but it's good to have a spare in case the first gets wet or soiled.

BINOCULAR The best binocular you can afford. You'll spend most of your day behind this glass.

SLEEPING BAG A sleeping bag rated at least for -40°F (-40°C). If the weather closes in, you'll be spending a lot of time in a tent, cuddled up in this bag.

EYEWEAR A face mask and tinted snowmobile goggles cut the blinding glare of the snow and ice.

CARIBOU

NO ANIMAL better embodies the wide, wild north than the caribou. Its downy-white neck looks like early snow in the high country, and its flank—ranging from slate-gray to supple brown—resembles frost-touched tundra in September. But it's the caribou's towering, impossibly branched and pointed and palmated antlers that captivate hunters. How such a rack can sprout from an animal the size of a mule deer has prompted many a first-time caribou hunter to simply gawk at a line of passing bulls, looking for all the world like a grove of willows on the move.

One constant is that caribou are always on the move. It's their defining characteristic, marching from calving grounds to wintering range, seldom stopping for more than a few hours to bed and feed. Most hunters encounter any of the half-dozen subspecies of caribou in the midst of their fall migration, and their incessant, plodding pace is deceptive.

No human could hope to keep up with a herd of 'bou in their regimental formation, nose up, oblivious to danger, guided by some beacon that remains invisible to those of us who long for a landmark to spot where it is on the trackless tundra that the caribou live—or rather, where they are making their home today.

The empty land and this restless behavior define caribou everywhere they live. Caribou are really North America's reindeer. Northern Canada is home to six distinct subspecies of the family, though taxonomists quibble over some of the branches off the trunk. The family is circumpolar, and includes the tundra reindeer of Scandinavia and the woodland reindeer that extend across the expanse of northern Russia.

The most remarkable racks belong to the mountain caribou of northern British Columbia and the Yukon. But numbers have always defined the woodland subspecies of northern Quebec and Labrador, where a hunter might count thousands of animals in a long day of monitoring a migration trail. Barren-ground subspecies extend west across northern Manitoba, Saskatchewan, Alberta, and into Alaska, where the famous North Slope Porcupine Herd has stymied energy development on the North Slope.

WITLESS OR NAIVE?

Caribou have a deserved reputation as the bubbleheads of the North. One moment, they can be sensibly avoiding danger and acting wild and wily; the next they may run directly toward the threat. Many hunters have cited this capricious behavior, describing caribou as either goofy or stupid. But that doesn't credit either the animal or its habitat. It's entirely possible that the double-shovel bull that runs right up to the muzzle of your gun has never seen a human before, and doesn't recognize your erect profile as being particularly dangerous. That's the best reason to hunt the wild North—human presence here is so temporary.

On the other hand, caribou are inspired to truly odd and erratic behavior when the black flies become especially bothersome. I've seen a docile herd suddenly blow up like a covey of quail and run great distances when the wind quit and the flies started biting.

No matter where they live, whether in the cloudberry bogs of northern Quebec or the stunted-timber taiga that extends in an immense lonely arc from Hudson Bay to the Arctic Ocean, caribou are hunted according to the same basic tactic: getting in their way.

If you can find a string of migrating caribou, chances are good that you'll find a mature bull as long as you're patient. Rifle hunters should prepare for shots out to 300 yards, but standard deer calibers will handle caribou just fine. Bowhunters set up along ancient migration trails, typically in those spots where caribou pause to shake after swimming across lakes and rivers.

A SERIOUS DECLINE For generations of American hunters, caribou were the polestars that guided first international trips. Quebec and Manitoba herds were close enough that hunters could clock out of work on Friday, bag a couple bulls, and be back home by Sunday, with meat in coolers and those remarkable racks strapped to the roof.

But over the last decade, caribou numbers have declined range-wide. Biologists can't agree on the cause—climate change, gas and oil development, and habitat degradation are all possible culprits—but the outcome is significant. No longer are migrations robust and predictable, with two-bull bags the standard. Most outfitters, if they still offer trips at all, limit hunters to a single bull.

The declines are especially sharp in the eastern Canadian habitats,, especially in Quebec and Labrador, where the famous Leaf River and George River herds once sustained annual harvest well into six figures.

Will herds recover? Possibly. But for now, hunters are better off heading west, to British Columbia and Alaska.

LANDING IN KUUJJUAK

The largest village on Quebec's Ungava Peninsula, Kuujjuak is accessible only by air, and the tundra edges so close to town that the jet that flies in once a week from Montreal circles before landing—to be sure the runway is clear of caribou and polar bears.

On my first flight into Kuujjuak, I was gratified to see people waving energetically as we buzzed the terminal and runway. I waved back, out my little airplane window.

"What a friendly town," I said to myself as we squared up to the grass runway and bounced down. As I exited the plane, the waving continued.

Minutes later, the first black fly bit my cheek. Then a dozen attacked. I flailed my hands in a futile effort to beat back the flesh-drilling vermin. It was then that I understood. Those people weren't waving. They were swatting these insidious flies.

My trip improved greatly after this. Later that day I stepped off a floatplane to begin a self-guided hunt. I took two remarkable caribou, the first by spotting a string of migrating bulls and sprinting to get within a long rifle shot. Later, I belly-crawled across the soggy tundra to a bedded bull and shot him when he stood up to stretch.

KNOW YOUR TERMS

ANATOMY OF A CARIBOU RACK

[A] MAIN BEAMS The long antler that erupts from the skull and extends outward and back, then sweeps forward, usually showing palmation at its upper reaches.

[B] SHOVELS Also called "brow palms," the usually palmated antler that extends from one main beam perpendicular to the bull's face, sometimes as far as the nose. Occasionally these palms grow out of both main beams, creating what is called a "double shovel."

[C] BEZ STRUCTURE The forward-extending lower portion of the main beam, the bez typically branches into two or more fingers, and may be palmated.

[D] REAR POINT The unbranched rearward-pointing spike that grows out of the middle of the main beam.

[E] TOPS The series of distinct points that erupt from the top of the main beam.

MOOSE

WITH THEIR BULBOUS NOSES, squinty eyes, and galumphing gait, moose might be considered intellectually—or at least evolutionarily—challenged. But underestimate this largest of our deer species at your peril. Moose possess keen senses of smell and hearing, the latter amplified by their oversized, paddle-shaped antlers. A global species, moose of various races range from Maine to the Yukon, west through Alaska and across Russia to Scandinavia. What they all share, however, is a preference for willow bogs, low-slung brush, and mixed-age forest.

A GLOBAL FAMILY If you doubt the possibility that Asia and North America were once connected, the moose family tree should convince you. The same rangy animal that fishes cress from marshy bogs in Maine is kin to the tag-alder giants of Siberia and Norway, and has relatives at the same latitude around the globe. Moose races extend from the Czech Republic to Mongolia, and from the wild Kamchatka Peninsula of Russia over to Alaska and down south to Colorado.

Even the name of the animal reflects this circumpolar distribution. The dewlapped ungulate we call moose is dubbed "älg" in Swedish, "eland" in Dutch, "einu" in Russian, "alnis" in Latvian, and "khandgai" in Mongolian.

Evolutionary biologists think moose originated in Siberia, with one branch heading west to Scandinavian Europe and another heading east, where some ancestors of North America's subspecies walked the Bering land bridge and then spread south and east over the next millennium. But despite differences in size, the world's moose look a lot alike, and they certainly behave like one big, extended family. And hunting them involves the same strategies from Alberta to Finland.

The defining attribute of moose—their enormous stature—can be a liability. Their size obligates them to specific geographies, mainly the cooler northern latitudes, and it makes them a target for apex predators. Where moose share habitat in the American West with reintroduced wolves, the ungulates have experienced sharp declines as packs pick off vulnerable calves. Adult moose rarely flee attacks by wolves and bears. Instead, they back into a defensible space and fight with their long legs and antlers.

BIRCH-BARK MOOSE CALL

Just as a felt packer hat and a lever-action Marlin are synonymous with Canadian moose hunters of a certain vintage, so is a birch-bark call slung across a shoulder with a rawhide cord.

The call is basically a rustic version of a megaphone, intended to amplify the guttural groans and coughs that mimic a rutting bull.

You can make your own call out of a 1-by-4-foot (0.3-by-1.2-meter) swatch of green bark rolled at an angle and stitched with leather or strips of bark soaked in water. Better yet, pick up a commercially made call at just about every store in moose country.

ALWAYS HUNT THE WATER Where to start your hunt? Guides will tell you that moose are never found far from water, partly because they crave the sort of succulent foods that grow in swamps and bogs, but also because their long-legged bodies and wide-splayed hooves are built for wading shallow ponds and navigating muddy terrain.

The moose's habitat preferences, in combination with their huge, coal black to rust brown bodies, make these animals easy to see in the wild. And, happily for hunters, moose are relatively tolerant of inspection. Unlike most other members of the deer family, they don't flee to cover the minute they sense a human. Instead, they're more likely to wait and watch, a behavior that gives hunters time to size up the trophy quality of bulls or to work in for a closer shot.

Moose are relative loners. They will gather in small herds during October's breeding season, but during the rest of the year, you're more likely to see solitary bulls or family groups of a cow or two along with their calves.

Bulls gravitate to cows, rather than vice versa, and because females are relatively sedentary, if you find a group of cows in early October, it's worth waiting with them for the arrival of a bull. Or, if you prefer to dice the odds in your favor, you can try calling bulls.

FIELD JUDGE A MOOSE

For most of us, a mature bull moose is a trophy regardless of the numeric score of his antlers. But most hunters want at least a quick answer to that eternal question: Should I shoot or not? Here it is: If he's heavy and tall, shoot! That said, here are some finer points of field-judging.

SPREAD [A] While spread (expressed in inches) is used as the rule of thumb for the quality of a bull, it's actually one of the least reliable predictors of trophy quality.

PALMATION [B] The amount of antler material in the paddles (height times width) is a big determinant of final score. Look wide and tall palms. Generally speaking, taller antlers will be wider than you think.

FRONT POINTS [C] These tines, which erupt from the base of the palm and run parallel to a mature bull's snout, are another crucial ingredient. You want at least two front points, and preferably three or more.

TOP POINTS [D] Most trophies earn one inch of trophy score for every point on the perimeter of the antlers. But mature bulls typically rub off these secondary points to a blunt nose, rendering them as something less than an inch. These points only count as scoreable if they're 1 inch or longer.

A British Columbian guide, Derek Mohr, once told me that rutting bulls sound like an obese man in a truck-stop bathroom, grunting with the effort of relieving himself. A deep, guttural moan with a sort of gasping crescendo is a fair way to describe a rutting bull. Many hunters add a sort of caricature to their calling, spreading their hands—or even holding up their rifles—to look to weak-eyed bulls like a rival male. You can add to the charade by raking brush and snapping limbs to complete the mimicry of a rut-addled bull.

USE MODEST FIREPOWER For animals of their size—big Canadian and Alaskan bulls will get to 1,800 pounds (816 kg)—moose are fairly easy to kill. Modest magnum calibers or even elk-sized standard calibers will do, as long as your shot selection is good. The important thing is to shoot good-quality bullets that will remain intact after punching through thick hide and massive bones.

Count on follow-up shots, even if the first round was true. Moose have huge circulatory systems and even a vital hit can take time to show effects. Just don't shoot too high. Like many African antelope, the shoulder hump on a mature bull contains no vital organs, and if a seemingly well-hit moose gets away, it's a good bet it's because your bullet hit the vacancy of gristle north of the shoulder blades.

BOAT HUNTING

Since moose are never far from water, hunting from a boat can be highly effective. Whether you paddle a canoe or captain a jet boat, here are some aquatic considerations:

BRING WINCHES AND ROPE Moose rarely drop in their tracks when shot, so count on having to ratchet quarters through dense streamside vegetation.

PADDLE SILENTLY Learn the slice stroke with a canoe paddle so you don't make moose-alarming splashes. Turn your paddle 90 degrees following your power stroke so that it never leaves the water. Slice it forward in the water, then turn it to begin the next stroke.

WEAR WADERS Whether chest or hip waders, make sure you can stay dry as you slog through bogs and swamps.

PACK A CHAINSAW You'll likely need the saw to clear sweepers from the current or to clear a trail to deliver your fresh moose meat to the boat.

BEST MOOSE GUNS AND LOADS

THE ALL-PURPOSE RIFLE Moose hunting is often cold, wet, and dirty, and you need a rifle that can handle the elements. A synthetic, all-weather model like the Remington 700 XCR—it stands for "Xtreme Conditions Rifle"—is built for bad weather. Chambered in .300 Win. Mag., it can precisely place long-distance shots.

THE SADDLE GUN In much of northern Canada, moose hunting happens from horseback, and the Browning BLR is a great scabbard rifle. Outdoor Life's Jack O'Connor killed plenty of big bulls with his beloved .270, and untold numbers of trappers made moose meat with their modest .25/35s and .30/30s. Shot placement is everything.

THE SLUGGER Knockdown power is a key consideration for moose, which can commonly weigh 1,500 pounds (680 kg). For close-quarters hunting, it's hard to beat a 12-gauge slug. Consider one of the new saboted projectiles, like Federal's Trophy Copper.

BROWN BEARS

THE COASTAL ALASKAN brown bear and the grizzly bear are the same species, *Ursus arctos horribilis*, which as a name is pretty descriptive. Large bears are North America's only true dangerous game and, out of all of them, the grizzly might well be the most cantankerous. These bears are mean tempered, tough as granite, and always a challenge to hunt. The grizzly bear is a creature of the wilderness, and he does not thrive where there is civilization. He lives on his own terms, takes no guff from anything or anybody, and is my favorite North American animal.

The coastal Alaskan brown bear was once thought to be a separate species from the interior grizzly, but they are now known to be the same species. The difference is the coastal bear leads a much easier life, has plenty to eat, and has evolved into a larger bear. The interior bears are much smaller and usually are more aggressive. (Small bear syndrome, maybe?)

The bears of the Kodiak Archipelago are the largest brown bears and are classified as a distinct subspecies *Ursus arctos middendorffi*. Typically, the coastal and island bears are called brown bears while the interior bears are called grizzlies. Although rivaled by the polar bear, the Alaskan brown bear is said to be the largest meat-eating mammal in North America. These bears can run up to 1,600 pounds (726 kg), which is a lot to deal with if you encounter one in a foul mood. More commonly, a big male will run 1,000–1,200 pounds (454–544 kg), which is still a lot of bear.

Regardless of which variety you hunt, at some point every bear hunter asks this question: How do I tell a big bear from a smaller one? It's difficult to answer because it depends, mainly on the area. Alaskan guides claim that a 9-foot (2.7-meter) interior grizzly squares wider and shorter than a 9-foot (2.7-meter) coastal brownie. Same dimensions, but the measurement isn't achieved the same way.

In general, the best way to judge a bear is by its behavior. Larger boars act differently, deliberately. They move slowly and powerfully while smaller bears are nervous and keep watching larger bears. If you doubt the size of a bear, wait. You'll know a block-headed trophy boar when you see him.

THE BACK-UP GUN

S&W 500

I believe in carrying a big handgun when living in bear country. Rifles get left behind when you are going to the outhouse or to the river for a bucket of water. You can also lose them in an altercation and they can be unwieldy inside a tent. Rifles get set down, left behind, or lost, but a pistol is attached to your body and should be with you at all times.

The .44 Magnum, .454 Casull, .500 S&W, or comparable cartridges can all do the job. Load your revolver with ammo using heavy, hard-cast, non-expanding bullets for deep penetration—and hope you never have to use it.

BROWN BEARS In the spring, brown bears are fresh out of their dens and looking for food to prepare for the coming breeding season. Hunting along the coastal beaches is very productive, as the bears search there for washed-up food. Hunters may also venture back into the mountains, often on snowmobiles and snowshoes, to find newly opened bear dens—following tracks in the snow to locate them or glassing the snowline where the bears will be foraging for food.

In the fall, the bears are on the move, looking for food in an effort to fatten up for the long winter hibernation. During a typical day, the hunter will climb to a high point overlooking a lot of prime bear territory and then will sit and glass for hours at a time. Often this will include a salmon stream where the bears might be feeding on spawning fish. Once a bear has been located and judged to be of trophy quality, the hunter will attempt to stalk close enough for a shot.

Because these bears live in some of the toughest country on earth, stalking is often not easy. The lower lands are choked with thick alder bushes or, if it's open, the swampy tundra is littered with ill-spaced hummocks that are never the right distances apart for stepping on. There are deep rivers, marshy bogs, and even steep, rocky, cliff-infested hills to navigate. Nobody goes anywhere fast in coastal Alaska.

If the bear is feeding, a stalk is pretty straightforward. But if the bear is traveling, the only hope is to get ahead of him and wait. Either way, due to the thick brush and rough terrain, brown bears are often shot at relatively close range.

BEST GUNS AND LOADS FOR BROWN BEARS

Brown bears are true dangerous game, and, in Alaska, they hurt or kill people just about every year. They are big, incredibly tough animals, and you must take them seriously.

I'll never forget the first big boar I saw. I was sitting on a hill on the Peninsula, and the sun had just broken through the clouds. The big boar was about a half a mile from us, walking down a steep hill. Every time he took a step his shoulder muscles would bulge in the golden sunshine. I can promise you, no rifle will ever feel too big in your hands under this kind of circumstance.

While a lot of bears fall each year to the various .300 magnums, I believe a true bear gun starts with the .338 Winchester. The .338 Remington Ultra Mag is another good choice, as is the .338 Weatherby and .338-378 Weatherby.

The .358 Norma is also good, and I have hunted brown bear with my wildcat .358 UMT, based on the Remington Ultra Mag case. I have used the .375 H&H for brown bear more than any other cartridge, though any of the .375 cartridges will also do very well. The .416 cartridges are favored by many brown bear guides for backing up clients, and are a good choice for the hunter as well. The .458 cartridges will work, but lack the flat trajectory for a possible longer shot.

Use only premium quality bullets like the Barnes TSX, Trophy Bonded, Nosler Partition, or Swift A-Frame. Pick a heavy-for-caliber bullet weight, 250-grains in the .338 and .358 cartridges. In the .375-cartridges, a 300-grain is best. In a .416, pick 400-grain bullets.

Most of what applies to brown bear hunting in terms of cartridge selection also applies to grizzlies, and none of those rifles suggested for brown bear are inappropriate. However, keep in mind that the size of the bears can vary a great deal. If you are hunting coastal bears in British Columbia, they may well be as big as a brown bear, so stick with the bigger guns. But if you are hunting the much smaller inland grizzly that may run half the size of a brown, you might think about downsizing a bit.

Also, grizzlies are often part of a multispecies hunt including moose, caribou, sheep, or mountain goats, so a rifle appropriate to all the game being hunted is a good idea. Any of the various .300 Magnums or .338 Magnums would be a good choice.

PREPARE FOR BAD WEATHER

Coastal Alaska has some of the harshest weather on earth, so come prepared. Until you have experienced Alaska's "horizontal rain" you have not truly seen a storm. I have actually seen the wind blow a river back up a mountain and off the top like a geyser.

Bring two sets of Gore-Tex, one to dry and one to wear. A large rubber parka is a good idea too. Hip boots are a must, although there is a trend now to the lightweight, Gore-Tex waders with good, hiking style wading boots.

The easier hunts are conducted from large boats where you can sleep in warmth and comfort at night. In daylight you will venture out with a smaller boat to the hunting areas, then back again at night.

Other hunts are even rougher, but definitely have their own appeal. For example, you might be flown in and dropped off to live in a small tent with your guide. In this case, you'll live on freeze-dried backpacking food and filtered river water.

GRIZZLY BEARS The grizzly bear has a distinctive hump above his shoulders and a dished out face, which distinguishes him from the black bear.

The northern Rocky Mountain states have good populations of grizzlies these days—perhaps even too many, but political issues have prevented the return of grizzly hunting in these areas.

Canada has grizzly bears in British Columbia, Alberta, Nunavut, Yukon, and the Northwest Territories. Hunting has become increasingly restricted in recent years and nonresidents can hunt only in British Columbia and Yukon at present. Alaska has good populations and allows hunting throughout much of the state.

While the same species as the brown bear, the grizzly is a much different creature. For the most part, they live a hardscrabble life in the far north, where they struggle to find enough to eat. As a result, they have evolved into a smaller bear than the brown. But at the same time, they have also developed an attitude. On the average, the grizzly bear is much more aggressive than his bigger brother, the brown bear.

The inland grizzly is smaller than the brown bear by about 30 percent, but size varies a great deal from region to region. Some bears in Alaska or British Columbia may be nearly as large as a brown bear, whereas the grizzlies in the Yukon River or in the Northwest Territories tend to be much smaller.

Hunting is usually spot and stalk, often in conjunction with another species like moose or caribou. Often a hunter will sit on the gut pile from a moose kill and wait for the bear to show up to feed. Bears are also hunted along mountainside slides where, particularly in the spring, they come to feed on the fresh green plants. —*Bryce Towsley*

WILD SHEEP

MAYBE IT'S THE MASSIVE, curling horns or the regal, powerful stance of a mature ram. Or maybe it's the stunning places they inhabit—high, snow-stunted meadows and towering ridges—that make wild sheep so appealing. Or maybe it's because hardy rams are synonymous with the backcountry, the game-rich wilderness that requires time, intention, and logistical support to access. It is said that there are no easy sheep, but the corollary is equally true—there are no forgettable sheep, either.

For most of my life I resisted the consuming obsession with ovis, the family of wild sheep. Sure, I was aware of the romantic appeal of rams, mainly because of my affection for Jack O'Connor's dispatches in the pages of *Outdoor Life*, which elevated sheep to a pedestal above other game species—above moose, elk, and even mule deer.

For years I applied for bighorn tags in every available jurisdiction in the country. But I confess to missing a little of the gravitational pull of wild rams—they seemed too far out of reach for mortal hunters like me—until I drew my first sheep tag, in Wyoming's alpine wilderness east of Yellowstone National Park.

It was on that hunt, the creak of bridle leather keeping time with the stiff gait of balky pack mules, and the crenelated jags of sawtoothed peaks just suggested in the feeble light of September's stars, that I finally got sheep hunting. O'Connor was right: It's not like other hunting. It's richer, more elemental, and simply more romantic than any other hunt I have experienced.

Maybe that's because there's more at stake. In most areas of the West, where bighorn tags are distributed by lottery, you have better odds of drawing a Powerball ticket than a ram permit. So when you finally draw a license, as I did for Wyoming Area 2, you recognize that it's truly the hunt of a lifetime. Don't blow it.

Equally rare is the charm of sheep country. It might take you all day to grind to where rams loaf and graze, but when you finally reach these wild pastures, you marvel at their flowers, their alpine grasses, and their stunning views. It's hard to reach these places, but it's even harder to leave them—especially without sheep meat in your pack.

REVISITING THE .270

Jack O'Connor, *Outdoor Life*'s shooting editor, waxed poetic about wild rams and the absolutism of the .270 Win. as the perfect sheep caliber. And though I still love to read his spare text, I'm not sure his ballistics advice continues to hold water.

That's because he never met either the 6.5/284 Norma or the .280 Ackley Improved.

Based on the short-action .284 Winchester, rifles chambered in 6.5/284 can be built on smaller frames, making them lighter. The .280 Ackley Improved is a standard long-action round that performs like a magnum caliber without the punishing kick, as well as accurately delivers wind-bucking bullets for longish shots.

SCARCE OPPORTUNITIES If you'd rather not rely on luck of the draw in the western United States, you can still find places to hunt wild sheep. In the western Canadian provinces, principally British Columbia, the Yukon, and Alberta, it is possible to hire an outfitter to take you to big rams. These are expensive undertakings, but once you start sheep hunting, it can be hard to stop—luckily, you don't have to. Sheep are found around the northern latitudes of the globe, from the Canadian Rockies to the Himalayas to the Gobi Desert of Mongolia.

North America is home to four species of wild sheep. In the far north, the two races—snow white Dall's sheep and slate gray Stone's sheep—occupy remote mountain ranges that typically require a pack train to access.

These two varieties of northern sheep, smaller in stature than their southern cousins, are called thinhorns because the headgear of the rams tends to be more slender and curling than the heavier, more massive horns sported by their southern cousins. Together, these four species of wild sheep—Dall's and Stone's, and the southern species, the Rocky Mountain bighorn, and the California (or desert) bighorn—constitute the grand slam of wild sheep, and hunters who have collected full-curl rams of each race have attained a remarkable feat. They've also probably paid dearly for their trophies, too—in money, time, and expectation.

Hunters who get the bug for more far-flung adventures can pursue their world slam of ovis from the Himalayas to the contested highlands of the former Russian republics to the far corners of Mongolia's Gobi Desert. These adventures require more money and logistics than nearly any other variety of hunting in the world. It's a testament to the magnetic attraction of these animals that every sheep hunter I know, physically whipped and monetarily depleted by their last ram hunt, is already planning their next.

OPTICS FOR SHEEP HUNTING

More than any other gear, light, bright optics are your most critical tools for finding sheep, judging rams, and even assessing your approach. Not all optics are created equal, especially for mountain hunting. Durability and optical clarity are just as important as weight on a sheep hunt. Buy the best glass you can afford, even if you have to borrow to do it.

 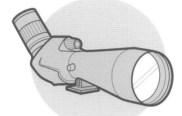 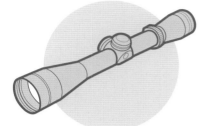

RANGEFINDING BINOCULAR A new generation of high-end binoculars combines bright optics with an accurate laser rangefinder. Get a model that allows you to enter your ballistics data into its "brain" so you'll know precise holdover for any distance you range.
Good options include the Leica Geovid 10x42, Swarovski EL Range 10x45, and Zeiss Victory RF 10x45.

SPOTTING SCOPE In sheep country, you'll spend more time behind your spotting scope than you will in the saddle. It's tempting to settle for 65mm scopes because of their light weight and packable configuration, but opt for the brighter, crisper 85mm scopes instead.
Consider Zeiss 85mm Victory DiaScope, Meopta 82mm MeoStar S2, or Swarovski 80mm ATS.

RIFLE SCOPE Pick a durable one that can handle knocks on rocks, bumps in a scabbard, and big swings in temperature. Choose a modest magnification range, ensuring it has adjustable focus for long shots. Opt for duplex reticles or crosshairs with just a few holdover references.
Look into the Leupold VX-2 4-12x40mm, Bushnell Elite 4-16x40mm, and Nikon Monarch 3 4-16x42mm as good options.

From the urial rams of Pakistan to Siberian snow sheep to the desert bighorns of Mexico's Baja, wild sheep occupy much of the high, wild country north of the Tropic of Cancer. Here are some of the wildest rams the world has to offer.

MARCO POLO ARGALI (Central Asia) This ram with spiraling, corkscrewing horns is the best known of several subspecies of argali (also known as central Asian mountain sheep).

EURASIAN MOUFLON (Mediterranean) These ancestors of our domestic sheep roam an arid strip from Iran, through the Caucasus Mountains and then around the Mediterranean.

SNOW SHEEP (Eastern Russia) A Russian relative of the Dall's and bighorn sheep, this stocky, massive-horned ram lives in Siberia and throughout the Kamchatka Peninsula.

FANNIN SHEEP (North America) This white sheep with black highlights is thought to be a hybrid of Dall's and Stone's sheep and is found in isolated areas of the Yukon and Northwest Territories.

CALIFORNIA BIGHORN (North America) Also known as the desert bighorn, this subspecies ranges from Nevada's Great Basin south and west into Mexico's Baja Peninsula. These rams are defined by heavy, curling horns atop a relatively slight body.

FIELD JUDGE A RAM

The goal of any wild sheep hunter should be to kill a mature ram. There are sound conservation reasons for this—the oldest males are at the end of their reproductive lives and are most susceptible to predators and winter kill. But estimating the age of a ram and the size of his horns is also great sport, and in areas with minimum age or size restrictions, correct field judging is also a legal matter. There are so many variables—the length and circumference of the horns, the mass at its base, the arc of the curl, the size of the skull—that any serious sheep hunter should study as many field photos as possible. Here are four elements to consider:

CONTEXT Get a copy of the latest sheep records for the unit you're hunting, as trophy qualities may differ significantly from area to area. In Wyoming, for instance, alpine bighorns tend to have tighter curls that start from less substantial bases than the lower-elevation rams of Montana's Missouri River Breaks rams, which have massive bases and more open curls. If you hold out for a 180-inch (457-cm) ram in Wyoming, you may be disappointed, while that benchmark is regularly obtained in the Breaks.

AGE With good optics and the right light, you can often count the annuli, or age rings, that define ram horns. Growth rates differ by range, but generally a 6- to 7-year-old ram is considered mature.

BASES The circumference of a ram's horns tells you a lot about his overall score. Look for horns that rise high from the skull but don't show a lot of light between the skull and the inside of the curl.

SUSTAINED MASS Mass is the least appreciated aspect of a trophy ram. Look for heavy horns that carry their weight around the curl. My friend and taxidermist, Dale Manning of Missoula, Montana, applies the "three-finger rule" when judging rams. If a ram's horn is at least three fingers deep at its terminal end, he's probably a good one.

GEESE

JUST A GENERATION AGO, the hunter who bagged but one goose—be it a Canada, snow, or white-fronted—had cause for great celebration. A goose was the epitome of success, as worthy of showing off as any heavy-racked whitetail. In modern times geese have largely forfeited this panache, owing to a population boom and, in turn, more consistent hunting. Do not be fooled: Geese remain one of the savviest, most challenging birds in the world. They are smarter than ducks, perhaps equal in wits to wild turkeys and, above all, they are still trophies.

Given that the prolific Canada goose is now considered a nuisance in many areas, it's easy to forget that market gunning and other factors nearly led to its extinction in the early 1900s. Fewer than three decades ago, population expansion efforts were underway, which included reintroduction of Canada geese to many areas of the country. Suffice it to say, no municipalities want extra geese today. Thanks to conservation efforts and the Canada's ability to adapt, resident populations now exceed 3 million nationwide. Management goals have thus shifted to control, affording waterfowlers a unique opportunity: nearly six months of semi-uninterrupted hunting.

Special resident goose seasons occur as early as August and as late as March, and limits are quite generous. In many states, seasons for migratory populations open soon after the first resident season closes and end prior to the second—it's like three seasons in one!

Then there are the snow geese, which are hunted practically from the time they migrate into the United States until their return north of the Canadian border. Why? Despite an early 20th century population crash, snow geese have multiplied to the point they're a threat unto themselves. The season is long, limits are liberal, and, in certain seasons, even digital calls and unplugged shotguns are legal—yet hunters practically can't kill enough to please biologists.

Much has changed since the days when shooting a goose might've resulted in a local newspaper reporter knocking on your door. A diverse number of species are widespread and offer ample hunting opportunities. It may be human nature to glorify the past, but not for the goose hunter. This is the greatest era in which he has ever lived.

WHEN TO CALL (AND WHEN NOT TO)

The decision to call—and how aggressively—is determined by the behavior of the geese themselves. If birds are approaching in a low, direct fashion, a few basic clucks to keep their interest may be all that's required, and decoys will do the rest. If the geese are soaring at great altitude toward a destination, you may as well save your breath.

But if the flock is flying lower, changing altitude or direction, and includes birds that seem interested in breaking from the group, the geese are often callable. A loud hail call—consisting of extended, repeated *kerrrrr-hooonk*s and best accompanied by flagging—will gain their attention. With any luck, a bird or two—usually juveniles—will peel away. Your mission is to keep their attention so as to draw the rest of the flock along with them.

Above all, read the birds. Their moods vary, and a well-developed hunter's instinct is required.

There are a variety of ways in which to hunt geese, but all share a commonality: The hunter who wishes to enjoy consistent success must find where the birds are eating or where they're loafing— and ideally both. Therefore, goose aficionados spend nearly as much on gasoline as steel shot, checking areas geese are known to frequent and even chasing after airborne flocks to find their destinations. One clever trick is to grab a pair of binoculars, head into known goose country and find the highest nearby elevation. Your vantage aids the search for feed and roost sites, and in many cases geese will reveal themselves as they loudly, excitedly take flight. The mission is then to pursue the birds and find where they're going while avoiding traffic citations.

Once geese are scouted, diverse strategies— ranging from casual to complicated—may be employed. Pass shooting is among the simplest, but it requires a knowledge of the geese's most recent daily travel routes for any modicum of success. Assuming the birds cooperate, hunters need only a trusty, tightly choked shotgun, a box of shells, and perhaps experience with the Churchill shooting style in order to bag passing geese. Preferred loads often consist of B-shot or larger in a velocity sufficient to carry lethal energy at altitude.

More commonly, however, decoys are employed, generally in larger spreads than for ducks because geese are found in such congregations. A sizable spread often appears more natural to the birds and is a more visible draw, but be sure to tailor the size of your spread to the flocks you've scouted. During resident seasons, especially, a dozen or two may better mimic real birds on the ground.

Full-bodies are perhaps most realistic, but they're also the most expensive and require a large amount of transport space—even a specialized trailer. Windsock-style decoys are easier on the wallet and offer the advantage of motion, but generally require a slight breeze for optimal performance. Traditionally silhouettes used to be wildly popular and, in fact, still offer advantage.

They're comparatively inexpensive and when faced in a variety of directions, they offer the illusion of motion to circling birds.

Geese of all species have adapted well to modern farming practices and may be decoyed in corn stubble, wheat, soybeans, and other crops. Such feed sites likely result in the most consistent hunting. However, there remains something special about shooting geese in classic fashion—over water—as the splash of a 20-pound (9-kg)

bird provides quite an exclamation point to a fine shot. Unlike ducks, geese go to water not to feed but to rest, so a relaxed-looking spread of full-body floaters accompanied by a few land-based decoys can be greatly effective.

Regardless of how you hunt geese, returning home with a bag justifies maximum satisfaction. You have conquered the wariest of waterfowl species, and you hold in your hands one of the sporting life's great trophies. —*Kyle Wintersteen*

A THREAT UNTO THEMSELVES

The recovery of Canada and snow goose populations is among North America's great conservation success stories. Unfortunately, the story may be too good to be true: Segments of both populations are booming to the extent that they risk their own demise.

This is particularly true of the lesser snow goose subspecies, which exceeds 5 million birds—a three-fold increase since the 1970s—and continues to grow by about 5 percent per year. Biologists credit available waste grains and years of mild nesting conditions for this artificially inflated, nonsustainable population. Simply put, the birds are eating away their wintering and nesting habitats. So in 1999, special spring seasons began in the United States and shortly thereafter in Canada.

Resident Canada geese, too, are a concern. Exceeding 3 million in the United States, they do quite a bit of harm to soil banks and water quality as they linger in home areas. Resident geese also beget more residents by attracting migrating birds to their comfortable lifestyle. This is rather concerning given the more fragile nature of migratory populations.

A variety of management tools are employed to combat these issues, but hunting is easily the most affordable and effective method. Fortunately, many waterfowlers are happily answering the call.

THE BEST GEESE ARE UNEXPECTED

For many hunters, a limit of geese is a prerequisite to any favorite tale, but my most cherished memories have nothing to do with high volume. Rather, many of my favorite experiences hunting involve geese I simply did not expect to kill or even see. Given the smarts and survival instincts innate to the birds, such surprises are rare and exciting.

One such morning began on a favorite mallard slough outside State College, Pennsylvania. Two friends and I had assembled a modest duck spread, not even fussing with geese given we'd never seen them at the location. As a result, it initially seemed like a trick of the mind when we heard the lonely honks. Six giant Canadas crested a line of oaks and slammed on the brakes, audibly slicing the crisp January air. After a quick pass, they promptly landed to our right before thumbs could reach safeties. My friend Jake had never shot a goose, and conveniently the small flock had lit nearest him.

"Go ahead and shoot your first goose, Jake," I offered, to which he nodded.

With a quick "Hey, geese!" Jake flushed the birds and promptly dumped one. Then something truly bizarre happened: Instead of taking any number of easy escape routes, the confused geese flew directly at us. We felled the lot of them.

Per our tradition, Jake had to carry his first goose—plus all of ours—out of the field. Never has a hunter smiled so broadly with 90 pounds (40 kg) of goose slung over his shoulders.

NORTH AMERICA'S DIVERSE GEESE

Goose hunting offers a rich diversity of birds, but the differences are often subtle. For instance, the seven subspecies of Canada geese include the Atlantic, Hudson Bay (or interior), giant, Moffitt's (or great basin), lesser, dusky, and Vancouver. A 20-pound (9-kg) giant Canada is easily distinguished from a 6-pound (2.7-kg) lesser, but others require coloration, size, and regional clues. On average, the farther north a subspecies nests, the smaller it is; and while Atlantic populations tend to have light gray breasts, those farther west are incrementally darker.

Considered Canada geese until 2004, the four subspecies of cackling geese include the Aleutian, cackling, Taverner's, and Richardson's (Hutchins'). Most are found in the Pacific Flyway, while the Richardson's winters in the Central.

The snow goose population is dominated by the lesser subspecies, but also includes the big-bodied greater. The "blue goose" is not actually a subspecies, but rather a color-phase of the lesser.

Ross's geese are very similar to lesser snows, but quite smaller. Average weight is only 3–4 pounds (1.4–1.8 kg).

Pacific and Central Flyway hunters are treated to the white-fronted goose or "specklebelly," a lovely bird with a barred chest that's also superb on the table.

Lastly there are brant—dark-plumed, seafaring birds divided into two subspecies: the Atlantic and Pacific.

Canada Goose

Snow Goose

Brant Goose

Cackling Goose

Ross's Goose

WILD CANINES

EVER SINCE THE FIRST CAVEMAN threw a spare bone to a curious jackal, wild dogs have shadowed us. But they also infuriate us. Hunters who would risk their lives to save a fawn deer or rescue a turkey poult shoot on sight every coyote they see. Our persecution of wolves is even more intense and personal. But wild canines have thrived in our prejudicial midst, and their expansion has given hunters additional seasons and opportunities to pursue what may be the smartest and most adaptable of our wild quarry.

"Coyotes are the price we pay for living here." That's the way my neighbor, an old-school rancher, explained why he carried a dented-and-scarred Husquevarna .243 rifle in his pickup, which he used to fling hot lead at every coyote he saw.

My neighbor was reflexively acting on an ancient antagonism we have for wild canines. It's not just a ranch-land grudge. Our antipathy extends around the world—to north-woods wolves, sub-Saharan jackals, the dhole (or "devil dog") of India, dingos in Australia, the curious raccoon dog of Japan, the Abyssinian wolf of the original Bible belt, and even the furtive foxes of the high arctic.

We simply have it out for wild dogs, the equal and opposite counterbalance to the huge doses of hospitality and compassion we extend to our domestic canines. But a growing group of hunters is recognizing the value of hunting coyotes, foxes, and wolves not just to protect livestock, but for sport.

These are smart and cagey animals that exhibit great capacity for recall and adaptation, and they can live in nearly every habitat on earth. That makes them nearly perfect critters to teach us to be better hunters, because only when we do everything right—watch the wind, exercise extreme stealth, call correctly, and then shoot straight—will we consistently kill wild canines.

By that measure, North American hunters have more canine teachers than ever before these days. Coyotes, perhaps the most adaptable and widespread of the world's wild dogs, have grown in number and distribution over the last 50 years, generally following the growth curve of the white-tailed deer.

PLAYING THE WIND

Whether you're hunting foxes, coyotes, wolves, or jackals, the wind will either put fur on the ground or make you look like a chump. Of all the defenses canines share, their sense of smell is the sharpest, and you should be prepared when hunting a wild dog.

If you are calling, set up in an area where you have good visibility downwind of your stand. Canines will almost always try to circle downwind of you to get a sniff of your identity. Expect to get a shot just before the dog cuts your scent and turns himself inside out trying to get away.

CLASSIC CANINE CALLS

DISTRESS CALL These calls mimic the death screams of wounded rabbits, deer fawns, birds, and other prey species.

CHALLENGE CALL These sharp, aggressive howls and barks communicate a range of various emotions, announcing that you are ready to fight and raising the hackles of local canines.

GATHERING CALL These long, baleful invitation howls speak to a canine's desire to coalesce as a pack.

CURIOSITY CALL These piercing, high-pitched calls sound like peacocks, woodpeckers, or magpies and are designed to pique the curiosity of scavenging canines.

HUNTING THE HUNTERS Wild dogs all share a number of traits that make them appealing targets. For starters, they are pack animals, so where you find one, you're likely to find more. Because they are carnivores, they respond to calls that imitate prey species, and because they are social animals, wild dogs respond to challenge and bitch-in-heat calls. And because they are so ubiquitous, a hunt for any other animal—antlered game, small game, upland birds—can instantly transition to an opportunistic canine hunt.

THE COYOTE BOOM Coyotes have always lived in the Western plains and foothills and shared with foxes the woodlands of the Midwest. But their spread into the Eastern seaboard and Southeastern states is a relatively recent phenomenon. DNA evidence suggests these coyotes, which are prodigious killers of white-tailed deer, hybridized with Canadian wolves, and their expansion is especially vexing to hunters who cultivate food plots to enhance their local deer herds only to see a favorite buck taken out by coyotes.

TIMBER WOLF (N. America) Huge, yellow-eyed, and carnivorous, this woodland species preys on moose and deer.

GRAY WOLF (N. America, top left) Fast reoccupying its historic range across the Rockies, the gray wolf can travel thousands of miles to find a mate.

ARCTIC WOLF (N. America, Asia) This scrappy canine migrates with caribou herds, and is equal parts predator and scavenger.

COYOTE (N. America) Capable of making a home in just about any kind of habitat, coyotes are smaller than most people think, topping out at about 35 pounds (16 kg).

ARCTIC FOX (N. America, Asia) Small, furtive, and hungry, this little fox preys on hares, ptarmigans, and voles.

RED FOX (N. America, Europe, Asia, Africa) One of the most widely distributed canines, red foxes' primary prey are mice and birds.

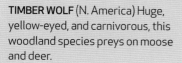

GRAY FOX (N. America) Smaller and more compact than the red fox, grays have been known to climb trees for food and refuge.

SWIFT FOX (N. America) This small, nocturnal canine of the American plains and desert feeds mainly on birds and insects.

PAMPAS FOX (S. America) Think of this South American dog as the swift fox of the gaucho country.

BUSH DOG (S. America) This packing dog of the jungle herds large prey into swamps and rivers.

FENNEC FOX (N. Africa) The fennec's huge ears help it dissipate heat and hear prey sneaking underground in the deserts of northern Africa.

ABYSSINIAN WOLF (N. Africa) Similar in size to the coyote, this canine lives in the highlands of Ethiopia.

BAT-EARED FOX (S. Africa) Primarily an insectivore, this fox uses its ears to locate prey. Its diet is mainly comprised of harvester termites.

BLACK-BACKED JACKAL (S. Africa, top right) The most widespread wild canine in sub-Saharan Africa, the black-backed jackal hunts and scavenges in the bushveld.

GOLDEN JACKAL (W. Asia) Another coyote cousin, this adaptable canine is spreading into Europe from its native Middle East.

DHOLE (India) Sometimes called the Indian wild dog, this packing canine runs down blackbuck and axis deer on chases that can last for days.

RACCOON DOG (S.E. Asia) One of the evolutionarily oldest canine species, this omnivore feeds on insects, fish, and rodents—much like the North American raccoon, though it hails from an entirely different taxonomical family.

DINGO (Australia) The iconic wild dog of Australia, the dingo preys on nuisance rabbits, rats, and kangaroos, but is considered vermin by ranchers.

MOUNTAIN GOATS

THEY CLING TO CRAGGY CLIFFS. They stick landings on tiny jags of slippery shale. And they endure endless winters in the high, wind-strafed roof of the continent. They're mountain goats, and hunting them requires the gear and determination of a mountaineer, the lungs of a Sherpa, and the balance of a gymnast. Ounce for ounce, mountain goats are the toughest, most athletic, and least appreciated of North America's game animals. And they live in the continent's most formidable and achingly beautiful real estate.

If there is a freer animal than the mountain goat, I don't know it. The alpine goat is never lured to lower elevations by succulent alfalfa, has never tasted a kernel of corn, and can spend its lifetime without stepping across a road or jumping barbed wire.

Even its surroundings are liberating. With only a couple of exceptions, North America's population of mountain goats lives on public land, most of it in designated wilderness areas, where access is free, even if it's not always easy.

In that fragile, alpine environment, the mountain goat makes a living by grubbing for lichens and cold-stunted plants, escaping predators by climbing to places that no animal without its specialized splayed hooves could go, and by growing a luxuriant coat that insulates it from the wind and cold.

It's that wind that enables goats to live in the high country, places where snow is measured in yards and meters. The wind blows ridges bare of precipitation, exposing the lichen and mosses that sustain them through months of winter. That's where you can expect to find goats, on the knife-edges of ridges, on the shoulders of high peaks, and in the rims above bowls and cirques, anywhere food and escape routes converge.

In nearly every Western state, you must draw a special permit to hunt goats, and the handful of hunters who get the opportunity must be in top physical shape, able to reach the high country and stay in the field for days at a time. It's the ultimate backcountry hunt, where lightweight and weatherproof gear, GPS units, and immunity to vertigo are important considerations.

BRITISH COLUMBIA

For numbers and trophies, British Columbia's remote coastal range is the top destination for goat hunters. The mountains have relatively low elevation, receive extensive precipitation, and grow abundant food, while the relatively longer growing season promotes horn growth. Populations of goats tend to be more accessible here than in the Rocky Mountains, especially for hunters who begin their treks from boats on rivers or coastal inlets.

The biggest hazard, beyond the usual mountain perils, is the weather. Freezing fog, whiteout blizzards, and icy rain can turn a sure-thing goat hunt into a life-or-death ordeal.

IN ONE DAY

Back in 2001, everything for me came in pairs. Early in the year, my wife gave birth to our twin boys. The streak continued later in the spring, when I discovered I had drawn both moose and mountain goat tags in my home state of Montana.

The moose hunt took priority, and I killed a decent bull not far from my home. The goat tag was for the Crazy Mountains, a high series of crenelated ridges that glower over the prairie between the Yellowstone and Musselshell rivers.

I prepared to spend as long as a full week in the peaks, assessing many goats until I spotted the right billy. But as we were setting up a big tent at base camp, I spied a white animal on the cliffs above the campground. It was a billy, standing maybe 2,000 feet (610 meters) straight above us.

In what may be the only single-day goat hunt in history, I scaled the cliffs and shot that billy in his bed at 400 yards (or meters). I was back in camp with cape and meat well before midnight.

Good optics are important not only to locate goats from a distance but to judge their trophy potential as you close in. The final decision to shoot must be based on two considerations. First, can you anchor the animal where it stands, even if that requires shooting up or downhill at severe angles? And second, can you retrieve the goat? Too many mountain goat hunts have ended with the trophy of a lifetime either hanging up on an inaccessible ledge or tumbling all the way down to be dashed on boulders below.

If you have the luxury of picking your time, try to go as late in the season as you can. Early-season hunts have the benefit of decent weather—a serious consideration—but late-season goats have far better hair, and aside from their sharp, black horns, the luxurious coat of an October or November goat is a real trophy of the high country.

FIELD SKILLS

FIELD JUDGE A MOUNTAIN GOAT

Because male and female goats have horns of approximately the same length and shape, assessing sex and trophy status requires careful study and attention to these details:

[A] COAT COLOR Nannies typically have dazzlingly white coats, while the coats of mature billies are often stained ivory, light khaki, or as one veteran goat hunter told me, "the color of an old tooth."

[B] BODY SHAPE Mature billies exhibit a pronounced hump on their shoulders and appear to have thicker bodies than females do.

[C] HORN SHAPE The horns of mature billies curve backward along the entire length. Nannies' thinner horns tend to grow straight upward, curving only in the last third of their length.

[D] BLACK GLAND Billies have a donut-shaped gland at the base of their horns. Nannies do not.

[E] HORN BASES Thick horns of mature billies appear to nearly touch at the base; trophy goats retain that mass well up the length of the horns. If you see white hair between the two black horns, you are probably looking at an immature billy or a nanny.

GROUSE

WHEN EUROPEAN HUNTERS FIRST LANDED in the New World they were greeted with a sound with which they were well familiar. The echoes of ruffed grouse drumming in the old growth forests of the Northeast surely reminded them of the red and black grouse back home. As their covered wagons pushed west, sage grouse, spruce grouse, and prairie chickens sounded a thunderous welcome, and many a settler survived on grouse meat cooked over a campfire—if they were smart enough to pack a smoothbore for the trek.

Today, the distinctive drumming of the male grouse can still be heard across the northern hemisphere. After some difficult years, ruffie numbers have stabilized thanks to restoration efforts and smart management. Other forest-dwelling family members such as the dusky, sooty, and spruce grouse have also survived threats, though some subspecies that prefer more open country, including prairie chickens and sage grouse, haven't fared as well, with the heath hen disappearing altogether in the 1930s. European populations of red, black, and wood grouse (the largest of the family, and perhaps better known as Western capercaillie), are also closely managed by conservation-minded sportsmen.

Arguably, the ruffed is North America's most popular gamebird, and certainly the most romanticized, due much in part to the outdoor art and literature of the early 20th century. Firmly ingrained is the image of tweed-clad men and their long-haired setters wending their way through grouse coverts far from industrialized America. Like most members of the *Galliforme* order, grouse spend much of their life on the ground, foraging for berries and vegetation within a small home range, moving as their dietary whims dictate depending on the season. During winter, grouse subsist mainly on catkins, and are particularly fond of the emerging buds of fruit trees, making them a frequent visitor to orchards.

Male ruffed grouse stake out their turf through loud drumming—rapidly flapping their wings, often while perched atop a drumming log used year after year. They are solitary by nature, though more than one hunter has been shocked by a second, unexpected flush.

THE WORLD SLAM OF GROUSE

I swelled with my achievement: three grouse—sharptail, sage, and ruffed—on the same day. But that's strictly amateur for some grouse gunners. Here are some regional collections (often called "slams"):

SWEDISH SLAM In the forested Lapland, you can collect the capercaillie, black cock, hazel hen, and willow grouse.

FOREST SLAM One of the most achievable, you can kill spruce, ruffed, and blue (now called dusky) grouse on U.S. Forest Service land from Montana through Colorado.

ARCTIC SLAM In interior Alaska, you could take the willow, rock, and white-tailed ptarmigan.

PRAIRIE SLAM Hunt the grasslands of the Dakotas to bag sage, sharptail, and both greater and lesser prairie chickens.

The first ruffed grouse I ever encountered flushed at my feet and whirred directly away from me down a long, wide lane. Shocked, I didn't even raise my gun. My companion remarked I'd never have such an easy opportunity again. And he was right. Since then I've heard grouse flush as I crawled through thorny vine, caught glimpses of them beating their wings through the "popple," and generally been embarrassed by them. On occasion, a rushed shot and hopeful prayer have converged in a puff of feathers, and each time the dog brings one to hand, I marvel at the beauty of the plumage, the wild smell in their feathers and, later, the flavor of the forest in their succulent, white meat.

You can judge a grouse hunter by his clothes. A serious hunter's duds will be in tatters, torn and muddy from slogs through brush and bogs. The more casual grouse hunter, by comparison, looks clean, for he spends his evenings walking logging roads and picking the "fool's hen" from ditches as the birds come out to peck gravel. Neither technique is wrong, but it's the well-worn hunter who takes the most pride in his pastime, and holds the best coverts close to his game vest.

Discovering your own honeyhole means finding edge cover. As long as food (in the form of berries, green forbs, and flower buds) is nearby, grouse spend the majority of their days in the thickest cover they can find, such as overgrown clear cuts, young forests, and dense swamps. An abandoned farm, preferably one with an overgrown orchard, is like money in the bank.

When a grouse does appear, don't wait for the perfect shot—you're more likely to hear the bird flying than see it. Anticipate its flight line, swing past it, and pull the trigger, even if your target is not in view at the time. With any luck, you'll connect, but if not, you'll realize why experienced grouse hunters count a successful day not by birds in the bag, but in flushes heard. —*David Draper*

THE PERFECT GROUSE GUN

Naming anything but a double-barrel as the perfect grouse gun is likely to provoke angry e-mails. The uproar would be well justified, and not only for aesthetic reasons.

A classic stacked double with barrels 26 inches (66 cm) long is light enough to carry all day, not so long as to be cumbersome in dense cover, and quick to point at a grouse as it rockets away. Having only two shots shouldn't be considered a handicap, as the opportunity for a third is so rare as to be remarkable.

Grouse aren't notable for their durability, making 20 gauge more than adequate and shot size no bigger than 7 ½ preferred. Suitable grouse guns can found on used-gun racks, but they're often well worn. Of new models on the market, my pick for the perfect grouse gun would be a 5 ¾-lb (2.6-kg) Browning Citori Lightning Feather or, if budget shopping, the Franchi Instinct SL at just over 5 lbs (2.3 kg).

PICK OF THE GROUSE-HUNTING LITTER

ENGLISH SETTER With its head up, tail raised like flag, and a single paw lifted, the setter strikes a beautiful point and it couldn't be sweeter as a companion. Unfortunately, looks and demeanor have in some ways meant the breed's downfall, as many have had their nose and instinct bred out of them, turning them into pets rather than hunters. Do your research and buy from a line that's bred to hunt.

BRITTANY Formerly considered (and still sometimes referred to as) a member of the spaniel family, the Brittany is a pointing dog known for its excellent nose and ease of training. It's these traits, along with the Britt's eager-to-please nature, that makes it a preferred gun dog for many grouse hunters. Of the two types, the small, close-working French Britt gets the edge in tight grouse coverts over the bigger, faster American breeding.

GERMAN SHORTHAIRED POINTER Like the legendary UFC fighter that shares its initials, the GSP is a world-class athlete that seems to vibrate with energy and anticipation. Barrel-chested with long legs and a gazelle-like gait, the big-running shorthair might be a liability in thick cover, but it shines in the wide-open space of the West where sharp-tailed grouse and prairie chickens are found, thanks in no small part to the breed's best-in-class nose.

PRAIRIE CHICKENS

Hunters who chase (and *chase* is the correct term) prairie chickens are typically a rangy lot. Long of leg with wind-burnt faces and eyes squinting at far-off flushes, they're the product of the environment the prairie chicken prefers—huge landscapes of tall- and mixed-grass prairie, far from any signs of civilization. Studies have found the stocky, ground-nesting birds shun anything made by man, including roads, power lines, and wind turbines. These threats to their habitat, along with changing agricultural practices, have caused prairie chicken numbers to decline across their range, especially for the Lesser sub-species on the southern Plains. The Greater Prairie Chicken, known for its elaborate courtship rituals, survives in huntable numbers, mostly in Kansas, Nebraska ,and the Dakotas, where rangy hunters and their big-running dogs walk the grasslands each autumn, watching for a point, hurrying before a flush and, hopefully, making a long shot at these enduring symbols of all that is great about the Great Plains.

WHITHER THE SAGE GROUSE?

In the last century, sage grouse populations have plummeted from 16 million to as little as a quarter million recorded, depending on the source you believe. What is known: As goes sagebrush, so goes its eponymous fowl.

Every year, acres are lost due to energy development and changing land-use patterns. Sage grouse, known for beautiful courtship displays, now occupy a miniscule percent of their once vast range, making them a candidate for the Endangered Species Act. While there is hope for the bird, as conservation initiatives mitigate habitat loss, there's little chance the next generation of hunters will know what it's like to feel the heft of one in their game bag.

ELK

FOR EVERY AMERICAN whitetail hunter, elk are aspirational, calling to them the way Cooperstown calls to a Little Leaguer. The impossibly heavy and branching antlers of bulls are as alluring as the soaring mountains where they live, and the mythology of elk is filled with Western romance: canvas wall tents, the creaking leather of pack trains, and frosty mornings at timberline. And thanks to reintroductions and range expansion, an elk hunt is more attainable than ever. Even if Major League Baseball remains stubbornly out of reach of most of us.

More than the wild turkey or the bald eagle, the majestic elk should be considered America's national animal. Before we timbered and plowed the continent, elk roamed from sea to sea, inhabiting nearly every type of terrain in between. Material progress sent elk—sometimes called wapiti—to a few remote sanctuaries, where the pillars of our conservation movement recognized them as indicator species of wild lands. Folks like Theodore Roosevelt and William Hornady argued to preserve these remnants of backcountry, so elk and their allies would survive.

They couldn't have imagined the century since the establishment of the National Forest Preserve. Elk have not only come to define those Western public lands, but they've recolonized much of their historic range, including western Pennsylvania's hardwood forests and eastern Kentucky's coal country, where hunters have the opportunity to kill some of the largest bulls on the continent and hunt them under the changing leaves of an Appalachian autumn. Elk have been reintroduced into the Ozarks of southern Missouri, and there are huntable herds in northern Michigan, Minnesota, Nebraska, California, and every Canadian province west of Ontario.

The reintroduction of gray wolves to the West has impacted local elk populations, but ongoing research suggests that prey and predator cycles will likely achieve balance over the long term.

In their core habitat of the West, the restoration story has been almost too good. Populations have increased in some areas to the point that game managers are trying to reduce herds and increase hunting opportunity. In short, it's a good time to be an elk hunter.

BUGLE OR ROAR?

North American elk are known to bugle—a keening, nasally whine that changes in pitch and carries across open land. European stags bellow like lunatic cattle—accurately called a roar, it sounds like it came from an apex predator, not a prey species. Biologists think the low-throated roar evolved in woodland wapiti, because it can be heard well in dense cover.

AN INTERNATIONAL FAMILY Four distinct subspecies of elk currently roam North America. By far the most numerous and widely distributed of them is the Rocky Mountain elk, which can be found in mountains and adjacent habitats from Arizona north to the Yukon. The Roosevelt elk lives in the rainy forests of the Cascades and Washington's Olympic Peninsula. California's interior valleys and remnant swamps are home to the rare tule elk, which is creeping back from the brink of extinction. And the Manitoba elk lives in the northern woodlands of the Canadian shield and the St. Lawrence River.

Two North American elk races have gone extinct since Europeans settled the continent: the huge Merriam's elk, which was once found all the way from western Texas through southern Arizona, and the abundant Eastern elk, which was native to the hardwood forests of the Ohio and Mississippi river valleys until the early days of the last century.

American elk are part of a large and widely dispersed family. Until recently, biologists thought that elk and European red deer were a single species, but DNA research indicates that they are genetically distinct, though so closely related that they can interbreed.

The red deer, or stag, is native to much of Europe, from Scotland's bogs to the forests of northern France, through Germany, east into the Balkans, and across much of Russia. The species has been widely transplanted, as far as the foothills of the Andes in Argentina and the Southern Alps of New Zealand. An Asian species of elk, more similar in appearance and behavior to our North American elk than the stag, occupies forested habitat from Kazakhstan east through Manchuria.

HUNTING STRATEGIES While elk and stag can tolerate dense forest—and they will flee to the densest, most remote timbered pockets whenever they feel threatened—they prefer areas with frequent openings. Hunters should key on these edge habitats, where elk emerge to feed at twilight.

Setting up on these meadows is a good plan, assuming the animals arrive as scripted. If you prefer a more active type of hunting, climb to a lookout and use optics to find elk and then work out a stalk that gets you within range. Pay careful attention to the wind, always keeping it in your face. Shifting winds have saved the lives of more elk than all the habitat conservationists together.

Especially in the mountains, elk migrate along ancient corridors that deliver them from higher-elevation summer ranges to more hospitable winter ranges. Once snow piles up, intercept elk along these routes. Or you can bowhunt during the rut and call bugling bulls into bow range.

However you hunt your elk, plan on longish shots—out to 300 yards (or meters)—with a rifle, and shoot a bow-and-arrow combination that can deliver at least 60 foot-pounds (81 newton-meters) of energy.

BOWHUNTING RUTTING BULLS

There's a sound reason most archery seasons for elk open in early September. These short-range hunting opportunities are timed to coincide with the rut, the breeding season when mature bulls gather and defend large breeding harems of cows from interlopers.

This is a vocal business. Cows make their presence—and availability—known by chirping and mewing. Bulls respond by emitting the high-pitched keening cry of a bugle. Hunters who are able to mimic both these sounds can often call bulls right into their laps.

In practice, it's not quite so easy. Sometimes calling spooks elk, other times it attracts only immature bulls (called spikes or raghorns). But when it works, calling a bull into bow range is like conjuring a cage fighter. I know of nothing else in hunting that compares to having an 800-pound (363-kg) bull come running to your call, wild-eyed and heaving, thrashing brush with his remarkable antlers, calling you out to fight.

BONE OUT AN ELK

My elk-hunting strategy is to hike into backcountry areas as light as I can and to come out heavy, laden with meat and antlers.

But there's a limit to the weight I'll pack, and I draw the line at dense, heavy elk bones (and the bones of moose, caribou, and mule deer, for that matter). That's why canvas game bags, a good boning knife, and a frame pack are essential parts of my backcountry-hunting arsenal.

Once you get an animal down, the first thing *not* to do is to gut it. There are two reasons for this. First, many elk live—and die—in predator country, and you don't want entrails to attract claws and fangs as you take apart your trophy. Second, the real trophy of an elk is the delicious meat, and the faster you can get it off the bone and out of the field, the happier you'll be the rest of the year.

The trick is to lay the carcass out on its side, then fillet the skin off the front and rear quarters. Open a game bag and carve off big chunks of meat—roasts, hams, backstraps, neck meat—keeping them clean of dirt and hair. Once you've dissembled one side, turn the animal over and repeat. Then, once all the exterior meat is bagged, it's time to extract the tenderloins.

Do this by making a small incision in the flank, just behind the ribs, and reach up toward the backbone. You'll feel the tenderloin; make a cut at the forward end and carefully work it loose from the carcass. Turn the animal over and repeat.

If you're alone, you'll have to make several trips to pack out an entire elk; hang the bags in a shady tree to cool until you come back to retrieve them.

WHITE-TAILED DEER

WHEN THE AIR TURNS CRISP in November, hunters celebrate opening day of deer season as though it were a national holiday. In Pennsylvania, schools close. All across the nation, guns boom. Six million deer fall. Rites are passed. Traditions continued. Then, in the offseason, hunters buy gear, study how-to articles, and watch hunting shows. The animal's economic impact is measured in billions. Why? There is no warier, more adaptable, tastier, or more challenging game animal on Earth. In America, whitetail is king.

Odocoileus virginianus is purely American, ranging from Peru to Canada. While bespectacled men have attempted to classify whitetails into subspecies, DNA evidence suggests they are genetically identical. But that doesn't mean they haven't adapted to environments.

Any traveling hunter who's stalked a giant Canada whitetail knows they're bigger—and darker—up there. That's because whitetails follow Bergmann's rule, which states animals' body size increases with its distance from the equator. Coues whitetails of Mexico and the southwestern United States are ash gray in color and weigh 50-125 pounds (23-57 kg). While most whitetail hunters grin proudly with a 135- to 200-pound (61- to 91-kg) buck in the truck, Carl Lenander, Jr., reportedly killed a Minnesota whitetail in 1926 that weighed 403 pounds (183 kg), field dressed!

Savvy hunters know deer's preferred food changes with the season and crop availability, but less known is how adaptable their diet is. Deer have been observed eating bark, cactus, ants, chicks and eggs from nests, and other oddities. But a ripe acorn from a white oak tree remains the whitetail's caviar.

The deer gets its name from its flaglike tail that it raises when scared. This communicates danger to other deer—and tells the hunter he's not sneaky enough. Bucks grow antlers annually, beginning in late spring. The living tissue, covered by a velvety network of blood vessels, is thought to be one of the fastest growing on earth; by September they shed the velvet, revealing hardened antlers used for defense, territorial marking, and fighting. Antler size and configuration vary depending on age, genetics, injury, and nutrition.

THE SPIKE QUESTION

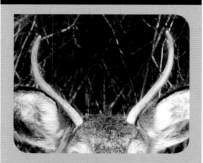

On properties where deer are managed for quality antler growth, a debate rages: Some hunters believe yearling spike bucks have inferior genetics and therefore aren't capable of becoming respectable bucks. They believe spikes are a waste of habitat resources and should be culled. However, research conducted by Texas A&M University suggests that while a yearling spike buck is unlikely to blossom into a Boone and Crockett-caliber trophy, a spike can become a respectable 8- or 10-point—if it's given adequate age and nutrition.

As wary whitetails expand their range, hunters expand their tactics. Yet the basic methods for hunting remain, with some local variations.

STAND HUNTING The vast majority of the country's 13-million-plus whitetail hunters use permanent and portable treestands to ambush deer as they travel, feed, and interact. Hunters employ decoys, scents, lures, and calls to bring whitetails into range of their stands.

STALKING AND STILL-HUNTING The most skilled hunters among us can find, stalk, and kill whitetails in wooded terrain. The Benoit family of Vermont has made their living doggedly tracking big bucks through snow. Other hunters "still-hunt," or ease through the woods while scanning ahead for deerlike shapes and movement. Damp, quiet ground and a favorable wind are important for still-hunting success.

SPOT AND STALK Western hunters employ this technique in which large expanses of country are scanned and scrutinized for desirable animals. Once they're spotted, a stalk is made using available cover to creep within gun or bow range. Where the terrain allows, this is an active, highly enjoyable method of whitetail hunting.

OTHER METHODS In the South, where swamp-land abounds, deer hunting with dogs is a very traditional method. Hounds are let out at one end of thick cover in order to roust hiding deer past hunters lying in ambush. Since most shots are taken while the deer is running, it's common to use shotguns with buckshot.

WHITETAIL ESSENTIALS

All ancient hunters needed in order to take a whitetail was patience, cunning, and skill with a homemade weapon. Modern American hunters don't live in the woods, however, and most only get a few days to hunt. As a result, our hunting skills have eroded, and we rely more heavily on technology for success. After acquiring an accurate rifle or bow, a few pieces of gear have been proven to make hunting more enjoyable and more successful.

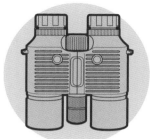  

OPTICS Quality optics are essential for finding and identifying deer. While hunters *can* spend thousands on a top-end binocular, they can also purchase an adequate unit for about a tenth of that price. Bushnell's Fusion binocular includes an integrated laser rangefinder—and the price is reasonable.

CLOTHING Modern clothing can make hunters quieter and more comfortable. Gore-Tex, or similarly lined clothing, stops wind and rain while letting body vapors escape so your own sweat won't soak you. Clothing containing wool, down, or synthetic-fiber insulation keep the head, body, and feet warm so hunters can hunt more and warm up in the truck less.

TREESTAND For ambush-style hunters, a commercially manufactured treestand is important for sitting comfortably and safely above the deer's natural line of sight. Homemade stands can be dangerous if not well maintained.

Where legal, it's an exciting and effective method. In some states, like Pennsylvania, "deer drives" are conducted wherein a group of "standers" sneak to line likely deer escape routes, while a group of "drivers" walk through targeted cover to push deer by the standers.

In Texas, corn feeders are used to bait deer into kill zones while hunters wait nearby in elevated "shoot houses." In the South, the same tactic is used, but distributed corn is substituted for cultivated bean fields.

—*Jeff Johnston*

URBAN HUNTING

As one of the planet's most adaptable mammals, whitetails have taken to lush suburban areas like sunbathers to Malibu. The suburbs of Washington, D.C., Atlanta, and similar areas offer mild climates, year-round flowery forage, legal protection, and a lack of natural predators. In fact, the whitetail's biggest threat in these areas is traffic.

Recognizing severe over-population, some game managers have instituted urban archery seasons. In Northern Virginia, homeowners and guests can bowhunt even in tiny backyards. Several counties have antlerless seasons extending nearly to the end of April.

BOWHUNTING MONSTER WHITETAILS

The United States's surplus of whitetails has afforded hunters the luxury of being choosy. As a result, a legion of hunters has emerged who are only interested in the biggest and most mature bucks—and only hunt them with self-handicapping archery gear. These big-buck fanatics might opt to pass by hundreds of legal deer before finally taking one that meets their standards.

These hunters obsessively pursue the species' biggest specimens for its challenge. Fact is, getting within 30 yards (or meters) of a mature, free-ranging whitetail is one of hunting's greatest feats.

Here's how they consistently put trophy bucks on their walls.

1. Don't shoot small bucks. If you do, your chance of seeing a monster is diminished, and that deer's chance to become a monster is destroyed.

2. Hunt areas where monster bucks exist and focus on heavy cover there.

3. Always use the wind to your advantage— and don't hunt if you think it's wrong.

4. Hunt the rut hard. Even wise deer make mistakes during this time.

5. Practice shooting in pressure situations to make the shot if/when it presents itself.

THE ULTIMATE HUNT

Conversation at deer camp often turns to the best places to hunt trophy bucks. There's Texas, where hunters sit and view 50 deer per day at a feeder until Mr. Big shows up. Some love it, but to me, it's more like deer shootin' than deer huntin'. Saskatchewan, Canada, where bucks can weigh 350 pounds (159 kg) and grow headgear to match? Odds for a giant are relatively good, but the Siberian style of hunting in which hunters sit in ground-blind prisons overlooking corn piles in –15°F (–26°C) weather just isn't appealing. Kansas, Iowa, Ohio, or Kentucky? Tempting. But a November bowhunt in Illinois's famed Brown or Adams counties is my deer-hunting heaven. Big bucks don't prance around in the open often, so you know they're in the thin fingers of woods and creek bottoms that lace the region's vast cornfields. Place a treestand in an oak funnel during the rut and get ready; it's likely your best chance to take a Booner. Bucks scoring over 200 inches (500 cm) are taken here each year. Problem is, finding land to hunt is virtually impossible unless you know someone or are willing to pay. Try Richardson Farms Outfitters of Mt. Sterling and hunt as long each day as you possibly can.

WHITETAIL WEAPONRY FOR EVERY SEASON

It's often said that hunters should respect the man with a single weapon. But for the modern whitetail hunter who must take up multiple arms if he wishes to take advantage of all seasons, the saying is grossly out of date. What follows is a list of weapons that are both efficient and cost effective for every major deer season.

RIFLE: REMINGTON MODEL 700 More than 5 million 700s have been sold—for good reason. Remington's flagship bolt-action rifle has seen duty in war and in the woods, and the common trait of all 700s is its accuracy. For deer hunters, that means venison.

SHOTGUN: SAVAGE 220F Several Midwestern states prohibit the use of rifles for whitetail hunting, so Savage Arms built a shotgun on the same basic design as its renowned rifles. It takes a bolt-action receiver and mates it with a 20-gauge rifled barrel. Add an AccuTrigger and it's a slug gun capable of 1.5-inch (3.8-cm) accuracy that's plenty for deer but without undue recoil of a 12-gauge.

MUZZLELOADER: CVA APEX This muzzleloader feels more like a modern rifle than any front-stuffer going. It sports lightweight, stainless steel for corrosion resistance, has a quality Bergara barrel for accuracy, and a glorious trigger. I like its rubberized stock that's quiet in the woods. Take time to experiment with various bullets and charges, and it might shoot 2-inch (5-cm) groups.

COMPOUND BOW: PSE X FORCE All of the top bow companies produce wonderful bows—Mathews, Hoyt, Bowtech, among others—but PSE's X Force technology revolutionized the industry. Engineers found they could take short little limbs and make them extend beyond parallel to produce the world's fastest arrow speeds. It's also quiet—and deadly accurate.

CROSSBOW: STRYKER STRYKEZONE 380 The Strykezone is ridiculously accurate thanks to its quality construction and light trigger. I shot some grapefruit-sized groups at 80 yards (or meters). It's more compact than most crossbows, and therefore less cumbersome in the woods—a huge attribute when hunting whitetails that have ears like radar beacons. With more states allowing crossbows for whitetails, it's a handy tool to have in the bag.

MULE DEER

IT'S A WONDER THERE ARE ANY MULE DEER LEFT ALIVE. Nearly everything about these magnificent open-country creatures courts their demise. Instead of ducking into cover, when startled they tend to run a ways, then stop in the open and look back quizzically at their pursuers. Their marginal habitat is squeezed by drought, brutal winters, and human development. But this icon of the West is very much alive, and a mature buck—with wide, deeply forked antlers and a regal square-backed stature—is one of the hardest-earned trophies of any deer hunter.

I've killed more mule deer than any other species of wild ungulate. It's easy to do if you're a Montana resident with more than enough public land out your back door. But a heavy-racked trophy still eludes me. In some ways, this is the conundrum of mule deer. In most areas west of the 100th meridian, they are commonplace, visible in alfalfa fields and open prairies, their characteristic stiff-legged springing run (called "stotting") familiar to anyone who drives Western highways. But old, big bucks are almost always products of the backcountry: deep canyons, desolate deserts, and subalpine basins.

Hunting techniques for mule deer are as varied as their habitat. Legions of Great Plains deer hunters don't walk far from their pickups to engage "muleys," as the deer are often called. Especially during the November rut, when otherwise elusive old bucks get spiral eyed and dull witted with lust's distractions, covering ground on back roads is a good strategy to find doe-tending bucks in the open.

In the Missouri River Breaks, near where I live, hunting deer is a hiker's game. I use powerful optics to spot interesting bucks, and then plan an approach that takes me within rifle or bow range. Mountain hunters either find velvet-antlered bucks above treeline in September or wait for deer to follow ancient migration corridors to lower elevations once heavy snow falls.

And in the vast, scorching deserts of the Southwest and Mexico's Sonora, hunters drive sandy roads until they cut a buck's track, then spend hours or even days walking that deer down. Hunters prepare for long shots in the shimmering heat or close-range snap shots when a buck flushes from cover.

CAN YOU CALL MULE DEER?

Whitetail hunters carry a veritable orchestra of noise makers: grunt tubes to challenge mature bucks, bleat cans to mimic the estrous wails of ready does, squeaks to sound like lost fawns. Mule deer hunters, on the other hand, are a relatively laconic lot.

Do mule deer respond to calling? Conventional wisdom says no. Because they inhabit wide-open habitat, muleys rely more on their eyes than their ears to make contact with their herd mates. But that doesn't mean you should never try to call mule deer.

Sometimes a fawn bleat will attract a curious doe, and especially as the rut approaches, a mature buck will follow the doe to your call. And high-pitched predator calls will sometimes prompt a bedded buck to stand up and look around, giving you a shot opportunity that you wouldn't otherwise have.

PUZZLING DECLINES Taken as an entire population, mule deer numbers are on a long, slow downward slide around the West. Some classic big-buck zones, such as the aspen-and-sagebrush ridges that fall away from Yellowstone National Park, have seen sharp declines. In areas with irrigated, succulent agricultural forage, the slumps have been shallower.

There's no consensus on the cause of the declines. A wildlife biologist in Montana once told me that he's documented 50 years of boom-and-bust population dynamics on a roughly 10-year cycle. Within each decade, you can expect a few lean years followed by a population rebound. The thing is, over the last 40 years, the booms have been shallower, and the busts steeper.

Some biologists think our resurgent elk population is to blame, outcompeting muleys in shared habitat. Others suspect a slow change in forage as the West warms. Still others blame the combination of wildfire suppression and energy development. Human development in the foothills of the mountainous West have undoubtedly fractured critical winter range and contributed to mule deer mortality in deep-snow winters.

Whatever the cause, the overall decline has made an ancient, white-muzzled buck an even scarcer trophy for Western deer hunters.

THE ULTIMATE MULEY HUNT

The Holy Grail for many Western hunters is a mule deer that breaks the 200-inch (500-cm) mark. This is a remarkable trophy indeed, combining antler spread that nears or exceeds 30 inches (76 cm), main beams that stretch over 24 inches (60 cm), and cumulative mass measurements of more than 16 inches (41 cm).

Consider that the world's record for a typical mule deer is 226 4/8 inches (575 cm), a Colorado giant killed in 1972, and that the minimum score to qualify for Boone and Crockett Club's all-time records is 190 inches (483 cm). Bucks wearing headgear this impressive need three main things: time to get old, sanctuaries where they can stay hidden, and good forage throughout the year, especially during harsh winters.

So where do these bucks live? Your best bet remains Colorado's Western Slope, but other trophy areas are Saskatchewan, northern Arizona, and southern Utah, where drawing a buck tag in some units is harder than drawing a bighorn sheep tag in most states.

A GREAT (AND CHEAP) MULE DEER RIFLE

Serious mule deer hunters spend thousands on high-end rifles and optics, but sometimes a more modest setup works just as well.

I killed one of my best bucks with one of my cheapest rifles, a USD $400 Ruger American, topped with a Weaver scope and shooting a premium bullet, Federal's Trophy Copper. I chose that rifle specifically because of its repeated precision and its ability to function in cold, snowy, and muddy conditions.

The buck, an ancient loner, had been shot in the jaw and front shoulder weeks earlier, which prevented him from moving much. Even during the rut, he bedded in a huge alfalfa field bordering my property. I couldn't hunt the field, and I think he knew it. For two days, I set up on a snow-covered hump, covered up with insulating blankets, and waited for him to make a mistake.

On the third day, he did. He bedded on the edge of my property, a long 410-yard (410-meter) shot from my hide. I knew I'd have to thread a shot into his vitals as he lay on the sidehill. I consulted my bullet-drop table. With a 200-yard (200-meter) zero, my 180-grain Trophy Copper bullet drops about 24 inches (60 cm). Knowing that a mule deer's ears are about 8 inches (20 cm) long, I factored the amount of holdover my shot required. I killed that starving old buck in his bed with a single well-placed shot, ending the suffering that had started with another hunter's poor shots.

BLACK-TAILED DEER

BLACK-TAILED DEER MAKE PHANTOMS SEEM POSITIVELY OBVIOUS. These rainy forest wraiths are cousins of mule deer, but nothing except their forked antlers resemble their open-country kin. Blacktails crave tangles of grown-over hemlock and cedar and foggy ridges of old-growth fir. The Pacific Northwest's Columbian blacktail roams the Coast and Cascade ranges from central California to British Columbia. The smaller Sitka deer clings to the coast from central British Columbia into Alaska, where it shares habitat with the ferocious brown bear.

When I think of black-tailed deer, I think of banana slugs. Both the shell-less mollusk and the forest deer occupy the same soggy, slant-lighted domain of dripping alders, spongy moss, and stinging nettle and both seem allergic to sunlight and open skies.

Given their preference for tangled cover, blacktails are among the hardest of all deer to hunt, and a trophy blacktail or Sitka deer is one of the great prizes of North American deer hunters.

You will earn every blacktail buck you encounter, with merit measured by the heights of elevation you attain, thickets of brambles you negotiate, and hours of drizzle you endure. Those few hunters who take multiple trophy blacktails typically do it by hunting the edges of recent clear-cuts, where the deer emerge in feeble light to nibble on nutritious shoots and needles of grass.

Optics don't really factor into blacktail hunts, and neither does traversing lots of ground. What matters is being in the right place at the right time, a sensibility that's gained through years of living in blacktail country, noticing subtle patterns, and anticipating the movements and seasonal preferences of these deer.

This is a close-in game, more akin to grouse gunning than deer hunting. Many Northwestern blacktail hunters shoot open-sight pump guns, lever rifles, and short-barreled, quick-pointing bolt guns that won't get hung up in the brush and can be deployed rapidly.

The other critical attribute of blacktail gear is its ability to function when soaking wet. You need a gun that's capable of shooting even after soaking in streaming rain, and outerwear that can repel water while remaining relatively quiet in the brush.

FOREST MANAGEMENT

Traditionally, blacktails thrived in the years following logging activity. Mosaic timbering—rather than clear-cutting—particularly benefitted deer because they fed heavily on brush that grew up in clearings. But some biologists say recent logging practices are detrimental to blacktails, especially the use of herbicides to kill the brush and brambles that can choke out the newly planted trees. Without that brush, deer lose both food and secure cover.

THE CASCADE CREST Evolutionary biologists report that black-tailed deer are the ancestors of both our mule and white-tailed deer, and where their ranges overlap, mule deer will interbreed with blacktails. For those who keep records of big game, that can be problematic, as deer that occupy the hybridization zone might exhibit qualities of either.

The Boone and Crockett Club settles the issue geographically. Generally, deer killed east of the Cascade Crest are defined as mule deer, and those killed west of the divide are considered blacktails. There are exceptions, and undoubtedly many trophy blacktails of central Oregon and California might be considered middling mule deer, just as outsize blacktails killed on the east slopes of the Cascades have been unfairly classified as mule deer.

Still, if you kill a heavy, deeply forked buck west of Interstate 5, you have grounded one of the great trophies of North America, a moss-country deer that required skill, persistence—and good rain gear—to obtain. There are also some anatomical cues to consider:

TAIL A blacktail has a wider tail than a mule deer, and it will be more solidly black, with a white fringe at the bottom and a white underside.

METATARSAL GLANDS A blacktail has smaller glands on the insides of its rear legs than a mule deer does, and those glands are located lower down on the leg.

FACE A black-tailed deer's face is shorter and darker than a mule deer's, and the ears of a blacktail are shorter.

ANTLERS The antlers of a blacktail buck are shorter and more compact than those of a mule deer.

FIRST PERSON: ANDREW MCKEAN

KODIAK ISLAND SITKA

You know Kodiak Island for its monster bears, but your reason for hunting here should be its abundant black-tailed deer. The deer of this rain-lashed, brush-covered island are of the Sitka variety, smaller and somehow even more elusive than the Columbia blacktails of the mainland.

I hunted Kodiak from a boat, a small tender that offered little comfort beyond a berth and a kitchen. But that passes for luxury in these sleety, white-capped waters in October. I motored to shore each morning on inflatable Zodiac rafts and spent soggy days hunting the bear-infested brambles and high ridges of the island.

Hunters have two choices here. They can either stay on shore, to take their pick of does and immature bucks, or they can soldier through an empire of devil's club and vine maple to the upper slopes, where older, roman-nosed bucks chase does during the height of the late-fall rut.

I chose the latter and shot a Sitka buck that just misses the Boone and Crockett Club records. I'll always remember the view from where he fell, patches of sun glinting on the saltwater, the Alaska Range looming. And I'll definitely never forget the return to the boat, dragging 150 pounds (68 kg) of fresh meat through the very gut of bear country.

DUCKS

TO THE CASUAL OBSERVER, duck hunting may seem more misery than recreation. It's too hot when teal season opens and darn frigid by the time the mallards arrive. The duck hunter spends more money on boats, decoys, and nontoxic shot than any mother-in-law would ever approve of—all to lather his pricey accouterments in cold December mud. He hunts in rain the likes of which no self-respecting duck would ever fly in. He sledgehammers holes in iced-up ponds just to position his decoys and wait. All of this, if he's lucky, to shoot the occasional bird.

Ah, but rewards are to be found for such efforts. Any given day in the marsh could result in a brace of mallards, a long-sprigged northern pintail, or even the king of them all: a bull canvasback. It is this diversity of species that so affects duck addicts. Most do not pursue waterfowl for the sheer volume of shooting, though, to be certain, all relish those rare days of duck-filled spectacle. Rather their captivation stems from the rich breadth of North American waterfowl, all of them uniquely interesting and beautiful.

There are the dabbling or "puddle duck" species, which in North America include the mallard, American black duck, wood duck, American wigeon, gadwall, northern shoveler, three kinds of teal, and more. There is much habitat variation, from the tree-cavity nesting, acorn-feasting wood duck to the wigeon, which nests on the ground and has a gooselike affinity for meadow grasses. But all share a commonality: an act known as "dabbling," which involves tipping their tails up to feed on aquatic plants and invertebrates just below the water's surface. Unlike diving species, their large wing-to-body ratios facilitate springing rapidly from water to flight—an ability that has spared many from the fowling piece.

That is not to say divers lack athleticism, as any hunter who's tried to match his shotgun swing to the speed of rocketing scaup well knows. However, their wings are proportionally smaller and their feet set farther back on their bodies—these are ducks built to dive deep for food. North American species include the canvasback, greater and lesser scaup, redhead, common and Barrow's goldeneyes, ring-necked duck, ruddy duck, and assorted mergansers, among others.

THE CHALLENGE OF MALLARDS

Hunters who bag but one duck after a long day on the water may return home plenty happy—assuming that duck is a mallard.

The mallard is a lovely bird, with an iridescent green head, chestnut breast, and brilliant blue speculum that must be examined in the hands to fully appreciate.

However, its trophy status owes more to its distinction as perhaps the most challenging species. Neither shovelers nor teal nor gadwalls possess its discerning eye for the tiniest glint of gun metal or out-of-place decoy.

Hunters who consistently bag mallards are doing something very right, as these birds aren't lucked into with regularity. It is our great fortune that mallards are also the world's most widespread, numerous duck. Otherwise, their inclusion in a duck strap would be a rare event indeed.

Duck-hunting strategies are as varied as the birds themselves, from jump-shooting ponds to floating creeks to—by far the most exciting—gunning over decoys. The basic puddle duck spread consists of at least a dozen decoys arranged over water in a loose U-shape. The curve is directed into the wind, providing a landing zone as ducks pitch in against the breeze. Include decoys you expect to target, but err on the side of mallards. The drakes' heads act as big green beacons to passing flocks, and, most importantly, all puddle ducks decoy to mallards.

Ducks known to dry-feed, especially mallards and pintails, can also be targeted in rice, corn, and other agricultural fields. Spreads generally consist of full-body or silhouette mallards and geese. Even if honkers aren't in season, their black-on-white contrast affords great visibility, and hungry ducks know that finding geese means finding food. The setup is best whenever ducks are starved for carbohydrates, such as during sudden, bitter cold.

Diver spreads tend to be larger—2–3 dozen decoys, minimum—simply because divers raft in substantial numbers. Ideally the spread is positioned over a sandbar, oyster bed, or other active food source. Whereas dabbler decoys are usually individually rigged, divers are often arranged using long-lines, in which a dozen or more decoys are strung across a single cord

CANVASBACK: KING OF THE DUCKS

No waterfowl species is spoken of in hushed tones in quite the same way that canvasbacks are. Rich in lore and history, canvasbacks were the most prized birds of the market-gunning era.

So tasty is a roasted canvasback that, until the early 20th century, fancy restaurants in major United States cities served them—for an expensive price. The consequences were disastrous. Canvasbacks were highly overgunned, and the destruction of their favorite food, wild celery, proved a double whammy.

The population never fully recovered, and for much of the '90s and '00s the season was closed. A new age of optimism is upon us, however, as rebounding canvasbacks—fueled by consecutive wet springs—have resulted in a nationwide limit of at least two birds daily.

It is a joyous hope that a new generation will now experience the rush of hunting North America's largest, fastest, and perhaps most beautiful duck. For me, it is the only bird that provides a sense of having shot big game.

anchored at each end. This hastens setup and saves cord when hunting deep, diver-friendly waters. Single decoys are pitched alongside the long-lines for a natural, nonlinear look. For an easy, effective spread, try a decoy-filled triangle with the nose facing into the current. If there's no current, face the nose into the wind. Divers naturally feed in this manner and, well, it really works.

No matter your target, you may become a naturalist of sorts. Learning about and observing never-before-seen species are thrills all their own. So why shoot them? In short, it is a hunter's paradox of the truest kind: The waterfowler hunts ducks because he loves them. —K. W.

CHOKES AND LOADS

Arguments over duck loads tend to center on pellet size, primarily whether No. 2 or 4 shot is the superior choice. It's a little more complicated than that, however, given the varied duck-hunting scenarios. Here are a few basic considerations.

For most hunts, the author's choice is a 12-gauge, 1¼ ounce load of No. 2 shot with modified choke. It provides enough oomph for reasonable pass shooting, yet patterns nicely on decoying ducks at 20–40 yards (or meters).

However, creeks, ponds, and sloughs tend to offer in-your-face action, so a 12-gauge load of No. 4 steel is the author's preference. No. 4's are plenty lethal at 25–30 yards (or meters)—why reduce pattern density by selecting larger pellets? Tight chokes are also, if anything, a handicap at close range. Consider improved cylinder for small waters.

The only time a larger shot size may be in order would be gunning decoy-shy canvasbacks. I recently found that B or even BB shot can add great lethality at 40–45 yards (or meters). And, given the large size of canvasbacks, the shooter can get away with fewer pellets.

THREE DUCK CALLS TO MASTER

There are truly only three essential duck sounds to master: The basic quack, greeting, and comeback calls. The quack should be learned first, as the others are derivatives of it. It's essentially achieved by saying "ten" or "qua-CK" into the call. Note that you must actually "talk" into the call from your diaphragm; simply blowing air over the reeds results in nothing more than kazoolike notes. Use quacks to keep the ducks' attention as they circle, coaxing them in.

The greeting call is employed when ducks are initially spotted and their attention is sought. It's a smooth series of 5–7 quacks, each descending in length: "*Quaaaaack quaaaaack quaaack quack quack.*"

If the greeting call doesn't elicit a response, or the birds circle and begin to leave, try a comeback. It's similar to the greeting, but the 5–7 notes make up a faster, more urgent plea.

Instructional recordings can help you perfect these calls and others, but there's no substitute for studying a performance by actual hens. Even listening carefully to those at a city park can improve your craft.

THE BEST DUCK HUNT IN AMERICA

How you define America's "best" duck hunt depends largely on personal taste. Arkansas is many hunters' default answer, as it's rich in duck-call history and offers uniquely thrilling, flooded-timber mallard hunts. Others propose the Texas Gulf, a major wintering area for scaup and redheads. Those who yet disagree may suggest the potholes of the Dakotas or Montana, an increasingly good opportunity for wigeon, gadwalls, mallards, and divers staging for migration. There's even Alaska, which offers hunts for goldeneyes and harlequins on lakes nestled among coniferous forests.

I've been fortunate to hunt some of these destinations, and yet I find no greater thrill than hunting my home state of Pennsylvania. No, it's no duck paradise, and the Atlantic Flyway is easily the poorest for dabblers. But that's part of the fun. While I'm happy to return home with a duck in each hand, on those days when I beat the odds—such as when four friends and I shot 20 mallards on a central Pennsylvania creek—well, a more satisfying hunt does not exist. With proper perspective, no matter where you're located, the "best" duck hunt may be found in your backyard.

PRONGHORN ANTELOPE

SWIFT AS THE PRAIRIE WIND and handsome as a June afternoon, pronghorn antelope are marvelous creatures. The only member of a family of ungulates that occupies the evolutionary territory between African antelope and European wild goats, a black-faced pronghorn buck is the goal of many a first-time Western hunter. You can't encounter these "speed goats" and not be impressed by their prodigious eyesight, kinetic velocity, marathoner's stamina, or ability to live off the continent's most expansive land: the wide, windy, desolate Great Plains.

For several years in a row, I have hunted the same million acres of Wyoming sagebrush for antelope. My friend Mark and I start at sunup, each toting a rifle and a frame pack. It is an unusual day when we don't walk at least 10 miles (16 km) and bring back antelope meat to our simple campsite under a lone, stunted cottonwood.

This is the gift of pronghorns, and the reward of hunting them. Compared to elk or even deer tags, antelope licenses are relatively inexpensive and easy to draw. In some states, such as Wyoming, you can often buy doe/fawn tags over the counter even after the season starts. Hunter success rates are satisfyingly high, and the weather in September and October is usually fair enough to make camping on the open plains both comfortable and an effective hunting strategy.

What's more, antelope occupy mainly public land—huge blocks of empty sage and cheatgrass administered by the Bureau of Land Management. Because they are herding animals, where you see one, you're like to spot dozens—or even hundreds—of the tan-and-white animals. And for selective hunters like Mark and me, it's great to belly-crawl in on a herd and pick out the best buck. If it's not one we want to shoot, we back out without ever alarming the hair-wire animals and stride off to find another herd.

Too many hunters describe antelope as "speed mutton" for their gamy taste. But those hunters ran the pronghorns down, then allowed the carcass to bake under the broiling sun. If you kill a buck that isn't shot-through with adrenaline, keep the carcass cool, and get the waxy hair off, you'll find the real trophy of an antelope is its sweet, tender meat—there is no more finely flavored wild flesh.

HOW TO FLAG AN ANTELOPE

For a short window in the fall—late September through mid-October—you can kill a pronghorn with a handkerchief.

This practice appeals to their curiosity, territoriality, and herd dominance. Just wave the fabric until you get his attention, then lower your flag, and periodically raise and lower it to keep him interested and coming toward you. I have my best luck tying a hanky (or white T-shirt) to the barrel of my gun and raising the muzzle; I can get the buck's attention without showing myself.

Many hunters prepare for an antelope safari by working up a long-distance rifle load. Favorite calibers tend toward the light side: .243 Win., .25/06 Rem., .260 Rem. But pronghorns can be effectively killed with well-constructed bullets from a .223 or with lighter bullets from magnum rounds in the 7mm and .30-caliber families.

Besides a rifle capable of long-range precision, you need good optics and bullets with high ballistic coefficients that are relatively unaffected by the nudges of the relentless prairie wind.

The great challenge of pronghorn hunters, however, is not making long-range shots but seeing how close you can get to the wary animals. Use terrain features—dry streambeds, heavy sage stands, and even the rolling hills of the prairie itself—to hide your approach, and then belly-crawl the last few yards until you can set up for a shot. I wear volleyballers' kneepads and heavy leather gloves for this ambush, since cactus and sharp rocks are abundant.

You can also effectively bowhunt pronghorns. Most archery seasons begin in early September and coincide with the antelope rut. During this window, bucks are abnormally curious but also highly territorial, so decoys imitating young bucks can be especially effective. Hunters typically work in pairs, with one holding a decoy in sight of a lone buck, moving or flashing the decoy up and down while the shooter prepares to make a snap shot at the incoming animal.

One of the biggest challenges of bowhunting antelope is quickly and accurately estimating range. On the prairie, you don't have trees, bushes, or fenceposts for reference, and most archers tend to shoot over antelope, thinking that the small-framed animals are farther away than they actually are.

FIELD JUDGE A PRONGHORN

Pronghorn bucks can be notoriously hard to judge in the field. Horn length, mass, and depth of the prong—or the triangle that juts off the horn about halfway up its length—all contribute to what constitutes a trophy buck.

[A] LENGTH Horns that reach 16 inches (40 cm) in total length are the threshold for trophy status. A buck's ears measure just under 6 inches (15 cm) in length. Determine where the tip of the ear meets the horn and then visually double that length. If the rest of the horn exceeds that 12-inch (30-cm) mark, pay attention, especially if the horn curves deeply.

[B] MASS You want to find a buck whose horn bases are at least as massive as the circumference of his ear. And you should make sure that mass is sustained up the horn, well past the prong.

[C] PRONG A buck whose prong, or cutter, juts forward or sideways at least twice the width of the horn is a trophy, especially if you detect cupping of the prong. The cutter should project from the horn at least above the height of the ear, and remember: the higher the prong, the better scoring the buck.

FOUR PRONGHORN CURIOSITIES

BEHAVIOR IN WIND When the wind kicks up on the plains, antelope become especially skittish. That's probably because the relentless wind dries out their eyes, impairing their prodigious sight. If you can wait for the wind to die down, you can expect antelope to become slightly calmer, if no less eagle-eyed.

HORNS VS ANTLERS Antelope have neither permanent horns nor annually shed antlers. Instead, they have something in between: a hard sheath made of hair that sheds each fall and a permanent blood-filled core that sprouts the new horn each spring.

SIGNAL HAIR Pronghorns have specialized hair on their rumps that flares when they sense danger. This white hair can shine like a tin pan, and the flash signals to other members of the herd that danger is nigh.

SENSING A LINK While pronghorns are apparently unrelated to the true antelope of Africa, one curiosity links them. The hollow hair of freshly killed American pronghorns and the common springbuck of southern Africa smell almost the same: exactly like sweet, dry corn husks.

BLACK BEARS

FROM NEW JERSEY'S SUBURBS TO THE CASCADE MOUNTAINS ABOVE PORTLAND, black bears shuffle about, making a good—and for the most part, quiet—living. With the dietary preferences of a Labrador retriever and the survival instincts of a whitetail, *Ursus americanus* occupies nearly every habitat niche in North America, and styles of hunting vary as much as black bears' range: hunt in spring or fall, walk down or use a stand, bait or chase with hounds. They may not have the headgear of our antlered ungulates, but black bears are very game, indeed.

Next to whitetails, black bear may be the most actively pursued big game in North America. In Alaska and the Pacific Northwest, black bears grow fat on a diet of berries and fish. Along the spine of the Rockies, they gorge on yarrow roots and elk calves. They range all across the Great Lakes country and north toward Hudson Bay. And in Pennsylvania, some of the continent's largest bears are pursued by parties of hunters who post shooters and push brush with the precision of field marshals and the collective intensity of grand juries.

Black bears roam from New England south to Florida and across the Southeast. Bears are returning to their native habitats in the Ozark Mountains and the piny ridges of the Great Plains. But wherever they live, black bears prefer dense timber, a variety of food available from spring through late fall, and enough room to allow them to avoid their main persecutors: humans.

If bears are our most opportunistic foragers, we are their most relentless predators. We tend to think the worst of a bear. It's going to break into our home. It's going to kill our livestock. It's going to eat our dog's food. It's going to maul our children. Yes, black bears will do all those things, but it's the rogue specimen that intrudes on our settled world. Most black bears exist on our periphery without causing a spectacle or a problem.

But when we enter their world as hunters, our antipathy toward bears turns to something approaching admiration. How can they grow to such remarkable dimensions—a bear killed in New Jersey weighed 829 pounds (376 kg)—and live on such a varied diet as acorns and roadkill, wild mushrooms and whitetail fawns?

COLOR PHASES: THE NOT-SO-BLACK BEAR

Though its name suggests otherwise, color is the least reliable identifier of a black bear. *Ursus americanus* comes in browns, blonds, reds, and chocolates. Because they are often hunted for the quality of their hide, a color-phase bear is a trophy, indeed.

In one camp I hunted in Alberta, half the bears killed were as chocolate as candy bars. The prettiest black bear I've killed is a blonde with white highlights that looked like a silvertip grizzly as it sluiced through the spring woods of Saskatchewan.

Color is a hard attribute to predict or sustain in a population, but generally, you'll find more colorful bears inland and in southern latitudes than along the coasts. That may be because in the warmer, more open habitats of the West, black hair may make bears more susceptible to heat stress than their lighter-colored kin.

It's an unusual bear hunter who doesn't at some point make a connection between ourselves and our prey and pursue them with a mixture of fear and curiosity.

Many states and provinces offer spring bear seasons, and hunters who frequent food sources find bruins hungry from hibernation. In the West, hunters drive forest roads, where greening clover attracts bears, or glass south-facing avalanche chutes to find black bears gleaning the first succulent growth of spring. But if you are interested in better quality hair and meat, fall's the better time to hunt, as bears are foraging widely in front of their winter-long slumber.

To stalk a bear is to employ every hunting skill you possess. You must play the wind, as black bears have prodigiously sharp noses. You must walk silently, as their triangular ears are keen and stereophonic. You may fool a bear's myopic sight, but if its other senses detect your approach, you won't get close to these remarkably adaptable, hardy, and savvy animals.

THE ETHICS OF BAITING

To bait or not to bait? That is the question that many black bear hunters ask themselves at least once in their careers. More than half the jurisdictions that allow black bear hunting also allow hunters to set out baits that lure bears into specific spots. Is that sporting? Is it ethical?

The answer, like most matters of ethics, is situational. In many areas where baiting is legal, the habitat is dense, boggy, and largely inaccessible. Baiting may be the only consistent way to reliably see bears, especially later in the spring—when leaves and underbrush obscure much of the forest.

On the other hand, many hunters feel that using bait is an inappropriate crutch that habituates bears and makes them dependent on the handouts of humans whose only interest is in killing them. These hunters prefer to pursue bears in their unaltered habitat, either by tracking them in tight cover or by glassing them as they move across the vast landscape of their home.

This latter method is my favorite, and in my home state of Montana where baiting is prohibited, glassing high-country meadows and avalanche chutes can be effective for mobile hunters. But I see the value in baiting bears. Fundamentally, baiting ensures both positive identification—reducing the chance that a hunter will kill a sow with cubs or a young bear—and a quick, killing shot, since encounters are at close range.

HOW TO JUDGE A BLACK BEAR

Because they don't have distinctive antlers or other obviously measurable attributes, black bears can be among the hardest big game to judge in the field. Add long, dark-colored hair and their habit of hanging around densely foliaged, shadowed habitat, and you can understand why "I thought it was bigger" is one of the most frequent refrains of successful bear hunters as they approach their trophy.

Here are five elements to consider as you size up your next black bear.

IDENTITY First, are you sure it's a black bear and not a grizzly? In areas where their range overlaps, know how to distinguish the species. Grizzlies often have shoulder humps, concave faces, long claws, and tend to be larger than black bears. Hair color is the least reliable way to identify a bear. Once you've positively identified the bear, ensure that it does not have cubs—either roly-poly yearlings or larger, blockier two-year-olds.

CONTEXT Is the bear in the very midst of prime forage? The center of the berry patch or the best fish-catching riffle in the river? That's probably a dominant boar. Black bears that lurk on the periphery likely are juvenile or smaller specimens.

ATTITUDE Does the bear walk with a swagger? Does it seem to own the meadow and intimidate other bears? He's probably an older, bigger male. But if it shies away from its fellows, or acts nervous and edgy, it's probably a young, submissive bear.

SCALE One of the arguments for baiting is that hunters can compare the size of a bear to known items, such as the large drums that are often used to distribute bait. But bears can also be judged relative to each other. The bear most frequently misjudged is the solo bear.

ANATOMICAL FEATURES Lastly, judge a bear's ear size, the length of its legs, and how saggy its belly appears. The ears of large, old boars tend to look small and jut from the sides of his head while a younger bear has pointed ears that appear close together. An older bear looks like he has short, squat legs, because his body is so muscular. And a bear whose belly sags close to the ground is probably an older, well-fed boar.

TEMPERATE SPECIES

40° NORTH – 30° NORTH

40° NORTH – 30° NORTH

THE SETTING SUN WAS IN MY EYES, WHICH MIGHT EXPLAIN WHY I THOUGHT someone was carrying a stepladder over their heads, striding quickly through the oak forest of eastern Bulgaria. Why a worker would be in this remote patch of hardwoods at sunset didn't occur to me at first, but neither did the reality, which came into sharper focus as the object approached through the obscuring trees.

You can probably guess that I had not, in fact, spotted a rustic craftsman. It was a red stag, and what I thought was a ladder was the most impressive set of antlers I'd ever seen. Heavy. Wide. Long tines and crowns of points flashing in the last of the sun as this lord of the forest looked over his shoulder at the sound of baying dogs.

I stood statue-still against an ancient oak, but I must have gasped, because the stag spun his remarkable head my way and then vanished. The only evidence that he had been there was a faint trail of disturbed leaves—and his image burned permanently on my retinas.

I didn't have long to consider his departure, because another movement soon caught my eye. It was a sounder of bristle-haired boars, six or seven trotting like little pony kegs through the leaf litter, with brindled hounds hot on their trail. The pigs were too small, and the dogs too close, for me to shoot, so I watched them pass by into the darkening evening.

This is the essence of hunting the best European game areas: the surprising abundance of species and diverse opportunities to take them. And the ability to hunt them in this traditional manner, with keen-nosed dogs pushing through brush and timber, elevates driven hunting to an electrifyingly kinetic experience.

You simply never know when an animal will pop into range and, when it does, it's almost always moving fast, giving you scant seconds to identify it, swing your rifle, and place a killing shot. This is the land of centuries-old hunting traditions but also quick-shouldering, quick-shooting semiautomatic rifles, a region of ancient castles and modern hunting lodges, and a place where a jaeger's horn might date from 1200 AD—while his jacket features space-age fabrics.

Europe doesn't own this variety of game or hunting opportunities. The temperate zone, which we roughly define as stretching between Scandinavia and Pakistan, or Saskatchewan and Alabama, is among the most biologically rich on the planet. The climate is generally favorable, the terrain and habitat are diverse, and the game animals—from hares to bison—are scaled to the habitat. This is the land of the oak tree and the cornfield, the Black Forest and the Central Asian Plateau. And it's not just mammals that thrive here. The bird life in this zone is equally diverse. Whether you're discussing the grouse family or the dozens of species of ducks to be found, it's no wonder that the world's great shotgun manufacturers—from the Berettas to the Brownings—hail from these latitudes.

So, too, do the world's great hunting traditions. Not only in the Old World beats such as Bavaria, Scotland, and Spain's Basque region, but also in Mongolia's Gobi Desert, the elk lodges of the Rockies, and the sheep camps in the headwaters of the Black Sea.

Not to mention the forests of Bulgaria's Black Sea region, where I hunted for that one indelible stag, with a rack like an incandescent stepladder.

CRANES AND SWANS

FROM THE PERSPECTIVE OF A BIOLOGIST, tundra swans and sandhill cranes have very little in common—aside from their hefty wingspans, that is. To the hunter, however, there is a great deal of similarity, as they each make for a challenging trophy. Few states have sandhill crane seasons and swan hunting is an even rarer opportunity; the birds' vision, wariness, and intelligence are well documented; and, as North America's largest waterfowl, more than a glancing shot is required to bring them down to earth.

Starting with the arrival of European settlers and lasting until the 1916 Migratory Bird Treaty Act, cranes faced severe wetland drainage and were overshot for their delectable meat. By 1936, only 25 breeding pairs existed in Wisconsin, plus a few in the other Great Lakes states. Tundra swans were likewise shot in huge numbers for their meat and feathers but fared better than their cousin, the trumpeter swan. Trumpeters nest in the northern United States—far south of the tundra's arctic breeding grounds—which allowed year-round decimation, the lasting effects of which endure a century later.

But cranes and swans proved to be a resilient lot, once afforded conservation. Individual sandhills now number 400,000 to 600,000, making them the world's most populous crane. Tundra populations, meanwhile, have at least doubled since the 1960s.

Sandhill hunting resumed in 1961 when New Mexico, Texas, and Alaska added 30-day seasons to their calendars. It's since become a fixture of the Central Flyway: North Dakota, South Dakota, Oklahoma, Colorado, Kansas, Wyoming, and Montana all have seasons, as does Arizona. Several Mississippi Flyway states have also added crane seasons, including Minnesota, Kentucky, and Tennessee. Cranes are also hunted in Mexico, Manitoba, and Saskatchewan.

Tundra swan seasons remain rare and require special permits. The strict rules are largely intended to protect other swans (such as trumpeters) from misidentification. Utah, Montana, and Nevada have held seasons for more than 35 years, and permits for many areas are sold over the counter. Only North Carolina (5,000 permits) and Virginia (600 permits) offer swan hunting in the east. —*K.W.*

DECOY AND CALL

If you know how to arrange a goose spread, you can set a crane spread. Six to 10 dozen cranes positioned in small family groups as dictated by the wind can work well, as can 2–4 dozen on the downwind side of a goose spread. Geese provide visibility and confidence to cranes, and the seasons often overlap. Crane decoys are expensive; windsock-style dekes are most affordable and quite effective. Scout for cranes feeding on wheat, corn, and other waste grains, ideally with a marshy area nearby.

Swans are increasingly found in agricultural areas, but many prefer to hunt their traditional aquatic habitats. In pothole-rich regions, a careful spot-and-stalk can provide excellent jump shooting. In the east, full-body decoys are more often employed, generally as a half dozen at the edge of a duck or goose spread. Swans respond surprisingly well to loud "woops" and other vocal chord–only calls.

BISON

THE WORST THING THAT HAS HAPPENED TO AMERICAN BISON since their systematic decimation more than a century ago is that they have been reduced to mascots. Bison are emblems: an ascendant empire (the Buffalo Head Nickel), the promise of abundance (the U.S. Department of the Interior), and nostalgia for a closed frontier (Montana's license plate). Lost in the iconography is the fact that bison, once the most populous bovines, are slowly returning to their original range. And a lucky few hunters have the opportunity to pursue them as our ancestors did.

It's hard to understate how important bison were to Americans of the 19th century. In terms of sheer biomass, it's been estimated that 5 billion pounds (2.3 billion kg) of them roamed the continent at the time of the American Civil War. Bison populations were concentrated mainly on the tall- and short-grass prairies between the Mississippi River and the Rocky Mountains. Subspecies of the curve-horned mammal occupied the oak forests and river valleys of the Ohio River, and a larger specimen, the wood bison, made a living in the stunted birch forests of northern Canada. But it was the plains bison that fed, clothed, and defined an entire culture of Native Americans.

Indians hunted bison any way they could. They used rock cairns to funnel stampeding herds over cliffs, where butchering parties hacked their way through the shattered windfall. They ambushed them with spears and drove them into blind canyons. And, once they acquired horses, Plains Indians moved with the herds and hunted from the bare backs of sprinting steeds, burying arrow after arrow into the woolly flanks of heaving bison. They learned, as does anyone who sets out to hunt a buffalo, that even with perfect shot placement and sufficient ballistic energy, barrel-chested bulls take a lot of killing.

The removal of bison from North America, to starve warring tribes and to make way for European settlement, is one of the darkest stories of wildlife mismanagement. But the reason we can discuss the species in the present tense today is that a handful of foresightful conservationists, Teddy Roosevelt among them, intervened, and provided protection for a remnant population inside Yellowstone National Park and in various other conservation herds.

BUFFALO OR BISON

We tend to use the terms *buffalo* and *bison* interchangeably, but if you're talking about American bovine of the wide-open West, *bison* is the correct noun.

Shaggy grazers were tagged as buffalo by early settlers who confused them with the oxlike Old World buffalo. But our bison are a distinct species, more closely related to the forest-dwelling European bison than the Cape buffalo of sub-Saharan Africa and water buffalo of Southeast Asia.

Unfortunately for those of us who cherish wildness in our wildlife, a number of other bison were interbred with domestic cattle, and the alternative livestock industry has given hunters the most reliable exposure to these woolly mammoths. A couple years ago, as the bottom dropped out of the volatile bison-meat market, ranchers sold off their brood stock, and for a few hundred dollars, latter-day frontiersmen could walk into a corral and shoot a dull-eyed buffalo.

Opportunities are increasing to hunt free-ranging bison as our ancestors did, and the next generation of American hunters may get the chance to experience buffalo at their resurgent best—as the wide-ranging, stampede-prone occupants of our most expansive lands. An ambitious effort is currently underway to reintroduce wild bison to the prairies of eastern Montana. They might be established on public lands, or large conservation herds might roam private lands.

ANATOMY OF A BUFFALO RIFLE

In order to find favor with the bands of self-promoters, felons, Army deserters, and adventure addicts who collectively encompassed the vast majority of buffalo hunters, a rifle had to have three qualities. It had to be dependable in all kinds of weather and conditions. It had to be accurate at long range. And it had to be of sufficient caliber to take the wind out of 1,500-pound (680-kg) bulls.

A few rifles of the brief golden age of buffalo had those attributes. They included the Remington Rolling Block chambered in .50-70 and later .45-70; the "trapdoor" Springfield chambered mainly in .45-70-405; and the famous Sharps Rifle, favored by market hunters for range and accuracy.

Modern bison rifles share their

predecessors' attributes, but modern bullets allow hunters to size down their bore and increase downrange performance. Good choices are the .338 Win. Mag, the .30-378 Weatherby Magnum, and the .300 Win. Mag. with premium bullets, like the Barnes TSX or Federal's Trophy Copper projectile.

BUFFALO TODAY

We'll never see the sprawling herds of bison that defined the wild West, but a few modern opportunities to hunt the wild ancestors of this iconic American original do exist.

YELLOWSTONE PARK Both Montana and Wyoming offer limited permits to hunt the wild bison that roam outside the park's boundaries in winter.

HENRY MOUNTAINS This range in Utah boasts a bison herd of about 350, and the Division of Wildlife Resources issues a few dozen coveted permits per year.

CUSTER STATE PARK A handful of trophy bull (10+ years old) and cow permits are offered through lottery in South Dakota.

INDIAN RESERVATIONS In Montana, the Blackfeet, Crow, Fort Peck, and Fort Belknap reservations offer hunts, and others are offered in Oklahoma, South Dakota, and Utah. Check with the Intertribal Buffalo Council for details.

WOOD BISON One of the best hunting opportunities is for free-ranging wood bison in northern Alberta.

MOUNTAIN LION

NOW THAT WE HAVE FAR-SHOOTING RIFLES, AND AUTOMOBILES, and tractors capable of tilling a township in a day, we don't need mountain lions quite like we used to. Before we became such efficient killers and manipulators of deer and their habitat, the only real thing keeping deer numbers in check with their food supply was the mountain lion. Slowly, lions are repatriating their original range, which includes every region occupied by deer. Whether we will be able to live with predatory cats is a moot point: we already do, though few people ever see them.

The closest I've come to a mountain lion—besides the one that my elk-hunting buddy and I discovered high in a ponderosa pine in northern Utah, its cold yellow eyes staring holes in us until we walked away, nervously looking over our shoulders, arrows nocked on our bowstrings—was while hunting whitetails in ankle-deep snow.

I wasn't far from Seeley Lake, Montana, and I was tracking a good buck. As I followed his splay-hooved trail through fir stands and around slash piles, I cut smoking-fresh lion tracks on the path of the same deer. So I joined the parade, my eyes sharpened by the forensic drama that pulled me deeper into the woods. Soon I noticed the lion's tracks peeling off to the right. I was determined to find this deer, so I kept tracking the buck.

Then something made me turn around, and there he was, an unblinking gray shadow frozen in mid stride, about a house-length behind me. Before I could get my rifle to my shoulder, the lion was gone, leaving me trembling and absolutely forgetful of that big buck.

That's the nature of lions. They are the most elemental of our predators: stealthy, patient, silent, and quietly terrifying. They are not barking, howling, charging canines. Instead, imagine a housecat, 40 times larger, without the cuddle. Cougars are ambush predators, preferring to wait in cover for their meal to walk past, preferably in the night, or to slink after it on big, soft, clawed feet.

Weighing about the same as a mature deer—anywhere from 120 to 170 pounds (54 to 77 kg)—mountain lions have powerful shoulders and forearms. They prefer to pounce on a prey species, snap the neck, and then drag the carcass into cover to devour it.

DO MOUNTAIN LIONS SCREAM?

It's one of the staples of Old West novels, of fur-trappers' journals, and of Hollywood: the "blood-curdling," "womanlike," "hair-raising" screams of a mountain lion.

Really? I've spent a lifetime in the mountains and woods of the West, and I've never heard any scream of the kind come from a cougar. Neither have any of the biologists I've worked with or the hardcore mountain lion hunters I've talked to.

I'm not saying that lions never make noises. They growl and chirp, and their kittens purr. But it's out of character for an elusive, secretive predator to suddenly emit high-pitched screams that call attention to itself and scare away prey.

Maybe females occasionally do it to attract a breeding partner, but until I hear one with my own ears, I remain dubious, and suspect the screaming is more poetic license than reality.

Mountain lions are sprinters and climbers, but they are not built for endurance, which is why an earnest pack of hounds can soon tree even the cagiest lion.

Mountain lions—you may also call him puma, cougar, panther, catamount, painter, or, in the Southwest, *el leon*—were the most widespread mammal in prehistoric North America, and they ranged through Central America and the length of South America. Over the last century of settlement, the strongholds of lions have been in the wild mountain country of the American West, Pacific Northwest, and Southwest.

But even in areas with high lion densities, they are scarce. That makes even a fleeting glimpse of these elusive felines one of the great experiences of an outdoorsman's life.

Luckily for those who like wildness in their neighborhoods, sightings are becoming more frequent in places that haven't seen a lion since America was a collection of colonies. In 2011 a juvenile male cougar was hit by a car just north of New York City, and confirmed sightings have come from Iowa, Illinois, Maine, and New Hampshire.

Many of these sightings are probably young males, roaming widely in search of mates and suitable habitat. They are not, as some rural mythologists insist, planted by game wardens and insurance companies to control deer populations.

If you see a cat, make yourself look as large as possible, grab a stick or a gun, and aggressively approach the lion. Cougars are almost never confrontational, and if given an escape route, they will take it. Once the cat is safely gone, you may cherish the rare experience of an encounter with one of the wildest animals of North America.

ON THE PROWL FAR FROM HOME

In 2011 a mountain lion was hit by a car just outside Milford, Connecticut. DNA extracted from the carcass indicated that the cat was native to the Black Hills of South Dakota, some 1,500 miles (2,414 km) west.

Lions that have been killed across the Ohio and Mississippi river valleys have been traced to the same geographic area. A study of 24 cougars captured in the Black Hills and fitted with radio collars indicated that juvenile males disperse widely, presumably to find available mates. One male walked 663 miles (1,067 km) to Oklahoma, and on average juvenile males dispersed 280 miles (450 km) from the capture site. Juvenile females in the study, on the other hand, traveled an average of only 30 miles (48 km).

The results indicate that the Black Hills, which feature a relatively abundant population of cougars, is an important incubator for satellite populations of lions that may become established in the Midwest.

HUNTING WITH HOUNDS

Every year in my home state of Montana, I hear about some deer or elk hunter who blunders into a cougar in broad daylight, makes a snap shot, and comes home with a new rug and a tale for the ages. But it's hard to anticipate that kind of luck. If you're serious about killing a mountain lion, you need to employ their most ancient adversary: dogs.

Consistently successful mountain lion hunters drive remote roads at night just after a light snow, logging quite a trek in hopes of finding a fresh cougar track. When they do, they assess the direction of travel and then unleash their hounds. These dogs aren't so different from the Andalusian scenthounds that Spanish settlers brought to Mexico in the 1600s, or from the Walkers and blueticks that American coon hunters have used since about that same time. These are boisterous athletes, capable of pursuing a hot lion track for miles of deep snow, and likely to bellow and bark about it with every eager stride.

The idea is that the hounds will follow a hot trail to its end, which is usually the base of a large tree, the lion looking down from the branches above.

When the hunter arrives (no easy or quick thing when the snow is deep and the terrain is steep, as it almost always is in lion country), it's a simple task to determine the age and sex of the cat and then make a well-placed head shot with a small-caliber rifle, handgun, or even bow.

But as any veteran lion hunter will tell you, the killing is anticlimactic. The thrill of the hunt is in the chase of the hounds, and the song of their enthusiastic baying in the mountain morning.

DEER OF THE WORLD

HUNTERS HAVE BEEN FASCINATED, FRUSTRATED, AND BEFUDDLED by deer since our ancestors sharpened their first spears and tried to stick one. In almost every culture and on nearly every continent since then, we've pursued a dizzying variety of cervids (as the deer family is known to science). Because they provide more meat than a rabbit, deer have long been high on our grocery list. From Scandinavian reindeer and Virginia whitetails to tiny brocket deer of the Yucatan and the sambar of India, cervids are as ubiquitous as they are delicious.

To discuss all the species of cervids across the globe would occupy an entire book. Many are obscure, scores are classified as endangered, and the dozens that are important to hunters are further divided into subspecies, hybrids, and geographic variations. Consider the common North American white-tailed deer. Many zoologists classify the species into as many as 40 subspecies, from the rangy Dakota whitetail of the Great Plains to the diminutive Florida Keys deer.

A better way to distill the members of Cervidae into logical—or at least recognizable—units is to divide them by antler size and type. Deer generally conform to Bergmann's Rule: the farther away from the equator an animal lives, the larger the body (and headgear).

So, what makes an animal a deer? How in the world can an immense moose and a tiny brocket deer share a family tree, if not a literal one? First off, all deer are ruminants, meaning they have a four-chambered stomach. This allows them to feed intensively when conditions warrant, and then retreat to a safe spot, regurgitate their roughly digested forage, and spend time chewing cud. Also, they're browsers, meaning they feed primarily on leaves and shrubs. Then there are the antlers. Nearly all deer sprout antlers in the spring and shed them early in the winter.

Consider the family tree, starting in the northern branches with the (immense-antlered) reindeer and caribou (opposite, bottom), moving south to moose, then wapiti and its close cousin, the European red deer, which has defined big game in the Old World and, through translocations, in Argentina and New Zealand. Other temperate species include the mule, black-tailed, and white-tailed deer, and the paddle-antlered fallow deer along with the shy roebuck of Europe.

JAPANESE DEER ON THE CHESAPEAKE

You don't have to travel to Japan to hunt the spotted sika deer of eastern Asia. You can find them in a most unlikely place: the eastern shore of the Chesapeake Bay in Maryland, where descendants of sikas released on large estates early in the last century exist in huntable numbers.

Maryland awards sika permits by lottery, and hunters who draw one learn quickly that chasing these diminutive cervids is far different from hunting the Old Line State's native whitetails. Sika, sometimes called "mini elk" for their tall, branching antlers, are primarily nocturnal, and often swim to densely vegetated islands to spend the day, meaning that chest waders are a critical part of a sika hunter's arsenal. But during the fall rut, when the stags bark and the hinds whistle in response, calling can be an effective hunting tactic.

In Asia, the family includes the rare white-lipped deer of the Tibetan Plateau, the spotted sika deer (opposite, bottom left) that ranges from northern Japan and Korea across China and Southeast Asia, the Indian sambar, and the antlerless but curiously fanged water deer of China and Korea (page 118, top left). Other species include the shadow-dwelling axis deer and the omnivorous muntjac, or "barking deer," of the Indian subcontinent (opposite, top left). Cervids aren't limited to the Northern Hemisphere. They also occupy southern latitudes (the only continents where the family is not native are Australia and Antarctica), though their body size tends toward the diminutive.

You'll find brocket deer in Mexico's Yucatan Peninsula and south through Central America, and then the tiny, spike-antlered pudus (the world's smallest deer, about the size of a lapdog) take over in the highlands of Ecuador, Columbia, and Peru. The pampas deer, or *gamas* in Spanish, occupies the east-draining uplands of South America. Still farther

south, the larger marsh deer (page 118, top right) live in the boggy delta habitats of eastern Brazil, Uruguay, and Argentina.

Hunting strategies vary as much as the stature and habitat of the species of deer. While big-bore rifles may be required for northern moose and elk, nocturnal "high-seat" hunting often defines European stag and roebuck hunting while dogs, baiting, and calling can be very effective for various other species.

Plenty of critters in this family could lay claim to being the most oddball, but my money's on the tufted deer, a medium-sized specimen that lives in almost every part of China that has both trees and ample rainfall. What makes it unusual—besides the fact that its numbers are fairly robust in a country experiencing such meteoric development—is twofold: the shock of black hair on its forehead and its pronounced fangs. It's like Boy George as a vampire.

The tufted deer, which also sports tiny antlers under that topknot, is solitary and extremely shy (again, think Boy George), lives in high forests, and is prized for its pelt, which is reportedly used in native textiles. But if you ask me, it's the sharp, distinctive canine teeth that earn it my title as the most curious of deer.

PHEASANT

THE FLUSH OF A ROOSTER PHEASANT OFFERS THE COMPLETE PACKAGE: the rush of beating wings, a raucous cackle, plumage so colorful as to be almost gaudy, and a long, waving tail that, once focused on, all but guarantees the hunter will miss. Oh, and they're considered a king's feast. No wonder the beautiful pheasant is one invasive species you'll never hear complaints about. An emigrant from Asia, the ring-neck pheasant has carved out an ecological niche everywhere from the steppes of Asia to the European countryside even to the lush highlands of Hawaii.

American pheasant hunters owe their gratitude to Owen Denny, America's consul to China in 1881. Judge Denny released 26 pheasants in Oregon's Willamette Valley—the first successful stocking of the birds in the United States, and sportsmen encouraged the birds back eastward in a kind of avian Manifest Destiny. After reaching both coasts in the middle half of the last century, pheasant populations have since retreated, and hunters on the East coast now routinely travel to the Plains to find wild birds.

Although the pheasant's flush and speedy flight are primary reasons why we hunt them, the pheasant actually likes to use its legs to evade predators. In fact, pheasants spend much, if not all, of their life on the ground, roosting in trees only when deep snow or persistent predators drive them up. Instead, their preferred habitat is places where farmlands and mixed-grasslands meet, a unique ecosystem that offers abundant feeding in the form of grains, seeds, berries, and bugs, as well as plenty of tall, thick edge cover to provide protection from predators.

One might think the rooster's Technicolor plumage would make him stand out in such a monochrome landscape, but surprisingly, the 3–5 pound (1.4–2.3 kg) bird can fully disappear in the shortest of cover. Just ask any hunter who's had his heart momentarily stopped when one flushes underfoot in a field of short wheat stubble. The tan-colored hens and their drab clutch of as many as 10 gray poults are even better camouflaged, helping ensure their survival in the harsh world of the open prairie.

ASIAN PHEASANTS

As beautiful as he is, the common ringneck pheasant is just one member of a huge family found throughout Asia. Even the barnyard rooster is a relative. However, there are a few more sporting members that have been introduced as game birds throughout the world.

KALIJ A native of the Himalayas, the glossy black Kalij is a true trophy in Hawaii, where it lives in the Big Island's highland rainforests.

GOLDEN In terms of gaudiness, the Chinese Golden puts all the rest to shame. The canary-crested bird is rare on game preserves in the United States, but wild populations exist in the United Kingdom.

GREEN Trading the ringneck's golden breast plumage for iridescent, the green is Japan's national bird and, when flushed from cover in Hawaii and the United Kingdom, an emerald bonus for bird hunters.

Consistently successful pheasant hunters are like war-tested generals—they plan strategies before they even step onto the battlefield. Escape routes are identified, as are pockets of brush or weed-choked cover where pheasant may make a stand before flushing. Troops are deployed with terrain in mind and, just as importantly, with the utmost consideration for wind direction. Always hunt into the wind, not just for the dog's sake, but also to help mask movement from your quarry's keen ears.

The pheasant's superb hearing is its best defense, and defeating it requires the kind of stealth usually reserved for the whitetail woods. Approach every field quietly. Never slam truck doors or shout at the dogs. In fact, you're better off leaving a bad bird dog at home, as nothing will ensure a wild flush out of range faster than an uncontrollable hound dog.

A good bird dog isn't a necessity, but hunting behind an experienced one will significantly increase your odds of going home with a full game bag. In tall prairie and large fields, big-running pointing breeds such as German shorthairs are ideal, as long as the hunter can keep up—a rooster won't hold long at the end of a dog's nose.

In heavier cover, flushing breeds, particularly those that work close, excel. Many a Labrador has brought pheasants to hand, but a good springer spaniel is hard to beat.

THREE PHEASANT HOTSPOTS FOR YOUR BUCKET LIST

GREAT BRITAIN Introduced to the British Isles by Roman officers, the pheasant serves as a symbol of the pomp of English aristocracy. Rough, or walk-up, hunting does exist, but the drive, or battue, is the more popular pastime. Beaters push toward a line of butts or pegs, each manned with a double-gun toting, tweed-wearing sportsman who, with the help of his loader, does his level best to intercept waves of roosters rocketing overhead.

HUNGARY With castles rising from the fog and a ring of spicy sausages dripping fat into a nearby fire, it's not hard to imagine oneself a Hapsburg when hunting pheasants in Eastern Europe. The rich hunting tradition, incredibly friendly locals, and liberal bag limits reaching as many as 1,000 birds per day per group make Hungary a must-visit destination for serious wingshooters looking for the ultimate driven-bird challenge.

SOUTH DAKOTA Thanks to an aggressive stocking program, savvy landowners, and ideal habitat conditions, South Dakota hosts more pheasants, and more pheasant hunters, than anywhere else in the world. Harvest rates annually exceed 1 million birds, a majority of which are taken from wingshooting lodges. Hard-working hunters can find birds on public areas or lands managed under the state's walk-in hunter access program.

With or without a dog, solo hunters are at a disadvantage in typical pheasant country, for a wily rooster will often literally run circles around him before flushing well out of range.

When hunting alone, it's best to focus on hedgerows, windbreaks, and heavy marsh grass. Cold, snowy weather often offers the best opportunity, as wintry conditions will drive birds into thicker cover.

Like any seasoned battlefield general, always have a few tricks held in reserve for the late season, when roosters are apt to get particularly wary and wild. You'll need a trick or two—some favorites include approaching public fields from the opposite direction that you (and other hunters) typically would, and leaving the truck, radio blaring, at one end and circling around to the other in order to ambush fleeing pheasants. —D.D.

THE PHEASANT DRIVE

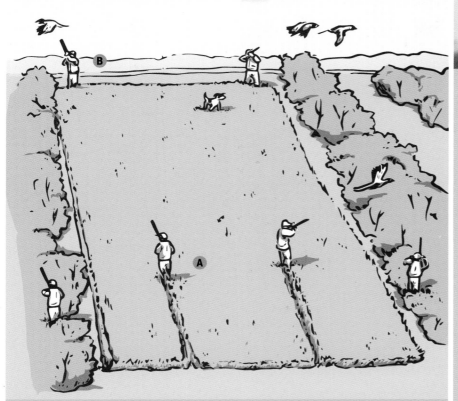

PHEASANT O'CLOCK

Any time you're facing an opponent, it pays to get inside his head. For pheasant hunters, that means understanding how roosters spend their days—particularly in the fall.

7:00 A.M. As the sun rises, pheasants will move from the overnight roosts. On cold or frost-touched days, they may stay tucked in deep cover, often on south-facing slopes, until temperatures rise or hunger forces them to move.

7:00 A.M.–11:00 A.M. Pheasants spend several hours each morning feeding. Catch them as they wander through agricultural areas, paying particular attention to recently harvested corn or bean fields bordering roosting cover.

11:00 A.M.–3:00 P.M. Just like you, pheasants need a nap after lunch, so they move into loafing areas to rest. In warm weather, they may loaf in tall stubble, but typically move toward tree rows, plum thickets, and other tall cover that protects them from hawks and other aerial predators.

3:30 P.M.–5:30 P.M. Just before sunset is the golden hour, when pheasants briefly feed before moving back to roosting cover. As dusk approaches, hunt the edges separating crop fields from roosting cover in the form of dense grass or brush.

No hunting technique is more effective on pheasants than a well-planned pincer movement, putting the birds between a line of drivers and several blockers posted at the end of a large field. Here's how to do it safely and successfully.

DRIVERS [A] Spread out an equal distance across the field, with no more than 25–30 feet (8–9 meters) between hunters, and walk slowly across the field. In large groups, the drivers on each flank should stay slightly ahead of the pack to keep pheasants from flushing out the sides. Shoot only when birds fly above the horizon line, and when approaching the end of the field, leave the shooting to the blockers.

BLOCKERS [B] After dropping off the drivers, blockers should make a wide circle to the opposite end of the field and take up their posts. As the walking group approaches, pheasants will be forced into the air, often toward the blockers. Flushes may come in flurries, so mark birds where they fall. Keep shots high and be ready to shoot behind you at escaping birds.

SAFETY Always wear eye protection. Hunter orange is a must. Stay alert and mindful of where other hunters are at all times. As they approach, make eye contact and, if necessary, wave your hand or hat to let them know where you are standing and make sure they notice your position.

RABBITS AND HARES

JUST AS BB GUNS AND .22S ARE GATEWAYS TO THE WIDE WORLD OF SHOOTING, rabbits are foundational game animals that build a hunter. Every skill you need to pursue a lion or a deer can be learned from hunting a cottontail: how to move quietly, how to watch for spoor and sign, how to notice the wind, how to wait, and when to go. How to direct dogs and guide hunting partners. How to shoot quickly and well. How to retrieve your prize and care for the meat and the hide. The fact that rabbits are so tasty simply adds to their abundant appeal.

You could plot the land-use history of the United States by the rise and fall of a single indicator species: the Eastern cottontail rabbit.

Populations of edge-loving rabbits weren't especially high at the time of early European settlements, but as homesteaders cleared land and piled slash, rabbit numbers increased. The small farms and brushy fencerows that defined rural America east of the Mississippi through the Dust Bowl created nearly perfect "rabbitat," along with an American original: the small-game hunter. Clad in red buffalo plaid, with a brace of brindled beagles at his ankles, an Ithaca 37 shotgun or a quick-handling .22 over his shoulder, the rabbit hunter could run any farm in the county and put up bunnies everywhere he went.

Roughly between the Wilson and Nixon administrations, two hunting generations chased rabbits—and squirrels and quail, too—with the intensity currently devoted to whitetails and turkeys. It's hard to imagine, but those bucks and gobblers were scarce back in our grandparents' day. Populations of deer have skyrocketed, but cottontails have declined as our agriculture has become more efficient, our fields larger, and our forests less intensively logged.

Today, rabbit hunting is considered almost quaint—a throwback activity to pursue between deer seasons, or as a gateway opportunity for a young hunter or a wild forager who knows that cottontail, whether fried or fricasseed or stewed, is a mild-flavored delicacy. That's fine with those of us who hunt cottontails anytime we can, as there's less competition for the best rabbit spots. And these rabbit spots are literally everywhere across the continent, even if populations are highly cyclical.

WALK UP A RABBIT

Hunting over a dog but a more effective method is simply to walk.

Pick a sunny day following a storm. A fresh snow is perfect, but hunting after any other sustained violent weather also works. The idea is to sneak up on cottontails that are basking outside their dens after being holed up for a few days.

This is a great game for two hunters, one carrying a scoped .22 rifle, the other swinging a light shotgun. For flushing rabbits, the shotgun is the best, but as long as you move slowly and keep an eye peeled, you'll get rifle shots at rabbits sunning at the edge of brush piles, fencerows, and stream banks.

Another effective strategy for walking shotgunners is to work in opposite directions around a large brushy area. As long as you know exactly where your partner is—blaze orange is critical for this game—you'll spook rabbits to each other, and both hunters can have fast shooting at flushing bunnies.

Eastern cottontails and their soggy-bottom kin, the marsh and swamp rabbits, occupy the eastern half of the United States, parts of southern Canada, and areas through Mexico and Central America into northern South America. Various other rabbit species have evolved in specific habitats as far south on the continent as Argentina.

In the western United States and into Mexico, the desert cottontail occupies the same type of edge habitat that Eastern cottontails do in farm country: brushy streams, arid grasslands, and transition zones in open pine forests.

Close cousin to the New World cottontail, the European rabbit is native to the Iberian Peninsula and northern Africa. This wild rabbit (which was probably the model for Beatrix Potter's *The Tale of Peter Rabbit*) has traveled the world as an introduced species, often with disastrous results. In Australia, where the rabbit has no natural predators, a pair was released as a Christmas present to a hunter. Populations have since escalated to such a degree that the pestilent bunny has degraded the local habitat of many native species.

And while rabbit hunting remains a rich tradition in parts of Europe—mainly Britain, Spain, and the Balkans—it's nowhere near as popular as it is (and was) in the United States.

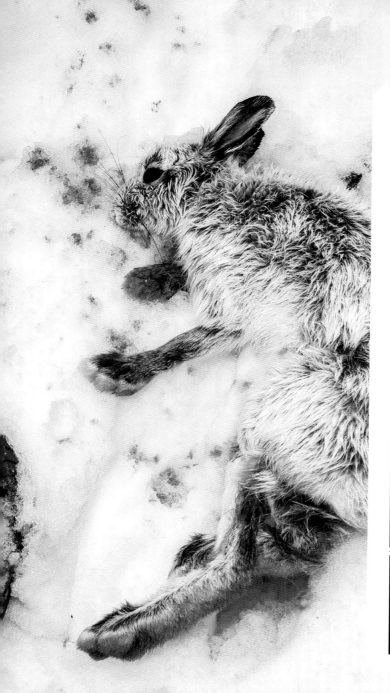

KNOW YOUR ANIMAL

They may belong to the same order—Lagomorpha—but rabbits and hares are markedly different, starting from birth. Rabbits are born blind and hairless; hare babies (called leverets) are born with hair and are able to see. And the differences don't end there.

	RABBIT	HARE
APPEARANCE	Compact body, smaller ears and feet, gray to brown in color.	Much larger ears and feet, hair turns white in winter, long and rangy body.
BEHAVIOR	Will circle back to den when pursued.	Tend to run in open when pursued.
HABBITAT	Social animals, prefer soft foods like grass or vegetables.	Solitary animals, prefer hard foods like bark and twigs. Associated with open barrens.
TABLE FARE	Tender, mild meat.	Tough, stringy meat.

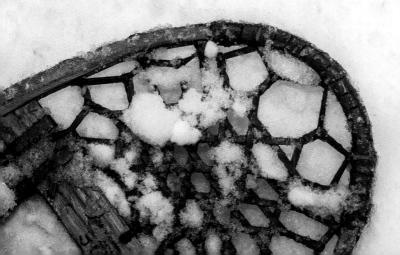

ESSENTIAL RABBIT GUNS

Rather than dividing this category into shotguns and rimfires, it's more educational to talk about classics and modern guns. The fact is, it's hard to go wrong with any walkabout gun you shoot well, as rabbits are not hard to kill.

CLASSIC On the classic side of the ledger, I prefer an open-sighted Remington Model 34, a fast-pointing tubular-magazine bolt rifle. For shotguns, the pump-action Winchester Model 12 was proven on the rabbit patches of the Midwest, but the Ithaca Model 37 is equally suited to this game. If you tend toward handsome doubles, either a field-grade L.C. Smith or a between-the-wars A.H. Fox will have you looking like a rabbit-hunting dandy.

MODERN Modern guns have a leg up in terms of functionality, and it's hard to imagine a more functional bunny gun than the Ruger 10/22 semiauto rifle. Other exceptional rabbit medicine includes the Weatherby SA20 semiauto shotgun and/or the slim, classy Ruger Red Label in 20 gauge. Or, if you want to mix eras and swing an exceptionally tasteful but functional side-by-side, look no further than Connecticut Shotgun's elegant RBL Reserve.

JACKRABBIT (top left) The iconic, rangy rabbit of the Great Plains and West, the jack turns white in winter and can be great game for varminters. As with other hare species, arid-country jackrabbits include many dozens of subspecies.

SNOWSHOE HARE (top right) This large hare occupies mountains and forests of the northern latitudes and turns white with the season. Its name comes from its large, furry feet that can course atop drifted snow.

ARCTIC HARE (bottom right) Even farther north, this large lagomorph eats alder-tree bark and dens in the tundra.

IRISH HARE Also called the mountain hare, variable hare, or tundra hare, this critter lives on the outer islands of Great Britain, through Scandinavia to Siberia.

EUROPEAN BROWN HARE The inspiration for our "mad as a March hare" phrase, this rangy animal roams the heath from western Europe through central Asia.

ASIAN HARE A mountain dweller, this race of hares roams from the northern islands of Japan across Mongolia. As with other northern-dwelling hares, the Asian hare turns white in the wintertime and dun colored from the spring through fall.

AFRICAN SAVANNA HARE One of Africa's most widespread mammals, this large lagomorph ranges from equatorial Africa south and east to South Africa's Eastern Cape.

BOBCATS
AND OTHER FURBEARERS

THE BOBCAT IS ONE OF THE TOP SPECIES SOUGHT AFTER BY PREDATOR HUNTERS both for sport and for profit. For the most part, there are two methods to hunt them: calling or chasing with hounds. I went hound hunting once. We found a track at daylight and released the dogs. We strapped snowshoes on our feet and started following dog tracks through the deep snow. It was dark again when we finally hit another road, a long distance away, and it was almost light again before we found the truck. I much prefer calling.

The bobcat (*Lynx rufus*) is a North American mammal and a member of the cat family Felidae. The bobcat ranges from southern Canada to northern Mexico, including most of the continental United States, and it has 12 recognized subspecies.

Bobcats can live just about anywhere there is a food supply, including wooded areas, semi desert, urban edge, forest edges, and swamplands. Their color is generally tan to grayish brown, with black spots and streaks on the body and dark bars on the forelegs and tail. The ears are black tipped and pointed, with short, black tufts. There is generally an off-white color on the lips, chin, and underparts. Bobcats in the desert regions of the American Southwest have the lightest-colored coats, while those in the northern, forested regions are darkest. The coloring is very effective camouflage. The name comes from the short, "bobbed" tail. (Get it? "Bobcat?")

Though the bobcat prefers rabbits and hares, it will eat anything it can catch, including insects and deer. Weights vary from region to region, but the males average 15–40 pounds (7–18 kg). Some northern cats will grow as big as 45 pounds (20 kg), but that is rare.

Bobcats prefer rough and broken terrain. Rocky escarpments or brush-choked ravines are good places to hunt them. They respond well to varmint calls like the sound of a dying hare, though they're notoriously slow to respond, so the best advice is to be patient. Stay put and keep calling for at least 45 minutes. The cats are very sneaky when approaching, and often the first time you see them they'll be sitting in the open, looking around—and you'll wonder how on earth they got there without you spotting them. —*B.T.*

BEST BOBCAT GUNS

Bobcats have thin and easily damaged skin, so it's best to avoid the destructive cartridges and bullets often favored for hunting other predators. Cartridges like the .22-250, .220 Swift or .243 Winchester are tough on the fur.

For a rifle, the .223 Remington with a 55-grain bullet is a good choice. These bullets expand but do not blow up, so they make an exit hole, usually one small enough to sew up and not damage the value of the fur too much. The .22 Hornet has also proven to be a good choice for many of the same reasons.

The other approach is to use something like a .17 Remington with a very explosive bullet that will not exit at all. The new hypervelocity .17 Winchester Super Magnum is another good choice.

A shotgun with No. 4 or No. 2 birdshot works pretty well, too, if you are hunting where you can call them in relatively close and where there's heavy cover.

THE FURBEARERS It's neither biologically nor categorically correct to say that a bobcat is a hunted mammal while a lynx is a trapped mammal—after all, those terms describing these close feline cousins refer to our sporting traditions and commercial perspectives of the animals, not to any endemic habit or behavior.

Any animal that can be trapped can also be hunted, though the opposite condition isn't always true. The elusive woodland weasel, the fisher, for instance, is rarely seen by humans, even by our hardiest hunters. But thousands are trapped every winter by smelly bait sets affixed to the trunk of a leaning tree.

Despite periodic legislative initiatives to ban it, fur trapping is alive and well in most northern latitudes, and furbearer numbers are healthy enough to support sustainable harvest. Here are the furbearers that are both trapped and hunted, depending on local regulations. —A.M.

COMMON FURBEARERS

LYNX Forest and subalpine cousins to bobcats, lynx are callable with rabbit-in-distress squalls.

WOLVERINE One of the toughest and most elusive mustelids (members of the weasel family), wolverines (top left) are solitary, roaming huge ranges.

BADGER Another tough mustelid, badgers (bottom left) are mainly shot as vermin or pursued by predator hunters.

WOLF In much of Canada and Alaska, more wolves are taken on traplines than by hunting.

FOX AND COYOTE In the old days, these were mainly trapped for sale to the trim-fur market. But the rise of predator hunting has tipped the balance toward hunting.

RACCOON AND SKUNK The fur trade still buys prime pelts from these two omnivores.

MINK AND OTTER Trapping of these wild aquatic mustelids (ermine and ferrets are also dry-land members of this tribe) still takes place, but most marketable fur is raised in captivity.

HIMALAYAN AND CENTRAL ASIAN SPECIES

IF YOU FIND YOURSELF ATOP THE BARREN TIBETAN PLATEAU, trusting a horse for your balance and fighting for your next breath in the thin air, you might be either a prisoner of the Taliban or on the hunt of a lifetime. Assuming the latter, you will endure hardship of your own making: sleeping on rocks, enduring searing storms, and scaling frighteningly steep terrain. But you will look back on it all fondly, hopefully while gazing at a trophy of this spectacular country, a horned ibex or a curling argali ram, savoring the memory of hunting high above the clouds.

Trophy hunting here at the roof of the world is a deliberate, expensive, often uncomfortable affair. Most hunts involve some combination of bribes to customs officials, terrifying rides in mechanically dysfunctional vehicles, ingestion of dubious foods, and language barriers that prevent the resolution of even simple problems. Yet those hunters who have chased the world's most remarkable horned game in the high plateaus of central Asia never hesitate to say they'd return.

This is home to the Marco Polo argali, among the largest of the world's wild sheep. Elsewhere in the peaks and valleys that stretch from central Kazakhstan west into China's Shansi Province and south into Pakistan, you'll find equally exotic animals: the stud-horned mid-Asian and Tien Shan ibex that is very successfully hunted in the Kyrgyzstan highlands (opposite, bottom); the urial sheep of the high steppe—kin to the curl-horned mouflon of Europe (and of game farms in Texas); and in the Caucasus Mountains that tip into Europe, a variety of hardy tur, the world's largest wild goats (opposite, top left).

To the east, the Nepalese blue sheep (actually a caprid, or member of the goat family, opposite, top right) hangs on cliffs beneath the world's highest peaks. Even farther afield, into the vast Gobi Desert and Mongolia's interior, you'll encounter Altai argali sheep and a mix of other trophies, including ibex, gazelles, and even elk and roe deer.

We tend to think of central Asia as all peaks and rocky highlands, member of the goat family) hangs on cliffs beneath the world's highest peaks. And even farther afield, into the vast Gobi Desert and Mongolia's interior, you'll encounter the Altai argali sheep and a mix of other trophies, including ibex, gazelles, and even elk and roe deer.

SNOWCOCKS IN NEVADA

Central Asia is known in hunting circles for its horned game, but it's also home to a remarkable game bird: the Himalayan snowcock.

But you don't have to get a passport and an interpreter to hunt these pheasant-sized partridge. In the 1960s and '70s, hundreds of transplanted snowcocks were released in the Ruby Mountains of northern Nevada, and a remnant population of the alpine birds still live above treeline, where they can be hunted by the hardiest wingshooters.

HUNTING IN ULTRA-ALPINE CONDITIONS

Mountain hunting strategies differ according to custom and species, but a constant is a flat-shooting rifle and durable optics. But hunting at 18,000 feet (5,500 meters) above sea level requires its own set of specialized (and some not-so-specialized) considerations, including:

GAMOW BAG This inflatable bag is large enough to fit a human, and is a fixture at many of the highest-elevation camps. When inflated with a foot pump, the effective altitude can be decreased by as much as 7,000 feet (2,134 meters), and hunters' elevation sickness—a potentially deadly condition—can be alleviated.

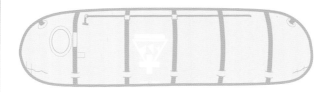

PRESCRIPTION MEDICINE Any hunter headed to central Asia should be familiar with the symptoms of acute mountain sickness (AMS) and high-altitude pulmonary edema (HAPE), which swells the brain and can be deadly. Consult your physician about the correct medicines (expect to hear about a glaucoma medicine called Diamox) and many of the classic warning signs, including ragged breathing, blue tingeing of the lips and fingernails, and dark urine.

NON-PRESCRIPTION MEDICINE Over-the-counter antacids can help reduce acidity in the stomach and bloodstream.

WATER AND PASTA Stay hydrated and eat as many carbohydrates as you can. Both have been shown to delay or minimize symptoms of altitude sickness.

TIME Plan to spend a full week prior to your hunt acclimating to the elevation. That's time you can get back on your return by keeping tales of your successful trip short and sweet.

Soon after a hunter encounters a Dall sheep or a Rocky Mountain bighorn, they begin to think about their next ram. It's usually not long before they realize that any mountain is more interesting if it is occupied by wild sheep.

The next realization is that ours is a world of rams, and many species live in remotest Asia. For those who are pursuing the Ovis World Slams—or those who are about to—you may consider the following a wish list.

SNOW SHEEP The Grand Slam Club/Ovis recognizes six distinct species of this ram native to eastern Russia and Siberia.

AOUDAD OR BARBARY SHEEP (top right) Native to northern Africa, this species splits the difference between sheep and goat.

MONGOLIAN ARGALIS Mongolia and northwestern China are home to the Gobi, Hangay, and Altay species.

CENTRAL ASIAN ARGALIS A dizzying (and frankly, confusing) number of argali rams roam across the highlands of Kazakhstan, China, Kyrgyzstan, Uzbekistan, and Nepal.

MOUFLON SHEEP (top left) This curled-horn ram is found in eastern Europe, Iran, Turkey, and N. Africa.

URIAL SHEEP (bottom right) A number of species are native to Pakistan, Iran, and Afghanistan.

TUR This family is native to Azerbaijan, Russia, and the trans-Caucasus region.

DOVES

AFTER A LONG, tedious summer, nothing reawakens the hunter's soul like mourning doves riding a cool autumn breeze. Doves are the most popularly hunted game species in the United States. According to surveys, more hunters are found afield on September 1—the traditional opening day of dove season—than any other day of the year. Mourning doves boast a population of approximately 475 million, their range includes every continental state, and any hunter with a shotgun and some shells may pursue them.

The reasons for dove hunting's popularity go far beyond simple mathematics. They are for many a first opportunity to get reacquainted with shotguns, friends, and out-of-shape retrievers. For others it's the challenge that intrigues: Finding a field that doves are hitting is no easy assignment, nor is centering the notoriously swift birds amidst a pattern of shot. Yet those who find success enjoy great rewards, as few birds deliver such culinary delight.

So what doves might you hope to pursue? The mourning dove is by far the most populous and widespread subspecies, but the southern United States is home to several additional bird species, notably the white-winged dove and the nonnative Eurasian collared dove. While the white-wing dove is typically included in daily bags, many states do not place a limit of any kind on collared doves—they're categorized as an invasive species and enjoyed by hunters as so-called bonus birds.

Both species are greatly expanding their ranges. Traditionally, the white-wing could be found in the southwestern United States, but its range now includes parts of Louisiana, coastal Mississippi, and most of Texas. The birds have a global breeding population of 8 million, of which about 4.5 million spend at least a portion of the year in the United States—half of them in Texas—before wintering primarily in Central America.

Nonmigratory populations also exist in Oklahoma, Kansas, Arkansas and more recently in Florida. In flight, the white-wing is easily discerned from the mourning dove due to—you guessed it—its brilliant white wing patches.

GET ON TARGET

How do you aim at a darting, speeding bird? You don't. Doves require the utmost commitment to instinctive shotgunning. Those who attempt to look at both bird and barrel, ascertain a lead, and pull the trigger will experience great frustration, despite how often more predictable birds will allow it.

Instead, focus exclusively on the dove and smoothly bring the gun to your shoulder—without looking at the barrel. Providing your mount is true and your eyes remain on the bird, the speed of your swing will match that of the bird. Instinct does the rest: At the opportune time, increase the speed of your swing so it overtakes the bird and pull the trigger. With repetition, you'll be amazed how well your brain calculates the acceleration and timing of the shot. And, should the bird adjust its trajectory, your eyes will guide your cheek-mounted shotgun to the path.

Truly, this is the way to gun doves.

The white-wing's cousin, the Eurasian collared dove, is thought to have originated in Florida via the Bahamas, where they were sold as pets and released. Their range extends across much of the country, excluding the northeast, but the estimated breeding population of 400,000 birds is primarily found along the Gulf Coast. Larger and less richly colored than the mourning dove, collareds are difficult to distinguish in flight, but the trademark collar is an easy identifier once in hand.

The most important skill set in the dove hunter's playbook has nothing to do with wingshooting but, rather, with the ability to scout effectively. Hunters often search for flocks of the ubiquitous mourning dove, as quite simply they're the easiest to find, but all subspecies have an appetite for seeds and tend to share fields. Recently harvested grains such as corn, sunflowers, millet, and milo tend to be good starting points. Once located, bring a binocular and scan the area for doves during their most active feeding times: before 9 a.m. or after 3 p.m. And keep an eye out at atypical hours, too. At midday or first/last light, look to pine stands to ambush doves intent on a siesta, or to gravel roads or sandbars to find doves filling their gizzards.

Doves are also greatly attracted to water. Check out farm ponds, especially with pebbly banks, or creeks. Water serves as a focal point, luring birds into gun range and also provides a convenient means for retrievers to beat the September heat.

Then there's power lines. Perhaps you don't relish the idea of hunting a field with a reminder of technological progress, but it's remarkable how productive a grain field can be due to a crossing power line. The doves seem to love the opportunity to eat, rest, and eat some more—who wouldn't?

Once an adequate number of doves are located and a firm handshake is exchanged with the landowner—private access still exists, especially with this species—find a good natural blind and avoid movement until it's time to shoot. Your hiding spot doesn't have to be elaborate, but doves' eyesight is largely underrated. If hunting agriculture, consider locating the highest point in the field. For some reason, the birds' flight paths often route over slight rises.

Now load up and get ready: You may just find yourself in the midst of one of the most challenging and fun wingshooting opportunities. —K.W.

DECOYS ADD EXCITEMENT

Pass-shooting or hunting a feed site is fine, but nothing tops the thrill of gunning doves over decoys.

The strategy can also be highly effective, grabbing the doves' attention and providing a point of focus across an otherwise large, nondescript field.

Spread decoys at least a foot (0.3 meters) apart on the ground and, whenever possible, across a nearby fence or dead tree (a favorite roost structure).

A variety of styles are available. Here are three to try:

MOJO OUTDOORS VOODOO DOVE This motion decoy simulates a dove coming in for a landing with great effectiveness. Combined with full-body decoys on the ground below, it's a deadly setup.

LUCKY DUCK CLIP-ON AND FEEDER DOVES These full-body decoys look great and won't break the bank. Clip-ons are available in four-packs and easily affix to fences and trees. Feeders come with handy bases, which lift them off the ground to maximize visibility.

CHEROKEE SPORTS INFLATABLE PHOTOPRINTED DOVES These photorealistic decoys are oversized to help ensure they're seen. Field stakes are included, or you can simply tie the doves to a limb or wire. Prior to inflation, half a dozen will fit in the pocket of your shooting vest.

LONE STAR DOVES

Every September 1, a quarter million Texans take part in one of the world's great sporting traditions: opening day of dove season in the Lone Star State. The Texas Parks and Wildlife Department estimates that 900,00 Texans hunted in 2012—generating an astounding USD $23 million for the economy—and doves start it all.

And why not? In terms of the volume and diversity of doves, Texas offers a seldom-rivaled opportunity. Mourning doves, white-wings, and Eurasian collareds are prolific throughout, while the southern corner is among the few places you'll find white-tipped doves north of Mexico. Bag limits are a generous 15 per day, plus unlimited Eurasian collareds.

If you bag all four plus a rock pigeon, congratulations: That's unofficially a Texas Grand Slam.

EUROPEAN SPECIES

IT'S CURIOUS AND INSTRUCTIVE that the most intensively settled continent on earth also has the most unexpectedly rich ensemble of huntable species. Rural Europe is simply gamy. From moose across Scandinavia to the shy, woods-loving roebuck of Central Europe to the brown bear, wolf, and red stag of the Balkans, Europe has maintained this biodiversity by conserving large swaths of forest and field and by carefully regulating who hunts. Europeans enforce a code of conduct that is reverential, deliberate, and steeped in tradition many centuries old.

You can easily see evidence of the ubiquity of European hunting as you fly into Frankfurt's airport, one of the busiest in the world. A short distance from the end of the runway is a hochsitz, or high seat, the elevated hunting platform that dominates pastoral landscapes from Helsinki to Istanbul.

The stands are used as American hunters might use tower blinds, strategically locating each to pick off roe deer (opposite, top right), mostly, but also red stag (opposite, bottom), wild boar, fallow deer (opposite, top left), and mouflon sheep, all creatures of European forests and fields.

These species crave edges, and on a continental basis, there may be no landform with more edge habitat than Europe. Stretching from the arctic to the Mediterranean and from the Atlantic to the Black Sea, dozens of ecosystems host a dizzying variety of huntable species.

Woodland species predominate, and across much of lowland Europe, jaegers who lease game-rich ground are also responsible for managing wildlife populations on that property. If they don't keep game in balance with habitat, the hunters—not the game agency or the landowners—are responsible for crop damage.

But a good deal of European hunting takes place in the wilder uplands. As you climb into the continent's picturesque mountains—the Pyrenees, Alps, or Carpathians—the game changes with the landscape. In mid-elevation pastures, you'll find subalpine stag, along with wolves, lynx, and brown bear in some of the wilder ranges of the Balkans and northern Italy. In the high alpine, you can hunt the cleft-clinging chamois and the handsome curving-horned ibex.

PURSUING ROEBUCK

The tiny, nervous roe deer may be the most widely distributed game animal in Europe—and its three-pronged antlers are the most common adornments of gun clubs and estate manors.

The somewhat larger Siberian roe deer ranges from Russia's Ural Mountains east into China. But the European roebuck extends from central Scandinavia all the way across the continent, from Great Britain and Scotland east through the Carpathian Mountains into Turkey and Iraq.

Sometimes called the reh, roe deer are as ubiquitous and energetically pursued in Europe as the whitetail is in North America. And just like the whitetail, the roe deer becomes more elusive the more it is hunted—and when on the run, it barks and flashes its white rump patch.

In forests where reh have been favorites for the past 2,500 years, they are rarely seen in the daytime.

To the north, Scandinavia is home to moose, caribou, polar bears, brown bears, and a few musk ox that are found roaming across Greenland and Canada's Nunavut.

Game populations in Great Britain are as extensive as they are on the continent, even if opportunities to hunt them are more exclusive. They include the royal red stag of Scotland, the roe deer that has spread to every corner of Britain,

fallow deer, and the introduced fanged water deer, not to mention the red fox that has been the object of centuries of choreographed equestrian fox hunts.

Then there are Europe's obscure critters, including the introduced white-tailed deer of Finland, wisent (European bison, above, bottom right), russian boar (above, left), the kri-kri ibex of Crete, and a variety of wild sheep and goats of the constellation of Mediterranean islands.

A DRIVEN HUNT IN GERMANY

It was the finest big-game trophy I'd ever laid my crosshairs on, and I couldn't shoot. It was a magnificent red stag, its impossibly heavy, crowning antlers looking like the ornate chandeliers that hung over the drawing room in the baronial castle where we gathered each evening to toast the day's hunt.

The allowable game of this day's driven hunt was roe deer does, red deer hinds (females), and wild boar. But because the roe deer had just dropped their daggerlike antlers, it took careful inspection of any reh (or roe deer) to ensure that it was a legal animal. And on driven hunts, in which the game is rousted out of cover by the *Jagdterriers*, or chase dogs, the animals are disinclined to stand still, waiting on an indecisive hunter.

Not long after I watched the giant stag glide off into the forest, I spotted movement from my hochsitz. It was a nervous roe deer, and I glassed it long enough to watch it squat to urinate. A doe! I can't recall being so excited to shoot an antlerless deer, but this was my first European game, and what it lacked in headgear and heft (it weighed about as much as my

Labrador retriever back home), it more than made up for in ceremony.

First, the jaeger who picked me up cut a green twig and placed it in the dead animal's mouth. This *letzer bissen*, or last meal, is a formal thanks to the game for giving its life to the hunter. Then the jaeger dipped another twig in the animal's blood and stuck it in my hatband before delivering a stiff salute: "*Weidmannsheil!*" The hunter is duty-bound to respond with an equally hearty "*Weidmannsdank*," the scripted congratulations and thanks for the hunt.

Then my deer was taken to a staging area, where game from the day's hunt was placed on spruce bows according to species and size. Bonfires were lit at the corners of the game display, horn players blew a memorial song for each of the species, and then the hunters sang song after song into the night, sparks flying above the scene, in a celebration of respect and tradition that links modern European hunters with their ancestors of centuries past.

LICENSING IN EUROPE

The expectation of European hunting is that it's expensive, exclusive, and extremely limited. That's true in some countries—primarily Britain and Italy—but in general hunting is accessible and egalitarian. But it is not casual.

Most countries require hunters to pass an extensive and time-consuming licensing program that is designed to test their knowledge of animal anatomy and behavior, habitat requirements, ballistics, veterinary science, and even hunting history. Proficiency must be proven in shooting, wildlife and plant identification, butchering, and forest management.

If a jaeger passes the years-long certification process, he is granted a license, which allows him to lease land, sell game he kills to butchers and restaurants, and help rural communities manage wildlife populations.

Think you could pass Germany's hunter-licensing program? Here are some sample questions from the *jagdschein*, or hunter test:

1) Which dogs are used for hunting fox in dens?

2) What is the minimum caliber and energy to hunt cloven-hoofed game?

3) How many teeth does a 3-year-old roe deer have?

4) On a sit for roe deer you see a mature doe with a yearling male and female alongside her. Which do you shoot first?

5) True or false: Bowhunting is illegal in Germany?

1) dackel and jagdterrier, 2) 6.5mm and 2000 joule, 3) 32, 4) the yearling female, 5) True

SMALLER GAME AND BIRDS The image of the gentrified wingshooter, clad in tweed, silk ascot beneath his square jaw, swinging a bespoke double gun from his designated peg, is a European (and chiefly British) construct.

While a whole culture has grown up around estate shooting for driven pheasants and grouse, the entire continent is a shotgunner's paradise, generally divided into northern and southern species. To the north, upland gunners shoot the large, purplish capercaillie (opposite, left), which shares habitat stretching from Scandinavia to Siberia with the smaller black grouse. And in the stunted northern forests, willow and rock ptarmigan mingle with the whistling hazel grouse.

Scotland's famous grouse is the red variety (opposite, bottom right), often flushed from the rustic moorland and driven past gunners' earthen

"butts" dug into the heather centuries ago. Increasingly, walk-up hunts are offered as a less-expensive alternative to traditional beaten hunts.

Farther south, Asian pheasants that were introduced a thousand years ago are thriving in areas of Britain, northern France, and Denmark.

Partridge hunting dominates southeastern Europe. Spain, Portugal, and Italy have abundant populations of the red-legged variety, and the gray partridge is found from eastern Germany through Hungary, Slovakia, the Czech Republic, and into Bulgaria and western Romania.

While woodcock, doves, and pigeons are all hunted locally, the culture of waterfowl hunting is, as you might expect, mainly limited to coastal Europe. Some species would be unfamiliar to North American waterfowlers. Diving species include the ferruginous duck, tufted duck, common pochard (similar to the redhead of North America), and the greater scaup.

European geese species include the white-front, the North Sea graylag goose, and the northern European pink-footed goose (above, top right). Coastal species include a variety of brants, the cackling goose, barnacle goose, and increasing numbers of Canada geese. But the prized (and locally endangered) waterfowl of the continent may be the striking red-breasted goose, which looks like a combination of a plumed wood duck and a spectacled goose.

FOXES

A BIOLOGIST FRIEND OF MINE once used breakfast breads to describe canine distribution. "Coyotes are like these donuts," he said, powdered sugar clinging to the corners of his mouth. He adjusted the half dozen confections so they covered the bottom of the pastry box. "Coyotes occupy these relatively large circles of habitat. But the fox . . . see those little places where the donuts don't quite meet? That's where the fox lives, the corners and the edges of other critters' habitats. And a few really smart foxes—they live in the holes of the donuts."

Every time I hunt fox, I recall my confection-loving friend's analogy. He's right. Foxes are nocturnal edge dwellers, picking out a living along fencerows, highways, suburban greenways, and woodlots, sniping mice and gorging on carrion, sleuthing in to poach the occasional housecat and barnyard fowl.

Living on the periphery of human activity has made the red fox an adaptable opportunist. There's a reason the fox is depicted as a conniving gambler (the Spanish call foxes "*zorros*")—they're smart, calculating, and omnivorous. Unlike coyotes and wolves, foxes are generally solitary. That means hunters are targeting an individual, not a collective, and that individual is a bundle of instincts tuned to survival. To hunt a red fox effectively, you must learn its food sources, its habits, its escape routes, and its responses to danger. A fox will always flee, will often circle and backtrack, and will never stray far from its edge of the donut. It prefers meat but will eat berries, fruit, grasses, and garbage. It is never far from human habitation.

North America is home to five species of fox: the ubiquitous red fox, the bashful gray fox, the open-country kit and swift foxes that roam the Southwest and the Northern Plains respectively, and the curious island fox that occupies a few islands off the California coast.

All foxes will respond to predator calls, but gray and red foxes are most callable with a variety of mouse squeaks, bird squawks, and rabbit distress calls. Foxes will steal through cover to watch for the source of the commotion, a behavior that lends itself to team calling, with one hunter on the gun and the other calling and watching for snatches of movement.

FOXES OF THE WORLD

It's a testament to the durability and adaptability of foxes that the family shows up in nearly every type of habitat on earth.

The scrappy canine chased by crimson-coated fox hunters in Great Britain is the same red fox that has colonized America. But the family extends across deserts (the fennec fox of the Sahara), mountains (South America's Andean fox), muggy tropical forests (the Bengal fox of India), game-rich savannas (the bat-eared fox of sub-Saharan Africa), the vast, empty Asian steppe (the lovely corsac fox), and even the high arctic (the white-plumed arctic fox). They're simply everywhere.

In each of these places, foxes exhibit the same tenacity. You won't see them often, and you'll rarely see them twice. But they are callable almost everywhere, in the first light of morning and the last light of evening, when foxes are most active.

A PROPER BRITISH HUNT

A century ago, if you were to tell a chap that you were going "hunting" on the morrow, it would be assumed, based on that generic mention, that you would be chasing fox, probably on horseback, and almost certainly after a sherry cocktail.

That's how central fox hunting is to the English sporting tradition, at least among the aristocracy. This is the sport that a character in Oscar Wilde's play *A Woman of No Importance* describes as "the unspeakable in full pursuit of the uneatable."

That tradition is under attack in Great Britain by animal-rights activists, but many of the terms from fox hunting have entered our wider language.

WHIP The parliamentarian tasked with garnering votes for a particular party (think majority whip, minority whip) descends from fox hunting. The assistant huntsman was called the whip, or whipper-in, and his job was to keep the pack of hounds together and on the scent trail of the fox.

STEEPLECHASE In Britain, where horseback hunters chased fox for many miles over stone walls and fallen logs, and across swollen streams, the only reliable landmarks were often the steeples of the village churches.

TALLY-HO A huntsman's cry to excite hounds when a fox is sighted.

LARK An unnecessary flourish, usually defined as a fox hunter who vaults a fence when a fox is not under chase.

BULGARIAN GOLDEN JACKAL

When I first saw the canine coursing through the weeds, I had to watch it for several seconds to ensure it wasn't wearing a collar.

I was on the receiving end of a driven boar hunt in southeastern Bulgaria and expected to see either a tusker or a wired-hair "*barak*," the scenting hound of the Balkans.

But the animal's snout was too sharp, and its furtive pace and behavior too feral for a dog with a name. I would recognize a wild canine anywhere. The fox hunter in me called my Sauer 101 to my shoulder, tracked the running jackal across the pasture, and downed it with a single shot from the .308.

It was a beautiful golden jackal, its luxurious prime yellow fur flecked with black and gray.

Back at camp, you'd think I had shot a gold-medal stag. Every European hunter in my group wanted a photograph with my jackal. It turns out that my prize canine is part of a leading edge of wild dogs that have been moving, over the last decade, from Turkey into southeastern Europe.

The arrival in Europe of jackals may be bad news for stockmen in the Balkans and Carpathians, but it's great news for roebuck and stag hunters who are eager to add an adaptable canine to their list of capable prey.

SEA DUCKS

THE PURSUIT OF ANY WATERFOWL SPECIES CAN PROVE A GRUELING TASK, but none inhabit such downright inhospitable waters as sea ducks. Those who target them face choppy surfs, freezing ocean spray, shotgun-disintegrating salt—why, it makes a mallard hunt seem perfectly civilized. As you may expect from birds that feel at home amidst such conditions, sea ducks are also likely North America's toughest ducks: This author has seen several absorb a load of No. 2 shot, wipe their brows in relief and rejoin their companions no worse for wear.

Even among sea ducks, eiders have a particular affinity for harsh environments. Common eiders, which include four subspecies, nest along the coastlines of Alaska, Maine, eastern Canada, and essentially all of Hudson Bay. Come migration time, the Pacific population rarely ventures beyond southern Alaska, while Atlantic eiders winter from Greenland to the Gulf of St. Lawrence and as far south as Virginia.

Their cousin, the king eider, is best recognized by the drake's orange-yellow frontal shield. Breeding across the arctic coast from Alaska to Greenland and the northern Hudson Bay, king eiders winter essentially as far north as open seas allow. They are most frequently shot along the Alaskan coast; those shot by Maine or New England hunters warrant special celebration.

Sea ducks found at slightly more temperate latitudes include the long-tailed duck (formerly known by the politically incorrect term "oldsquaw") and three kinds of scoters—the surf, black-, and white-winged. The breeding range of all four includes Alaska and northern Canada; scoters winter across much of the Pacific and Atlantic coasts, while the long-tail is most commonly found on the eastern seaboard from the Great Lakes to southern Maryland. All inhabit ocean waters, large lakes and bays, and deep, often brackish rivers.

Eiders, scoters and long-tailed ducks are thought to be in a slow yet steady population decline that began in the 1970s. Suspected culprits include a drop in the abundance and quality of their preferred foods, especially mollusks and crustaceans. However, the remote nature of sea duck habitat hinders definitive population surveys and studies.

CHATHAM'S EIDER PROBLEM

With an annual economic impact exceeding USD $2 million, the shellfish industry is an important source of revenue for the town of Chatham, Massachusetts.

But every year an unruly flock of common eiders sucks down more mussels and soft-shell crabs than the buffet line at a Kennedy wedding—an estimated USD $1.3 million worth. So in 2011 the town announced plans to install sound cannons along Chatham Harbor designed to shoo the birds away every 20 minutes.

The plan was initially scrapped when business owners and certain environmental groups protested, but the debate resumed in 2013.

Now, if the town is worried about money, why spend money on noisemakers? Hunters, America's original wildlife managers, would gladly scatter the eiders. We'd even buy licenses for the opportunity.

When hunting sea ducks, one must consider the potentially brutal and ever-changing conditions posed by North America's largest waters. There will surely come a time when you must end the hunt and head for calmer seas—immediately.

Many experienced sea duck hunters assemble a relatively small decoy spread, enabling it to be picked up quickly. Three or four long-lines are really all you need. Anchor the lines at both ends using sufficiently heavy weights—fishing weights or even red plastic cups filled with cement work great. Clip or tie about a dozen decoys to each line, spaced about four feet apart, as sea ducks tend to raft in closer quarters than other waterfowl. Space the lines 5–7 yards (or meters) apart, with the decoys' heads facing into the current or wind. The boat or blind should be positioned with the wind at the hunters' backs.

The spread should consist primarily of the ducks you're most likely to encounter. If scoters are on the menu, all three species may be mixed together in your lines. If targeting long-taileds, too, position three to five individually rigged decoys downwind of the spread—often that's all that's needed to draw these "bonus birds" within range. Then get ready. Sea duck habitat can be an adventure to reach, but the birds tend to decoy readily.

In scouting, look for sea ducks actively diving for shellfish, as opposed to those simply at rest. Loafing areas can change daily, but sea ducks hitting a food source are as close to a slam dunk as you'll find in waterfowl hunting.

When they do come, shoot, and don't be afraid to keep shooting. As long as a sea duck can move its feet, it's able to elude hunters and dogs with incredible might. —K.W.

DEFEND AGAINST SALT

I once asked a dedicated sea duck hunter how he keeps his guns in such pristine condition. "That's easy," he said. "Every year I buy a new one."

Saltwater is easily the worst substance a shotgun can be exposed to. However, preventative measures can be taken. Prior to the hunt, all parts should be wiped with a light coating of antirust gun oil. Note that powder solvents such as Hoppe's No. 9 are cleaners—they don't prevent rust. Take particular care to coat the barrel extension, which tends to trap moisture and can quickly pit. Choke threads are likewise a magnet for moisture; coat your tube's threads with gun grease, lest they rust and convert your gun to a fixed-choke model. After a hunt, break down your gun as soon as possible, and completely dry, clean, and re-oil it. Do not put it off until the next day.

If you're in the market for a sea-duck gun, consider a camo-dipped model. The dip conceals the shotgun, but more importantly it protects it from the elements.

THE MARYLAND SLAM

Unofficially known as a "Maryland Slam," the Free State offers one of the best opportunities to bag a long-tailed duck and all three scoters. Huge wintering populations are supported by the 4,479-square mile (7,208-square km) Chesapeake Bay and the Potomac River, particularly at its salty southern reaches. Completing the slam without a guide, however, is a daunting task. These are treacherous waters, and the often-confusing Maryland game laws are a challenge in themselves. All hunters are required to have at least one licensed Maryland resident with them at all times, and private blinds line most banks, relegating public gunners to hunting off-shore. In most cases, the law requires public Chesapeake hunters to be at least 800 yards (or meters) from shore. But with careful planning, the right equipment, and perhaps a call to the state authorities for clarification, your Maryland Slam dreams can become reality.

WILD TURKEY

"IN LOVE WITH A TURKEY? How could anybody be in love with a bird that looks like its head was boiled in acid?" That was my dad, circa 1995. I had just been anointed the Montana state president for the National Wild Turkey Federation, and I was feeling as reverential as a country deacon and as chesty as an April tom. "Maybe it's not love. But how could anybody not be in awe of a 20-pound bird that spends 10 months of the year hiding from everything and two months thinking it's an 800-pound bull elk? With claws?"

My dad was too stubborn to admit he knew exactly what I was talking about. A Missouri farmer, he had seen strutting gobblers from the seat of his tractor, tending harems of trip-wire hens, sparring with rival toms, and displaying their iridescent fan feathers like seniors at the junior prom.

And he had been stopped dead in his work boots by the explosive, astonishing gobbles of love-struck turkeys, the very sound of wild spring. But my father was a member of a lost generation of Americans, an age group of citizens who didn't hear a spring gobble or see a strutting tom until late in their lives.

Wild turkeys defined America long before our continent had a name. They fed Iroquois and Cherokee and Puritans. But they're poultry, and poultry love handouts. The wild turkeys that weren't shot were lured to the barnyard, and for most of the 20th century, the hardwoods and bottomlands of America were silent in the spring.

But a few reservoirs of turkeys remained, mainly in the remote hollers and ridges of the Ozarks, and thanks to far-sighted hunter-conservationists who recognized the forgotten resource, in the 1970s and '80s those vestigial flocks were systematically trapped and transplanted to habitat that had been vacant for my father's childhood. They are ancestors of the birds that wake us up each spring with their booming gobbles and brazen display. Thanks to this redistribution, North America's wild turkey population extends to every state but Alaska, and in nearly every type of habitat on the continent, from the swamps of Florida to the mountains of the West, and from the prairie states to the hot, arid Southwest.

GOBBLER LOADS

I once believed that only No. 4 shot was adequate to take down a big gobbler. But with new advances in shotshell wads and payload technology, I'm now shooting No. 6 or even No. 7 shot for wild turkeys out past 50 yards. A couple of brands have changed my mind. The first is Federal's Heavyweight lead load with Flitecontrol wad that keeps the pattern tighter for longer distances. The second is Winchester's Long Beard XR that uses resin to keep pellets intact and clustered.

Every turkey hunter has a favorite way to hunt. For some it's decoying gobblers into a ground blind. For others it's sitting in full camo beneath the same shagbark hickory each season and calling in an eager tom. But I like to walk and call, then walk some more until I strike a responsive gobbler. Then I improvise the final act, and sometimes walk home with a colorful, long-bearded wild turkey over my shoulder, its boiled-in-acid head dripping blood down the back of my legs.

I've hunted turkeys in the fall, ambushed them while they scratch in dry oak leaves and lain in wait as they filed past my deer stand. But there's nothing like hunting wild turkeys in the spring, as the earth wakens and the gobble of a dominant tom sunders the April dawn with the command of an Old Testament disciple.

The appeal of spring hunting is that you can call a gobbler into killing range, where his keen eyes can detect any motion or sign of danger—meaning that only hunters who employ stock-still stealth and woodcraft regularly kill turkeys.

And, like bugling in a bull elk or mouse-squeaking in a coyote, there's simply nothing more elemental than fooling a wild animal with its own razor-sharp senses.

A HARDWOOD ORCHESTRA: TYPES OF TURKEY CALLS

BOX CALL The simplest call to use, this is a thin-sided wooden box with a hinged lid that scratches across the opening. The friction of the lid (also called the paddle) makes high-pitched yelps and staccato cuts.

SLATE CALL Another friction call, the slate is sometimes called a "peg-and-pot" call because its sound board is any number of a friction surfaces (often slate, but also glass, ceramic, or aluminum) glued to a shallow cup, or pot. Imitations are made by scraping a striker (the peg) across the surface. Slates produce searching yelps, excited cuts, putts, and soft purrs.

DIAPHRAGM CALL Also generically called a mouth call, this is a thin piece of latex or other vibrating membrane that's held inside a horseshoe-shaped frame. The frame is sized to fit inside a human mouth, where it's held against the roof of the mouth while air is blown across the membrane. The air creates vibrations, which can be tuned to sound like yelps, clucks, purrs, and cackles.

PUSH-PIN CALLS These easy-to-use calls require hunters to push a plunger or wooden dowel over an internal striker, making clucks and purrs.

WING BONE CALLS Some of the most ancient and elegant turkey calls are fashioned from the hollow wing bones of wild turkeys. The bones are glued together to create a small trumpet, which is sucked on, or kissed, to create soft yelps and clucks.

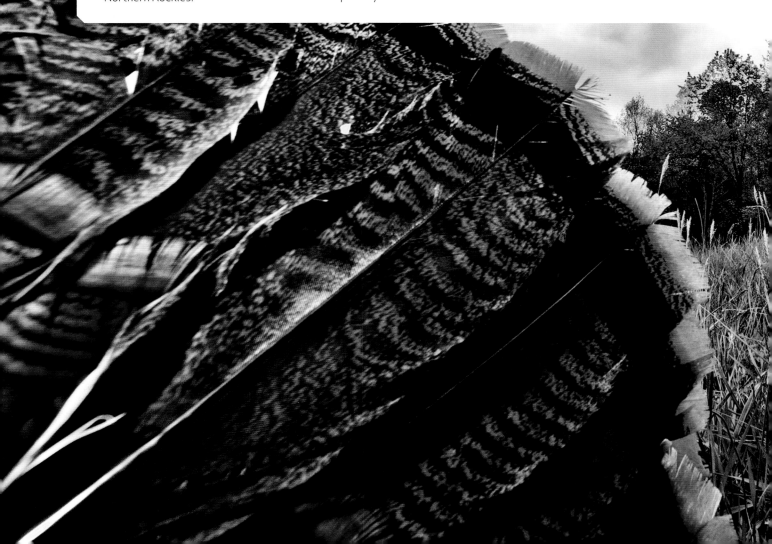

GO FOR THE GOLD

GRAND SLAM

EASTERN This subspecies, defined by an affinity for woodlands and its chocolate-brown tail feathers, is generally found in the East, Southeast, Midwest, and various areas of the West and Northwest.

MERRIAM'S Native to the Four Corners area of the Southwest, the Merriam's has distinctive, white-tipped tail feathers and is especially vocal. Merriam's have been transplanted to much of the Great Plains and Northern Rockies.

OSCEOLA Sometimes called the Florida turkey, the Osceola is native to central and southern Florida. It looks like an especially leggy version of the Eastern turkey, but has black wing feathers with little white barring.

RIO GRANDE This subspecies is native to Texas, Oklahoma, and a portion of Kansas. It prefers riparian corridors and has caramel-colored tail feathers. Rios tend to be especially vocal on the roost.

WORLD SLAM

OCELLATED This beardless turkey is native to Mexico's Yucatan and south into Belize. Long-spurred gobblers have orange nodules on their bright blue heads and prefer the edges of dense jungles.

GOULD'S The largest wild turkey in North America, this subspecies lives in Mexico's Chihuahua and Sonora states and north into the border country of New Mexico and Arizona. The Gould's white-tipped tail feathers resemble those of the Merriam's.

YUCATAN TURKEYS

I once suspected that the colorful, wart-skulled birds of Mexico's Yucatan Peninsula weren't true turkeys, but occupied a sort of evolutionary link between guinea fowl of South America and our North American wild turkey. I based that assumption largely on their appearance. Ocellated birds have iridescent eye-shapes on their tail feathers, just like peafowl do, and they don't have beards. They also don't gobble in the same way that northern birds do.

Then I hunted them. The mating whistle of toms was gobbling, only in a foreign language.

A generation ago, pioneering ocellated turkey hunters probed deep in the jungles of Mexico and Belize, located roost sites, and shot birds off the limb. They assumed these turkeys wouldn't respond to a call, and besides, the jungle foliage is so dense that seeing a turkey before it spotted you was nearly impossible. But a change in habitat and understanding of ocellated habits has made this more of a sporting hunt. I called my gobbler out of the jungle and into newly cleared soybean fields, where I had a clear shot.

On my drive back to the provincial city of Merida, I visited one of several Mayan ruins. There, carved in the porous limestone alongside depictions of leopards, ocelots, and human sacrifice, were carvings of wart-headed turkeys—evidence that jungle hunters have been pursuing ocellated birds here for a long time, indeed.

RAILS AND SNIPE

IF ONE HAS MERELY VIEWED PHOTOS OF THE VARIOUS MEMBERS of the rail and snipe families, he may think those who pursue them a curious bunch. The birds are small, long-billed, and rather gangly in appearance. But make no mistake: When they spring from the marsh, that whirring of wings is enough to awaken any hunter's heart. The small fraternity that pursues these birds is privy to one of hunting's best-kept secrets, indeed. The fact that these worm-eating shorebirds live mainly on easily accessible public marshlands further enhances their appeal.

As most hunters have never gone looking for rails, they're unaware of the abundance to be found. The rail family is quite diverse, with North America's key species including the king, Virginia, sora, and especially the clapper rail. While these migratory birds are found throughout the Atlantic, Mississippi, and Central flyways, they are most commonly hunted along the Atlantic and Gulf Coasts.

Rails are a reclusive bunch, hiding out in dense marsh vegetation and practically requiring contact from a boot to flush. Hunting techniques vary by region and personal taste. Some simply walk the soft, mucky ground hoping to force rails to take flight, while others employ close-ranging bird dogs. In Virginia, North Carolina, and other coastal states, poling boats through flooded marshes is a popular tactic. Florida sportsmen have adopted the ingenious technique of pulling a drag cord with a coin- or pebble-filled can affixed to it—creating a commotion to spring the birds. Once flushed, the challenge is mostly over: Rails exhibit a slow, low-altitude flight.

The woodcock-like snipe, on the other hand, flies like a ruffed grouse: swiftly, erratically, and without any apparent destination. And, also like the grouse, they often require long walks for the exhilaration of but one or two flushes. Jump shooting is common and pointing dog breeds are a fine asset. Look for snipe in marshy areas, swamps, and flooded agriculture such as rice and mud flats.

About 30,000 snipe hunters bag 100,000 birds annually, while 25,000 rail hunters take roughly 45,000 rails. Rather minuscule numbers, sure, but only because so many overlook this fine form of coastal outdoor recreation. —K.W.

ORIGINS OF THE TERM "SNIPER"

How much marksmanship is necessary to pluck a darting snipe from the air? Apparently enough that it led to the term *sniper*.

According to *Out of Nowhere: A History of the Military Sniper* by Martin Pegler, journalists popularized the term during the initial months of World War I as a reference to sharpshooters.

Comparing the skill required to bag a small bird to that of shooting an enemy soldier at short range is an interesting homage, but the term stuck. The sniper is now, of course, a specific military assignment, while accomplished snipe hunters quietly remain some of America's finest wingshots.

SQUIRRELS

THERE IS NO BETTER ATHLETE NOR GAME ANIMAL on the planet. Sure, they're members of the *Rodentia* order, but that doesn't stop millions of us from hunting and eating them. Tree squirrels—grays, reds, and variations—require woodcraft, patience, marksmanship, and a healthy dose of humility. Who's the best hunter you know? His teeth were likely cut staring into treetops. Looking for clarity in times of confusion? Seek out a hollow dripping with acorns and invite a hunter. There you'll find squirrels, hope . . . and truly, you just might find yourself.

Squirrels inhabit the entirety of the Americas and indeed are found throughout most of the world, with tree-nesting squirrels being the predominant species in the United States except out in the Mountain West. There, ground squirrels such as marmots, prairie dogs, and gophers colonize the earth and make challenging targets for long-range riflemen.

While there are more than 120 subspecies of squirrels, most American sportsmen focus on gray squirrels. State hunting seasons recognize this animal's proliferation and allow liberal seasons and bag limits. In the 2014 Squirrel Master's Classic hunting tournament held in Alabama, more than 200 squirrels where taken by 30 contestants in two days of hunting!

Squirrel hunting is the ultimate hunter's training activity; to be successful, hunters must employ many elements of woodsmanship—like moving with the wind, knowing when to sit and when to move, reading sign, using camouflage, and delivering an accurate shot.

Personally, I prefer still-hunting in the early fall, when squirrels can frequently be found among the leafy limbs of food-laden trees. Find a woodlot with good sign, slip in, and sit for 10–15 minutes until its creatures resume their natural chatter. Listen for the tell-tale grating sound of teeth upon acorns, the popping of shell cuttings falling to the ground, and the scraping of claws over bark—all the while scanning the limbs for movement and studying each trunk for the telltale hump of a tail or ear.

After I shoot at a squirrel or see none, I'll slip 50 yards farther in, lean against a broad oak, and do it all over again. —*J.J.*

PRAIRIE DOGGIN'

Want to get some marksmanship practice while doing farmers a favor? Go prairie dog hunting.

In the West, especially in prairie states such as South Dakota and eastern Wyoming, among others, thousands of concentrated prairie dogs can ruin farmer's fields and endanger livestock by lacing the ground with holes.

Find a colony, or call an outfitter for help locating one, and bring your most accurate rifle with plenty of ammo. A bolt-action rifle chambered in .22-250 Rem. is great, while a heavy-barreled AR-15 might even be better.

Mount a scope with high magnification and know your dope, because a 3-inch (8-cm) running, diving, and disappearing dog makes a darn tough target, especially at 500 yards (or meters) in a typical western crosswind. But it will also make you a better shooter—and make your local farmer happy.

GOOD SQUIRREL DOGS DON'T MISS

Danny Williams of Doniphan, Missouri, raises world-champion squirrel dogs. These tenacious, 15–30-pound (6.8–13.6-kg) Feists scamper through and bark when they spot, smell, or tree a bushytail. It's nothing for a hunter to bag a limit of squirrels in a couple hours of hunting, because good squirrel dogs don't often miss. "It's a great way to hunt squirrels," says Williams. "You don't have to be quiet; you can take a kid, talk, cut-up, and have fun." For more information, look up the American Treeing Feist Association.

GETTING SQUIRRELY

For best success in the squirrel woods, don camo or earth-toned clothes, a hat to shield the sun while looking up, and a game vest. Bring a knife, a small binocular, quiet boots, and a barking-type squirrel call. Most hunters prefer an accurate .22 LR rifle for headshots, while others prefer a 410-bore shotgun loaded with No. 6s, especially in fall months when squirrels are on the ground foraging food caches. Larger gauges are even more deadly but not as classy. For added challenge, try a bow loaded with a flu-flu arrow, a .22 LR pistol, or, best yet, a 32- or 36-caliber flintlock rifle. Aim for the head and prepare your ego for copious misses.

MISSISSIPPI-STYLE SKINNING

Here's a 5-minute method that minimizes contamination from hair and dirt. First, slice the underside of the tail just behind the back legs, and then cut through the tailbone to the off-side skin. Cut down the back of each thigh to the back of each knee. Then place a foot on the squirrel's tail to pin it to the ground, grasp the squirrel by the back feet, and pull up. The tail and skin should peel over the entire carcass to the head. Cut the legs at the knees, and with the squirrel suspended, gut it. Cut off the head and wash out the carcass.

THE MASKED BANDIT

Down around Columbus, Georgia, and a few other pockets of the Deep South, there's a color phase of fox squirrels unlike any other. Weighing nearly 3 pounds (1.4 kg), it wears a black mask over a white and brown face. After spying this curious creature, I discontinued my deer hunt and snuck back into the woods loaded with No. 6 shot. Today I'm as proud of that masked-face squirrel as any big buck on my wall.

PARTRIDGE

WARY BY NATURE AND AT HOME IN BIG COUNTRY, partridge are not a lazy man's bird. Hunters who chase the Eurasian imports (and *chase* is the appropriate word) need not only be fit but also borderline masochistic. In an all-too-common occurrence, chukars have a bad habit of leading hunters up rocky crags before pitching back to the bottom, while their gray counterpart, the Hungarian partridge, play catch-me-if-you-can with coveys flushing wildly across rolling grain fields at greater and greater distances from the hunters following behind.

In Europe, partridge hunting is a more civilized affair, in which red-legged birds fly high and fast over the heads of stationed gunners in grand, driven hunts. The chukar, Hun, and red-legged are just the three most commonly hunted members of what is a large group of partridges native to Europe and Asia. Part of the pheasant family, these birds spend most of their life on the ground, roosting and nesting in brush, grass, and other tall cover. Partridges prefer the company of others and live their lives in flocks of 8–12 individuals.

When flushed, their short wings provide a quick getaway, though generally not a long one. The flock will often come to rest within sight of the hunter—though unfortunately not within range of his shotgun.

Like their ring-necked cousin, both chukars and Huns staked a claim in the New World, the product of successful transplants by immigrant sportsman looking to continue their classic wingshooting tradition in America.

Although related, the two couldn't be more different in both behavior and appearance. The circuslike chukar, with its zebra stripes and clownish markings, set up shop in the Great Basin and high deserts of the West, where it lives today in rough, scrub country, drawing hunters ever uphill in steep terrain only to flush downward as the dogs and gunners approach. A minimalist beauty, the gray and brown plumage of the Hungarian partridge is well suited to the Huns' adopted home in the large grass- and croplands of the northern Great Plains and southern Canada's Prairie Provinces, where they flush out of wheat stubble and low-slung cheatgrass like stocky open-country quail.

IN A PEAR TREE

Knowing that the partridge is a ground-dwelling bird, it would be very odd indeed to find a single one sitting atop that famous pear tree your true love gave to thee at the start of that catchy carol, "The Twelve Days of Christmas."

The snows must have been deep during the holiday season when the song was written, forcing the flock to roost in an orchard.

All kidding aside, a more likely explanation is that the verse is a poor translation of "a partridge, *un perdix*," given that the latter term, pronounced "per-dee," is the French word for the bird.

In Greek mythology, Perdix, nephew of Daedalus, was tossed from a tower by his jealous uncle, but turned into a bird before landing. Despite this escape from death, the experience forever instilled a fear of high places— including pear trees— in his namesake, the partridge.

If you want to hunt chukars, you better be in good shape, for the little gray birds will make a mockery of all but the fittest of men. Dogs, too, take a beating in chukar country, as does a hunter's gear, begging the question as to why anyone would hunt the infernal things. That question is easily answered when you connect on one of the hardest-won trophies among wingshooters out West. The beautiful view rolling away from a shorthair hard on point at the top of cliff is just icing on the cake.

Just like glassing for big game, employing a good pair of optics to find birds can save miles of boot leather. Chukars tend to feed just after sunup, scratching out a meal from whatever seeds and greens can be found on steep hillsides. From there they move to shady rimrock and outcroppings where they're shielded from both the harsh sun and hungry eagles. Once you find birds, make a plan to get to them, which will almost always require hiking uphill.

Given the opportunity, chukars would rather run from danger than fly, but when they do flush they invariably do so downhill, using speed gained through gravity to their advantage. If possible, approach them from above in order to cut off their two-legged escape plans and force them into the air. When the covey does flush, pick one bird and shoot quickly. It's surprising how fast chukars are able to get out of shotgun range, and doubles are a very rare occurrence. —D.D.

THREE THINGS EVERY PARTRIDGE HUNTER SHOULD KNOW

STAY CLOSE Huns' wary nature all but guarantees they will flush wild, but birds tend not to fly far. Stick with the covey if you can. Eventually they'll tire and hold for a good pointing dog. Also mark any singles that may break away from the pack, as they have a tendency to sit tight, offering a closer, and thereby easier, shot.

FIND THE RIGHT HEIGHT FOR CHUKARS For whatever reason, chukars tend to favor a particular elevation, but it's not entirely predictable and may differ from day to day or depend on the time of year. Once you find a bird, make note of its level on the mountain. Chances are the rest of that covey, as well as others, will be at that same elevation, or close to it.

CHECK THE COVER Unless flushed, partridge tend to stay close to their roost, rarely venturing more than 100 yards or meters from it throughout the day. Concentrate your efforts around field edges or weedy patches in vast stubble fields. No cover is too thin for a Hun, so don't overlook close-cropped fields of oats, barley, or alfalfa.

QUAIL

THE BLUE-BELTON SETTER LOOPS DOWNWIND AND ARCS BACK INTO THE BREEZE with graceful ferocity. That is, until a covey of bobwhites wafts into his nostrils. The dog abruptly decelerates, lifts one leg slightly and locks his long, feathered tail at 12 o'clock. You approach with the butt of your grandfather's Parker tucked beneath your shoulder. Adrenaline flows. Your mouth runs dry. Bobwhites are about to take wing. Time stands still. This could be Alabama between the wars, or Oklahoma in the '60s. Or, for a few lucky quail hunters, right now.

There are no rules against hunting bobwhite quail while wearing jeans and toting a well-worn, pump-action shotgun. However, unlike most upland pursuits—in which necktie-adorned hunters exist only in vintage photos—southern quail hunting preserves gentlemanly tradition. Tweed and waxed cotton attire are not out of place, nor are 20-gauge sidelocks. Even the dogs seem dressed to the nines with their handsome coats and finely feathered extremities. Horses and off-road vehicles are further optional accouterments, as much ground may be covered behind a rangy pointer in pursuit of coveys.

Unfortunately, the pointer's task is a far greater challenge than when southeast bobwhites peaked from 1890 to the 1940s. A steady, drastic decline is ongoing—since 1990, the northern bobwhite population (the major subspecies) has shrunk by over 65 percent.

The tragedy is largely habitat related. Bobwhites depend on natural grassland habitats for nesting and protection from predators. When humans convert these habitats for their use—and don't undo the damage through prescribed burns—bobwhites are imperiled.

Despite their setbacks, bobwhites are still found east of the Rockies sporadically from Canada to Mexico, and they remain the most prolific quail species.

Mr. Bob is joined by five western cousins. Of these, the California (or "valley") quail is found in greatest numbers. Nesting in the western and northwestern United States, they may be found in massive coveys numbering hundreds of birds. Look for them in grassland valleys or foothill regions.

SHOW-ME QUAIL

Missouri's Department of Conservation has identified a number of plants that quail use for food and cover. If you want quail on your land, make sure you have at least a few of the following: American plum, shrub dogwood, common ragweed, foxtail, millet, lespedeza, partridge pea, and Illinois bundleflower.

The California quail's range overlaps with that of the mountain quail, a name derived from its affinity for nesting in the mountains before returning to lower elevations in the fall. Mountain quail are found in far brushier, forested habitat and smaller family groups than the bobwhite and California.

In the drier, more arid regions of the American southwest, you'll find Gambel's (or "desert") quail. Favoring habitat with desert shrubs, it occasionally interbreeds with California quail—the only known quail hybridization. They're known to covey by the hundreds near water sources.

Scaled (or "blue") quail are likewise found coveyed in southwestern desert-shrub habitats, as well as arid grasslands. They have an almost rabbit-like attraction to the shelter of brush piles.

If you're looking for a unique trophy, consider the Mearn's (or "Montezuma") quail, which has the smallest range of any species in the United States. Though widespread in Mexico, domestically they're only in the grasslands and oak-juniper mountains of southern Texas, New Mexico, and Arizona.

Regardless of species, the hunter who returns with a vest full is in for a fine treat. Lightly pan-fried, quail are pound-for-pound the tastiest of upland game. —K.W.

THE PERFECT QUAIL DOG

When the term *bird dog* is articulated with a southern drawl, rest assured it refers to an English setter or pointer that hunts quail. Such is the region's rich quail tradition and strict breed loyalty—but one would be hard pressed to argue that better quail breeds exist, regardless. Many breeds have good noses, but setters and pointers have the long legs and stamina required to cover vast tracts of open quail habitat. Many quail species also hold superbly for points, allowing hunters to approach their dogs and get in position for the flush.

This does not mean that flushing breeds such as spaniels and retrievers are never used. Some swear by them. But they must hunt within gun range, covering less ground per hour. And there's greater difficulty in getting on target, as even a close-ranging spaniel will flush birds farther ahead of the hunters than over a point.

Spaniels and retrievers are, the author contends, better at recovering downed birds. That's why many savvy hunters use them in tandem with pointers and setters. The pointing dog finds the quail and—at just the right moment—the flushing dog is sent in to spring the birds and fetch 'em up. It's the perfect team.

GET READY FOR A DESERT QUAIL HUNT

Given that the arid American Southwest is home to a diversity of quail including the scaled, Gambel's, Mearn's and, in rare instances, the California, it's a fine destination for mixed-bag adventure. However, desert hunting requires special preparations. Here are some items to help ensure a safe, enjoyable hunt.

WATER And lots of it. Keep a 2–3 gallon (7.5–11 liter) reservoir in your vehicle and carry canteens afield.

BOOTS (FOR YOU, AND FOR THE DOG) Wear light, comfortable boots. Consider leather to fend off cactus thorns. Specialized dog boots will likewise protect your dog's pads from cacti and sharp rocks. Don't worry; he'll get used to them.

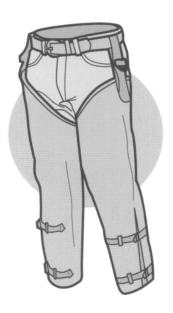

LIGHTWEIGHT SHOTGUN Carry a light 12- or subgauge gun for long, hot walks. They're also ideal for quick snap shooting.

BRUSH PANTS AND/OR SNAKE CHAPS Self-explanatory, no? You can also snakeproof your dog by using a fake or de-fanged snake and an e-collar. An Internet search will bring up plentiful opportunities in many regions.

VEST WITH OPTIONAL HYDRATION SYSTEM Many prefer the weight distribution of modern backpack-style or shoulder-strap style vests. Often they include hydration systems, the drawback being added weight and expense. The author prefers a traditional vest, but they get warm on hot days.

QUAIL AREAS MAKING A COMEBACK

The North American Wildlife Conservation Model is ripe with feel-good stories, but quail are among its saddest. Still, there are reasons for optimism.

Bobwhite quail appear to be on the cusp of a major comeback in some states, especially Oklahoma. Increased cattle sales in the Sooner State are decreasing pasture grazing, thereby improving grassland habitat. Meanwhile, several years of harsh weather have yielded to milder spring conditions and grass-replenishing rains. The impact has been swift, with state biologists reporting a decade-high bobwhite population. Still, Oklahoma's quail have a long way to go based on the current estimate of 750,000 to 1 million birds. It hasn't reached peak numbers since the 1990s, when the state had 7 million.

If it's mountain quail you're after, look for the highest densities in southwest Oregon. The Coast Range of mountains is considered the best choice, but ample coveys may also be found along the western edge of the Cascades. Mountain quail appear to be declining in other areas of Oregon, as well as Washington and California. Biologists have yet to fully ascertain why.

Gambel's quail, however, have fairly stable populations. They tend to fluctuate each year, a product of their dependence on weather conditions during the nesting cycle. An ample statewide population is found in Arizona, particularly the open desert terrain of the Sonora and Mojave.

TROPICAL SPECIES

30° NORTH – 15° SOUTH

30° NORTH – 15° SOUTH

IN THIS STEAMY LATITUDE OF JUNGLE AND DESERT, EVERYTHING EITHER BITES OR STINGS. Animals are armored, fanged, furtive, and camouflaged—sometimes all at once. Where there is water, it's brackish and malarial. Where there is none, animals congregate around succulent plants and canyon walls, waiting on the shade.

This is the land of the ferocious sun, and the intense temperatures and equatorial seasons affect both prey and predator species.

Take the apex reptiles of this region, those crocodiles and alligators found in the coastal estuaries. If there is a more sinister, ambush-minded predator, I don't know it. These water dragons may have the reactive, cold-blooded instincts of a ball peen hammer, but what makes them especially disturbing is that they combine homicidal impulses with the ability to reason, react, and decide.

I base that conclusion on the experience of a good friend. He lived in a subdivision along Florida's St. Johns River, and was training a six-month-old black Lab puppy, Homer, for the waterfowl season. Part of the training included dummy work, and one evening Doug launched his dummy in the backyard. It caught the wind and sailed over the dike into a canal. Of course, Homer pursued the dummy. But he never returned. A gator inhaled him.

Doug was naturally distraught, and determined that this wouldn't happen to any more puppies on his watch. He fished for that reptile with snagging hooks. He baited it with chickens and roadkill raccoons. He waited on the dike with his crossbow. He didn't see the gator for weeks, until his neighbor walked his terrier dog along the embankment. Something on the water's edge caught the dog's eye, and he went for it. Doug described the chaos that ensued.

"There was a boil, a big boil, like you rolled a piano into the water. That dog was just gone in the chaos. We called the gator folks and they basically fenced in the canal."

Animal control captured the gator, an 11-footer (3.4-meter) with barbed wire wrapped around one of its front feet, and got permission from authorities to kill it. Inside its distended stomach they found three dog collars, including Homer's. This was a mature predator that selected succulent young pups, not rank meat or opportunistic baits. And it confirmed my long-held certainty that I do not want to end up in the stomach of any reptile.

This is also the latitude of the hog and the javelina. As we'll discuss, feral hogs have become the scourge of the American South. But their presence there is complicated. Most hunters who don't have hogs in their area code wish they did, because they want limitless opportunities to gun for wild pork. Those who do have pigs would trade their big deer and even sacrosanct bobwhite quail for a future without rooting, grubbing, habitat-destroying hogs.

And this is the latitude of possibly the most efficient and least understood predator on earth, the jaguar. Do these ambush predators live in the American Southwest, or do they not? That's their nature and their appeal, to live on the obscure margins of human settlement, where they may (or may not) make a living on mule deer, desert bighorns, and the diminutive Coues deer.

So bring some breathable clothes, plenty of bug dope, and shoes that can handle sun-blasted rock and stagnant water, and hunt all the remarkable animals of this midsection of our globe.

JAVELINAS

IF YOU DOUBT the genius of evolution, then the pig and the peccary should settle it for you. On continents separated by oceans and millennia, the two species evolved to function and behave nearly identically, and even look so much alike that the New World peccary is routinely confused with the Eurasian hog. But the wilder, more bashful, and arid-loving peccary (better known as the javelina north of Mexico's Sonora) is by far the more polite of the two species, even if it's less adaptable and tasty than the voracious, invasive feral hog.

"Javelinas are fair game, and you're going to see some dandies," said Randy Morrison, foreman at the Texas Hill Country ranch that I was hunting. "But here's the deal: The limit is one, and you can shoot it only if you are going to mount it on your wall. Pigs? Shoot 'em all and leave 'em lay."

That seemed fair all the way around, and though I was covered up in nuisance pigs, I didn't fire a shot from my crossbow. I was holding out for a giant whitetail. My focus was broken only one time, as I rounded a bend of a gas pipeline in the middle of a huge cactus-infested pasture. A swarm of maybe 40 javelinas was jittering and snuffling toward me, snouts to the ground like bloodhounds. I tucked beneath a mesquite and watched them approach. They fretted prickly pear and rooted leaves, and one old male with a grizzled white mane caught my attention. He'd look great on my wall.

And that's where he might be if the wind hadn't shifted and blown my scent toward the herd, which scattered like quail into the Texas scrub.

I had experienced both the trip-wire senses and the communal nature of javelina, one of the most successful omnivores of the Southwest. Also known as collared peccary for the distinctive white brindle that decorates their shoulders and chest like a laureate's medal, javelinas grub scabland from southeastern Texas to Arizona and south through Mexico and Central America into northern Argentina.

They are often found in these gregarious gangs that I encountered, and when alarmed, they scatter. But a hunting technique that I didn't consider is to sit tight and make soft snorting noises. Often, the flushed animals will run to the sound.

CALLING JAVELINAS

While they are generally mild-tempered, javelina can be agitated by a distress call that imitates a trapped or injured member of their pack. The sound is similar to a distressed rabbit call, but with more screams, groans, and growls.

Calls are effective in short-distance situations, especially after you have busted up a sounder and want to regroup them around your location.

Many javelina callers say that adults will come charging in to their location, looking for the perceived persecutor, and may even bluff charge. But they will invariably stop short, giving you a close-in shot and a heady dose of adrenalin.

The collared peccary is the arid climate-loving member of this New World family. Its close cousin, the white-lipped peccary, roots in the rainforests of Central and South America, and a more obscure kin, the Chacoan peccary, lives in Paraguay and Bolivia.

But it's the javelina that gets the most attention from hunters, even if it is usually misinformed. These wire-haired grubbers have had an undeserved reputation for decades. Old magazines told sordid tales of peccaries mauling dogs, attacking hunters, and even taking down fawns. Their reputation isn't helped by the practice of most taxidermists, who mount javelinas with their mouths open, showing sharp, upjutting fangs. It isn't hard to imagine those root-digging teeth as flesh-rending tusks.

But it's all bunk. Javelinas are mild, shy, and almost entirely herbivorous, and their modest tusks point down and are hardly ever seen. These voracious trotters are, however, a lot of fun to hunt, and any Southwestern deer, coyote, or even hog hunter should keep an eye open for a javelina for the wall.

In the American Southwest, the best place to find them on public land is Arizona, mainly in the Tuscon area, though their range continues to expand north, and numbers are found as far north as Flagstaff. You'll find the greatest densities around concentrations of prickly pear cactus, for the spiny fruit is the javelina's favorite food. But these omnivores will eat the acorns of mature oakbrush, any fruit they can find, plus nuts, berries, and bulbs.

TOP JAVELINA GUNS AND BOWS

Without sounding too generic, any hunting implement that you would use for rabbit, deer, or predators will effectively handle javelina. A .22 rimfire might be a bit too light, just as a big .30 magnum might be too much for these animals, which average 30 pounds (14 kg) but have tough hides and a fairly small vital area.

The best rifles are the mild .25-calibers. An old .25/20 Winchester is nearly perfect for close-in shooting, and a .25-06 is about right for longer shots. Bows are well suited to javelina hunting, and crossbows are even better, since you don't have to draw your string as javelina sift in to your location. Any broadhead you'd use for deer will dispatch a javelina, though you should be prepared for a longish recovery through cactus, mesquite, and thorny chaparral.

HUNTING STRATEGIES In most of the world, the biggest crocs are either given a wide berth or are relentlessly pursued by visiting hunters with big-bore rifles, many of whom spend long days and nights baiting the brutes with tethered oxen and mutilated wildebeest. The sluggish and sleepy appearance of both alligators and crocs is misleading; they can move quickly in and out of the water with their webbed feet, and can snatch food and pull it under water in the blink of an (unblinking) eye. They also have prodigious olfactory and auditory senses, all of which make hunting an old trophy an intense exercise in surveillance and stealth.

In America, gator hunting is a more active sport, but most states discourage or prohibit shooting unless the animal is first hooked or caught, in order to minimize wounding loss. This means that most gator hunts more closely resemble fishing expeditions than hunting adventures.

GATOR HUNTING BASICS

Most alligator hunts begin after sunset, and primary tools are a shallow-bottom boat and a powerful floodlight. Hunters cruise lakes and marshes, shining the light along the shoreline, trying to catch the red reflection of a gator's eye.

Once located and sized up, gators are baited with a dead fish or chicken—something that is appealing to a predator and can hide a long, strong hook. Here's the typical gear that's deployed.

BAITED HOOKS Rotting chickens or other bait is fixed to large hooks and cast into likely gator water. When alligators take the bait, they hook themselves deep in the gut. Bringing the gator to hand is a matter of reeling it in, like playing a large and surly fish.

SNATCH HOOKS Snatch hooks, which are basically big hooks attached to broom handles, are used to try to snag the gator with the hook and bring it boatside.

HARPOONS AND GIGS Same idea as the snatch hook, these sharp objects are used to control the animal so that it can be dispatched. Harpoons are thrown; gigs are jabbed.

BANGSTICKS Also called "power heads," these are the simplest kinds of firearms, discharging a killing round upon contact. The hunter basically taps the tethered gator with the tip of the stick, detonating the cartridge and dispatching the animal.

GUNS AND BOWS In many states, shooting an untethered gator is illegal; instead, guns (often shotguns) and bows (either compounds or crossbows) are brought out to finish off a hooked alligator.

MEDITERRANEAN SHEEP

NORTH AMERICAN HUNTERS think of wild sheep as their own discoveries, the way a jeweler might fantasize that he mined the glittering diamond himself. The truth is that wild sheep have lived on the edge of human settlements even before (and happily, after) Noah gave their allegorical ancestors a ride on his boat—and long before we celebrated any ram slam. The crucible of the species is the dry, severe land around the Mediterranean Sea, the original Bible belt. Hunting them in their original habitat is a feat of logistics, endurance, and faith.

Just as many of the world's religions consider the Middle East their spiritual homeland, sheep hunters would do well to look to the creosote-dry mountains surrounding the Mediterranean as the biological and cultural epicenter of the species of their affections.

The genetic thread starts with the mouflon, a variety of wild sheep that features wide, curling horns and an affinity for vertical terrain. Mouflon range from northern Africa across the Islamist scablands of Iraq, into the timbered plateaus that extend from Turkey, west all the way to Spain. Transplanted mouflon are found as far north as Finland.

The urial sheep, a close cousin of the mouflon, ranges east through Turkey and Iran to the high, remote Central Asian Plateau.

The mouflon is probably the ancestor for our domestic sheep, and its acquiescence to the pen and ease of interbreeding made it a prime candidate for translocation. Subspecies of this wild sheep—and there are more than a dozen in the family—range from the rugged Atlas Mountains of Morocco all the way to the dusty foothills of Central Asia and central Europe's oak forests. But thanks to the mobility of game farms, varieties of the species have made their way to Hawaii and even Texas, where a hunter keen to add a "red ram" to their slam can chase them among the mesquite and prickly pear.

Barbary sheep, the wild goat-a-lope of northern Africa, enjoy the same internationality and can tolerate even harsher habitats. This is a curious critter, almost equal parts caprid (wild goat) and antelope, and hunting them requires a marathoner's embrace of hardship.

Barbary sheep, elsewhere known as aoudad (see sidebar), are spooky, hardy animals of the cliffs, rimrocks, and arid canyons.

WEST TEXAS AOUDAD

You don't have to travel to the Middle East to pursue Barbary sheep. Instead, book a trip to the Davis Mountains of West Texas, a terrain that doubles—visually, at least—for biblical lands.

Aoudad ("AWE-dad") were brought to Texas in the early part of the last century and managed to escape from confinement and establish robust populations.

These are mainly spot-and-stalk hunts, so any flat-shooting rifle you'd bring for mountain elk or mule deer will work. Plan on cross-canyon shots following boot-shredding hikes across sparse land that seems better suited to scorpions than sheep.

FIRST PERSON: ANDREW MCKEAN

A STRANGE SHEEP HUNT IN UTAH'S GREAT SALT LAKE

It was an enticing invitation: an offer to hunt wild sheep in Utah. Most hunters wait decades for the chance to draw a Rocky Mountain or desert bighorn tag in the Beehive State, but I was being invited to bypass the crowds and hunt on Fremont Island, the third-largest island in the Great Salt Lake.

Of course, there was a catch. These sheep, I later learned, were illegally brought to the island, and our host here was more or less slumming. Still, the variety of animals was as wild was it was international: shaggy merinos, Corsican mouflon, black Hawaiian mouflon, Barbary sheep, and an ivory-colored, full-curled variety of ram called a "Texas Dall," as well as huge, elusive Russian boars.

My group hunted hard (me with a .270 WSM), and we got an education in the survival strategies of these dry-land sheep species. When they found themselves targeted in the open, sheep gathered in huge, milling herds that made precise shooting impossible. On the ridges and rocky slopes where we stalked trophy rams, they had a habit of disappearing with one vaulting, well-timed jump. It took three days to kill a single sheep and hog.

Thanks to the critters being on the island illegally, the state has spent the last few years attempting to eradicate the populations. The fear is that if these transplant animals managed to get off the island, they could endanger Utah's native wild sheep.

WILD GOATS

WE CELEBRATE THE RAM as the very symbol of wild mountains, but a more suitable icon is the wild goat of Eurasia and Arabia. The hardy highland family includes the soaring-horned (and dropping-beard) ibex of various incarnations, the screw-horned markhor, and the alpine tur, a nimble goat that has stout horns like those of a stunted mouflon sheep. These agile mountaineers make a living in the planet's most desolate, weather-wracked places where hunters motivated by exotic experiences and completion of life-lists suffer to chase them.

The first ibex I saw took my breath, not only because of its remarkable headgear—sweeping horns studded with hard ripples that looked like knuckles on a fist—but also the location, the high, lonely, tinder-dry mountains of southern New Mexico.

What was this Eurasian wild billy doing in roadrunner country? Turns out, the same thing it does in its homeland, scraping a living off marginal habitat and surprising trophy hunters from Spain to Siberia.

The expansive family of wild goats, which includes a number of flavors of ibex and hard-horned tur, matches up neatly with early human civilizations. It's probably no accident that ancestors of wild goats and feral humans encountered each other from Mesopotamia to Memphis, and the goats that didn't become domesticated headed for the highest hills.

That's where these trophy species remain, in the most forbidding mountains of Europe, Central Asia, and Siberia. Both tur and ibex are hotly pursued by destination hunters, as many subspecies are ingredients in the grand slams recognized by various trophy-hunting organizations.

The ibex and the closely related wild goats are defined as much by their preferred habitat as by their appearance. They are almost always mountain animals, capable of surviving on bare rock and sparse vegetation. They are capable jumpers and, when pursued, almost always seek refuge in cliffy, dangerous terrain.

In fact, the Iranian ibex I spooked in New Mexico made two spectacular jumps and watched me from the safety of a rock spire that would have required either ropes or a helicopter for me to access.

THREE WORLD-CLASS GOAT HUNTS

MID-ASIAN IBEX Also known as the Tien Shan ibex, this is the largest member of the ibex family, with remarkable trophies that have been known to top 50 inches (127 cm). Many ibex hunts are add-ons to sheep hunts in Kyrgyzstan and Tajikistan.

BEZOAR IBEX A wild goat instead of a true capra (ibex), the Bezoar is sometimes called the Persian or Turkish ibex and is found across the eastern Black Sea plateau, with strongest numbers in Turkey and Turkmenistan.

CAUCASIAN TUR Possibly the hardest hunt in Eurasia is for the trophy tur of former Dagestan. This large-horned goat lives in the highest crags of the Caucasus Mountains of Eastern Europe. In record-keeping,, the tur is curiously classified as both a goat (capra) and a sheep (ovid).

EUROPE'S FORGOTTEN
CONSERVATION SUCCESS

American hunters like saying that we brought back imperiled critters through our funding of scientific wildlife management. That same model of conservation also benefited the European ibex.

The alpine ibex, which historically roamed most of Europe above about 6,500 feet (2,000 meters), was hunted nearly to extinction, and at one point was restricted to a tiny national park in the Alps between Italy and France. But a combination of hunting restrictions and recolonization efforts spread its numbers and its range.

Today the alpine goat is hunted across the Alps and the Pyrenean ranges and across southern Europe to the Black Sea.

WILD GOATS OF THE WORLD

Wild goats are never found in gentle country. They are creatures of the mountains and rugged canyons across Europe and the Middle East.

TUR (Caucasus Mountains, top right) The range that separates Europe from Asia is home to two species of this alpine goat-antelope. The West Caucasian tur has ridged horns like an ibex; the East Caucasian tur has lyre-shaped horns like a mouflon.

WILD GOAT (Europe, Asia, Middle East, bottom left) This wide-ranging, shaggy goat ancestor has long, arcing horns.

SPANISH IBEX Its range limited to the Iberian Peninsula, this goat has horns that curve up, then back and inward.

ALPINE IBEX (Central Europe, top left) Found in high country, this ibex has knurled horns that sweep back over its shoulders.

NUBIAN IBEX (N. Africa) This desert dweller is closely related to the Spanish Ibex, which is found just across the Mediterranean.

MARKHOR (Middle East, bottom right) The spiral-horned, bearded goat that once defined the Khyber Pass region of Afghanistan is also found in Pakistan, Tajikistan, and Uzbekistan. It's unclear how unrest in the region has affected population numbers.

WILD BOAR

THEY SAY DESOTO sailed swine over in 1539 to feed his men. Hardy and smart, some escaped and started living easy. Four centuries later, hunters imported wild Russian boars, and the two species bred like rabbits, with tusked armies of these omnivores marching west. The United States now has 6 million feral hogs that uproot native species and crops. Farmers are fed up; game managers are desperate for a solution. But hunters know bullets can stop these new-age conquistadors, and country hams hang from each leg. So get a good rifle and get to work.

Wild pigs might be America's perfect game animal—if only they were classified as such. In most states, they're defined as invasive species (vermin to be shot on sight) and that's one reason why pig hunting has become so popular.

Another is that they're a challenging quarry. They have better noses than bird dogs, good memories, and are able to quickly learn from past experiences. They'll pack up and move to areas of lesser persecution—or become nocturnal—when they start feeling the heat from hunters.

This intelligence, combined with the fact that they can eat anything and are one of one of the most efficient mammalian reproducers—often laying two to four litters of six piglets every year—make them nearly impossible to shoot out.

In Texas, hunters employ helicopters, spotlights, night vision optics, and anything else to get the upper hand. Still, pigs prevail. "There are two types of landowners," quip Texas cattlemen. "Those with wild hogs, and those about to get them."

Wild hogs are also formidable; sows with piglets and large boars can be dangerous when threatened. Boars grow tusks up to six inches (15 cm) in length and use them as weapons. Coveted as trophies by hunters, they're kept sharp by constant whetting against the boar's upper teeth.

Young, 30- to 150-pound (14- to 68-kg) "meat hogs" make for delightful pulled pork sandwiches and barbecued ribs, and many states allow procuring pigs with no hunting license at any time of the year. Wild hogs are the everyman's ultimate nongame game animal.

EUROPEAN BOARS AND THE HUNTER'S PARADOX

Hunters are thought to be responsible for first importing European hogs into northern states for the sole purpose of hunting them. Traces of this long-snouted, coarse-haired variety of wild hog can be readily observed among litters of feral pigs that closely resemble domestic swine.

As recently as the 1990s, it wasn't uncommon for enterprising individuals to capture wild hogs in the South and sell them to northern hunting operations that had none, thereby hastening their proliferation. The practice has been outlawed, but it's likely too late. Feral pigs have a foothold on most of the lower 48 states, plus Hawaii. While the impact of burgeoning pig populations on native ecosystems and game is negative, state game agencies have loosened laws on hunting them, and hunters are happy to oblige.

HUNTING TACTICS Plenty of pigs are taken as targets of opportunity while deer hunting from treestands, but due to their myopic eyesight, relatively slow running speed, their stand-and-fight nature, and lax laws on harvest methods, wild hogs are successfully hunted by employing a vast number of tactics and techniques.

A favorite one is to bait pigs with corn, crops, or other irresistible food. A pack of pigs will consume all the corn (and your pocketbook) in short order, however, so hunters must get creative. One cost-effective baiting technique is to dig a hole 2–3 feet (0.6–0.9 meters) deep, fill it with corn, pour a sweet soda over it to hasten its fermentation, then bury it. After a few days the pigs will find it, but it will take them a couple more to root it up—while you're ready and waiting nearby with a rifle and the wind in your favor.

In more open country, hunters readily employ the spot-and-stalk technique. After spotting pigs from a vantage point, the key to a successful stalk is to approach from upwind, as wild pigs have noses second to none. While they can't see detail well, they can spot movement, so use available cover to get within rifle or bow range, and move only when their heads are down while feeding.

A large and growing segment of American sportsmen employ the use of dogs to hunt pigs, especially in thick or swampy cover where other methods are rendered useless. Scent-hounds like blue ticks, walkers, and red bones find hogs, bay them, and bark to alert following hunters. Then "catch dogs"—often pit bulls, curs, or other fearsome types—are released to hold the bayed hog by the ears and legs, immobilizing it. Battles with large boars are brutal. Dog owners who tire of finding dead or disemboweled dogs fit their catch dogs with special Kevlar vests for protection against razor-sharp tusks. Finally, a hunter moves in with a knife, spear, or gun to deliver the fatal blow. —*J.J.*

FIRST PERSON: JEFF JOHNSTON

KILLING A WILD BOAR WITH A KNIFE ISN'T FOR THE FAINT OF HEART

It was midnight when the cutting dog began bawling and only a moment later when the catch dogs were released. I actually heard the smash of flesh as hound flew into hog. The din of combat—snarling fang against primal tusk—was as intense as life gets. Bayed boars often choose the thickest cover to make a stand, and the Tough Country Pratka Ranch west of Houston provided it in spades. It took us minutes of chopping through a wall of green to gain each step; meanwhile the sounds of warfare filled my ears.

Finally a whirlwind of hair and teeth flashed in a dancing beam of artificial light. The boar was the biggest I'd seen—perhaps 300 pounds (136 kg)—and wasn't about to give away his dreams. Honestly, I was hoping for a smaller one, but once those pit bulls are turned loose, there can be no turning back.

With one dog gashed and spilling innards, the dog handler lithely moved in to hold the hog's hind legs while Smiley latched onto the boar's face like a steel trap. I plunged the knife behind the boar's shoulder and leaned into the blade, probing for the aorta. Spurting blood turned white faces red. I felt the boar's pressure slow and then stop.

We pried the dogs from their death grips, and I sat down and thanked the boar. While he might not be classified as a game species, he was a game animal indeed, and for that I give him, and a tenacious pit bull named Smiley, due credit.

GEAR UP

THE BEST GUN FOR WILD PIGS

Although farm-fed feral hogs can reach obscene weights given enough age and forage, the average wild hog weighs 40–250 pounds (18–113 kg). Occasionally a boar may get bigger, but reports tend to be exaggerated. As such, any deer rifle of .25-caliber or larger is ideal, provided it's stoked with a premium, controlled-expansion bullet. Big boars have a shield of gristle around their shoulders and lungs that protects them from rival tusks—and cheap bullets.

While your .270 Win, .308 Win., or .30-06 bolt-action rifle will work wonders, hogs often run in packs. Perhaps the ultimate pig gun is an AR-10-style rifle. Chambered in .308 Win. these semi-automatics from Rock River, DPMS, Smith and Wesson, Ruger and others can deliver several shots accurately in seconds, piling up the pigs. Put a quality 3x-9x scope on your AR-10 for daytime hunting, or bejewel it with a night vision optic, thermal imaging device, or a flashlight for nighttime hunting, where legal.

INDIAN GAME

IN 1929 A SMALL HERD of large-bodied Indian antelope called nilgai was imported to the million-acre King Ranch in south Texas. These days, there are arguably more of these "exotic" antelope in that state than in their native India. It's the same story with axis deer, blackbuck antelope, and many other species. Now thriving stateside, they must be managed, and, in many cases, that means trophy hunting. So save yourself airfare to Mumbai, and instead hunt Indian game where your guide's accent will be, instead of subcontinental, deep Dixie.

YOU CAN STILL HUNT THE NILGAI (opposite, top left) across much of its native range in India, but there are so many impediments to the traveling hunter —importing rifles, finding a legitimate and knowledgeable outfitter, and then exporting your trophy—that your best bet is hunting these thick-bodied antelope on an exotic-game ranch in Texas, even if you're traveling from outside the United States to hunt. This is not an uncommon situation for a range of exotic game, and what the hunts may lack in on-the-ground authenticity, they make up for in ease of travel and exciting trophies.

You can expect to pay a decent fee for the opportunity, but in return, you get to take home the remarkable blue-gray hide, trophy horns, and some of the best-tasting wild meat on any continent.

The same can be said for blackbuck (opposite, bottom), the cork-screwing horned antelope of India that is closely related to northern Africa's gazelles. Populations in its native range are small and dwindling, but they are fixtures of many Texas game ranches, where even high fences don't always contain the prodigious jumpers. Exotic animals are purchased by ranchers, driven into desirable pastures that often span huge expanses, then raised to breed and thrive naturally, while providing venison, tourist attractions, and hunting opportunities for sportsman.

You can also hunt axis deer (opposite, top right) in Texas. Called "chital" in their native lands of India, Bhutan, Bangladesh, and Nepal's lower elevations, this dappled forest deer was introduced to Hawaii and, in 1932, to Texas, where they are carefully managed as one of the most desirable exotic game species today. —J.J.

STAND OR STALK?

In south Texas, exotics are primarily hunted like whitetails—from elevated "box blinds" near feeders (or natural food sources) that draw them from the thick mesquite. This often means waiting until the animal shows up in daylight, and then making a good shot. Traditionally this is the tactic most locals employ—and it's been proven extremely effective..

If you shop around, some outfitters allow clients to spot-and-stalk exotic animals on their land. While the average hunter's odds at taking a trophy animal are likely better in a box blind over bait, most agree that spotting and stalking is more challenging.

JAGUAR

SOME ARGUE the leopard is the most dangerous game on earth, but that could be because few have faced a wild jaguar. Ranging from South America northward, with rare sightings as far as Arizona, most *Panthera onca* live their lives devoid of human contact, in the world's most impenetrable region, the Amazon River Basin. Averaging around 225 pounds (102 kg), jaguars take to water and are listed as endangered, though many believe there are more in existence than thought. For now, hunters can only covet this predator via accounts of adventurers past.

While there have been cases of jaguars becoming killers of men, the instances are extremely rare—thanks in part to the fact that man isn't the jaguar's natural food. In addition, human presence is relatively sparse in the jag's rainforest range.

In the 1920s and 30s, however, one man killed over 300 jaguars in the Brazil's Mato Grosso region, a few of which were fought only with a spear. At least one of those cats was a notorious cattle-killer-turned-man-eater, named *Assassino* by a local rancher.

Alexander "Sasha" Siemel, a migrant from Latvia, was taught the art of *tigre* fighting with a 7-foot (2.1-meter) spear, called a sagya, by a native who later died at the fangs of a jaguar.

Because the "green hell" jungle was so hopelessly thick—often vision was limited to mere steps—he felt the sagya was a better weapon in some scenarios than a rifle, because it could physically hold a cat off him if it attacked. Using his trusted dog, Valente, to find and bay a jaguar, Siemel would move in and induce a charge. The cat would run or leap onto the blade, but was prevented from running all the way up it by a steel crossbar welded to the spear's shaft. Once the beast was impaled, a supreme battle of wills, balance, and strength ensued—where one slight mistake by either combatant would mean certain death alone in the jungle.

Siemel lived through several of these fights, and took many cattle-killing jaguars by other means. He eventually moved to the United States where the naturalist, hunter, and master of seven languages lectured students and spoke of his travels. He will go down in history as *Tigrero* (the Tiger Man). —*J.J.*

THE UNDISPUTED HUNTING CHAMPION

One viral Internet video shows a rare glimpse of just how skilled the jaguar is at killing.

Anyone who has hunted gators, crocs, or caimans knows how wary, strong, and tough they are. It's very difficult to get within rifle range of one of these sun-bathing reptiles before it senses movement and slides into the water.

In the video, a caiman sunbathes on a small island when the focus shifts to a floating object in the river behind it. Several seconds pass as a jaguar emerges from the water in a crouch, then stalks the caiman. In one frighteningly fast motion, the cat leaps, impales the 7-foot (2.1-meter) reptile's skull in its jaws—killing it instantly—and picks it completely off the ground before swimming with it back across the swift-moving water.

As good as a hunter as you think you might be, you'll never have the skills of a jaguar.

AN ACCIDENTAL HERO IN HONDURAS

The killer's work was done before rosettes of sunlight dappled the village in shadowy orange. Not long after waking, a poor Honduran farmer found that another of his family's precious cows had been ambushed on the edge of pasture and dragged into the jungle, where it was partially devoured. The size of the tracks pointed to the same tigre, and this baffled the man as much as it angered him. Why, if not for sheer pleasure, would it kill again so soon?

Dr. Charles Elliott had ventured south to seek Honduras' giant largemouth bass. After a few days of fishing and campfire stories, word circulated that Charlie was a keen big game hunter. Desperate, the farmer approached him.

Elliott readily agreed to hunt the cattle-slaying jaguar—but not without doubt when a wire-bound 30-40 Krag rifle was thrust into his hands. With a stone he pounded its iron sights until the rifle was passable at 25 yards (or meters).

Sacrificing an unweaned goat, the farmer led both bait and hunter to an area where the cat had killed. He pointed up a tall tree, and then tied the kid below.

Figuring the rickety machan made for him was far more dangerous than any jaguar, Charlie sat at the base of the tree, and waited only a short time.

A large jaguar sauntered down the jungle path, coming toward him as if in a dream, coaxed by the manic cries of the young billy. At 30 yards (or meters) the sportsman-doctor from Oklahoma eased the rifle up and fired, striking the big cat in the aorta, killing it as swiftly as a cat can be killed. Out of habit, he racked the rifle's bolt but remained seated for a few moments to survey. Mere moments later, he saw a second jaguar, identical in appearance to the first, sneaking down the same path.

Charlie fired again, and the village's cattle-killing problems ceased.

The doctor rose to celebrity status in the village, and although he couldn't take the cats' skins back home due to CITES (Convention on International Trade in Endangered Species) restrictions, he knows what many Central and South Americans know: There are plenty of jaguars left in the jungle, where they remain one of the world's most efficient killers.

SUBTROPICAL SPECIES

15° SOUTH – 60° SOUTH

15° SOUTH – 60° SOUTH

YOU COULD SAY AFRICA IS MADE OF GAME. From the desert gazelles of the Sahara and the sweat-weather goats of Eritrea down through the classic game ranges of Tanzania's Serengeti to South Africa's Cape provinces, this is a continent where the diversity of wildlife is matched only by the opportunity to hunt it.

Interested in a white-phase springbok in South Africa's karoo? That can be arranged. Or a Cape buffalo in the morning and then a kudu in the evening? There are places where that's entirely possible. The gift of Africa—besides its cheerful and welcoming people—is its dizzying diversity of habitats. Bush, savanna, forest, riparian marsh, desert, foothills, mountain, and coastal habitats are found across the continent, often within spitting distance of one another.

By my count, there are more than 90 species of antelope on the planet, and Africa is home to most of them. And a single species can be parsed into numerous subspecies, regionally distinct variations, and even local color phases—a distinct species like bushbuck, for example, boasts no fewer than 16 varieties.

The abundance of game animals south of the Equator extends to South America, with its keystone critters dove and waterfowl, and to Australia and New Zealand, which have—for better or worse—been recipients of other continents' benefaction. Can't hunt a tur in its native Himalayas? No problem—take a helicopter to one in New Zealand. Interested in shooting a trophy Cambodian cow? Consider Australia, where they're called water buffalo or banteng.

THE VALUE OF HUNTING In Africa, habitat constraints are rarely the limiting factor for wildlife. Instead, the main problems are humans, specifically some national governments and their disregard for the conservation value of managed sport hunting.

Take Zimbabwe, the unfortunate poster child. While the colonial oversight of Great Britain did no favors for much of the indigenous population of the eastern African nation, its system of fertile farms and game parks made Zim the gem of the continent for safari hunters. Game was plentiful, trophy specimens abundant, and hunting welcomed as a cultural expectation and an economic benefit.

Then Robert Mugabe's ZANU (Zimbabwe African National Union) revolutionaries overthrew the government, and the land reform that followed transformed much of the formerly lush landscape into a bleak zone occupied by subsistence villagers who killed buffalo and kudu for the pot. Even more damning, the lawless frontier favored poachers, who continue to kill elephants and rhinos. As this book went to print, Botswana, Zambia, and Congo were all mulling prohibitions on sport hunting.

As my friend Theresa Sowry, president of the Southern African Wildlife College, has noted, safari hunting is the golden bullet for wildlife conservation. "There are two things that are undeniable in Africa right now," she says. "The first is the wholesale loss of some species of wildlife through poaching. The second is that where we have managed trophy hunting, we don't have poaching." So sport hunting—not photo safaris or conservation parks—is the best tool we have at this moment to conserve African species.

Right now, the species most in need of conservation are the ivory-bearing mammals. But it's not a stretch to imagine most horned game in some sort of danger of poachers. And as we've established, Africa is full of game.

AFRICA'S BIG 5

THE AFRICAN BIG 5 is considered by most experienced hunters to be the Holy Grail of big game hunting. These five animals that have come to symbolize safari hunting in Africa: elephant, Cape buffalo, rhino, lion, and leopard. The name "Big 5" comes not from the size of these animals but from the difficulty and danger associated with hunting them. No hunter who pursues animals in this collection does so casually. They know that even with their big-bore rifles and telescopic sights, the odds are not always in the hunter's favor.

It's not unheard of for elephants to charge at the first sign of a human. If you try to escape, they will track you by scent. If they lose the scent, they will search until they find you. If you climb a tree, they push it over. If you find a hole, they dig you out. If they find you, it's all over—nobody survives a serious elephant attack.

Rhinos are big, powerful, grumpy, and stupid. That's never a good combination to run into.

Buffalo are sometimes called "Black Death." When wounded, they will lie in wait for the hunters tracking them. Then they charge out like a bulletproof freight train, intent on crushing anything in its path.

Lions have for eons considered man to be a food source.

Leopards are notorious for attacking with blinding speed, hitting every member of the hunting party in a bloody second, and leaving a path of destruction behind.

In short, the Big 5 are critters that can quickly turn the tables on a hunter; stomping, biting, clawing, or goring them into a bloody puddle, left to slowly seep into the dusty African soil—and therein lies the true appeal in hunting them.

Still, you might wonder, why in the world would hunters put themselves in such peril? For some, it's the simple, elemental challenge of it—the opportunity to match wits and abilities against primitive power. There's a thrill one experiences while holding ground against a charging buffalo that just isn't delivered by a fleeing pronghorn antelope. For others, it's the completion of a lifetime spent hunting more docile specimens. And for still other hunters, it's the very essence of the African experience. —*B.T.*

CONSERVATION HUNTING

Why in the world would someone hunt an elephant or a rhino? Aren't they protected?

Believe it or not, populations are robust enough to hunt precisely because they *are* hunted. If that logic seems circular, consider this: Everywhere in Africa where Big 5 animals are protected, populations decline, because poachers recognize that the animals have no defenders when armed hunters aren't in the area. That's the crux of the illicit trade in ivory. In areas with safari hunting, there is little illegal trade in rhino horn or elephant ivory.

But in protected parks, poachers kill without restraint or respect.

LEOPARD

THE AFRICAN LEOPARD (*Panthera pardus pardus*) is the subspecies of leopard occurring across most of sub-Saharan Africa and is the most common to hunt. The leopard is the smallest of the "Big 5" game animals, but that does not make it by any means the least dangerous. Tracking a wounded leopard in the tall grass is thought by many professional hunters to be the most dangerous situation in big-game hunting. I suspect that more professional hunters throughout Africa carry scars from leopard attacks than from any other big-game animal.

The leopard is a member of the Felidae family with a wide range across parts of Africa and tropical Asia, from Siberia, South and West Asia, to most of sub-Saharan Africa. They are endangered in much of their territory and are not hunted. Sport hunting is mostly limited to sub-Saharan Africa, where they are overpopulated and often cause problems with livestock.

The leopard is the smallest of the four "big cats" in the genus *Panthera*, which also includes tiger, lion, and jaguar. The loose definition of *big cats* is simply that they are the ones who can roar. If big cats were defined by measuring body size, the term would also include the cougar, cheetah, and snow leopard.

Compared to other members of the cat family, the leopard has relatively short legs and a long body with a large skull. Its habitat ranges from rainforest to desert terrains, and it adapts well and thrives in all of them. Leopards' coat color varies (by location and habitat) from pale yellow to deep gold or tawny. The skin is patterned with black rosettes while the head, lower limbs, and belly are spotted with solid black. The rosettes are similar to those of the jaguar, but the leopard's rosettes are smaller, more densely packed, and do not usually have central spots. Male leopards average about 130 pounds (59 kg) and can be as large as 200 pounds (91 kg). Females are smaller, averaging about 80 pounds (36 kg).

The leopard can run at speeds approaching 35 miles per hour (56 kph) and can climb trees even when carrying heavy loads. The leopard will eat just about any animal that it can catch, and impala, bushbuck, and baboon are among its preferred prey.

THE BEST BULLET

The leopard is not a big or toughly constructed animal. Any "deer" cartridge will kill leopards, but it's always best to go to the upper end of the spectrum with dangerous game. To insure a first shot kill, it's best to be a bit overgunned. With that thought, any of the .300 Magnums are a good choice, and the .338 Magnum cartridges are even better. In this case, fast-expanding, premium-quality bullets are called for, as they need to do maximum damage. And it's critical to have a high quality scope to aid in shot placement in poor light.

Once your blind is located, measure the distance to the bait. Then zero the point of impact for the rifle to exactly that distance. Shoot to break the off shoulder at an angle that will drive the bullet through the heart and lungs.

The leopard is covered by the International CITES Agreement, but the United States may not allow importing from all of those countries where hunting is legal. It is important that you determine the legality of hunting and importing leopards before you book your hunt. Also note that the hunting regulations change regularly in Africa and often without logic or reason. Leopard hunting is suffering from increasing pressure from Europe, the United States, and other countries to end cat hunting entirely and, as such, things can change rapidly. Remember, when hunting in Africa, nothing is set in stone.

Leopards are very secretive, moving mostly at night and under cover of darkness and vegetation. They are nasty tempered and, when pushed, will fight and attack even if they are not wounded. When wounded, they will wait in ambush, so well hidden that they are almost impossible to spot, and will attack with blinding speed. When they attack, they will often hit everybody in the party, grabbing a head with their forepaws and teeth while raking the length of the body with their powerful, sharp-clawed back legs, and then moving on to the next.

Hunting leopards with hounds is a very exciting and challenging way to pursue this big cat. It is not for the fainthearted or for the inexperienced hunter, as things move fast and it can be very dangerous. While this method grew in popularity very quickly, it has since come under scrutiny and is being regulated away—unfortunate for those skilled hunters who never had the chance to try.

The most popular and traditional way to hunt leopards is by baiting. The hunters will find travel corridors used by a big male and then hang baits in a tree. Typical baits are a zebra quarter or an impala, but many types of meat will work. We even used giraffe during one hunt; the leopards loved it. After placing the bait, the offal will be dragged on a string to lay a scent trail in order to aid the leopard in locating the bait.

The trees are carefully picked so that the leopard will come out on a limb to access the bait, giving the hunter a clean, broadside shot. Once a leopard is feeding, the hunters will build a blind about 50–75 yards (or meters) away from the bait.

EVERY HUNTER'S NIGHTMARE: A WOUNDED LEOPARD

For many years, a 12-gauge shotgun with buckshot was the gun of choice for tracking a wounded leopard, but after multiple failures to stop a charge, many professional hunters have abandoned that idea. A powerful rifle is now the gun of choice for those professionals I have hunted with or interviewed. They often prefer a heavy, big-game rifle used for elephant or buffalo hunting—and one loaded with expanding bullets. This will hit with enough energy to drive a bullet through the leopard, and do the most possible damage—which is necessary in order to stop the charge.

Following a wounded leopard is very high on the list of what most professional hunters least want to do. It's extremely dangerous, and all too often results in disaster. Many hunters wait until morning and follow when the light is good. The problem is that between the vegetation and the leopard's very effective natural camouflage, it's all but impossible to see a hidden leopard until you are very close to him—often you won't spot him until he starts his charge, giving you about a second to react and take your shot.

There are some professional hunters who believe that by following at night, the hunter actually has the advantage. The wounded cat will lay, well covered, waiting for an ambush. But his eyes will reflect the lights, which is a huge advantage. The cat will think he is still hidden and will stay still, giving the hunter a chance to finish things.

The secret is waiting in total silence until the leopard appears, which can be extremely challenging. Some places allow hunting at night with a light, but many other locations require that the leopard be shot in daylight. Because smart, old leopards move mostly after dark, this results in a very difficult hunt. It's not uncommon to hear stories about hunters spending 30 or more nights waiting patiently in the blind before getting the opportunity to shoot a leopard.

It's important to kill the leopard with the first shot as they rarely offer an opportunity for another—and a wounded leopard is extremely dangerous. You'll find it's very rare for any professional hunter with a lot of experience hunting leopards to have escaped without shedding some blood on the dusty African soil. —*B.T.*

TROPHY QUALITY

There are three ways to measure trophy quality: weight, length, or skull measurement. But weight can vary by how much the cat has eaten, and the skin can be stretched by the unscrupulous. So measure the skull by adding together length [A] and width [B]. That's how the record books do it.

The Rowland Ward minimum score to be included in the record book is 15⅜ inches (39 cm), and the all-time record is 19 inches (48 cm). The Safari Club International's minimum is 14 inches (36 cm), and their all-time record is 19¹¹/₁₆ (50 cm).

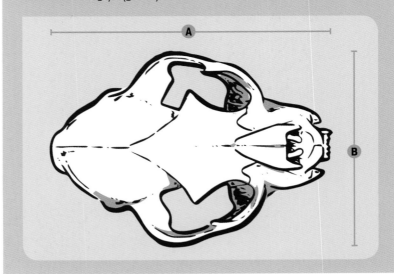

CAPE BUFFALO

THE AFRICANS CALL THEM Nyati or Mbogo. The Cape buffalo, *Syncerus caffer*, is the largest of the African bovine species and a bull can weigh up to a ton. Technically a prey animal, they don't carry the attitude expected from that standing. Africa is littered with the corpses of predators who have set their sights on a buffalo dinner. Some of them are lions, but more than a few are bipedal predators. The buffalo is by far the most common of the Africa's Big 5 species, and they are the most popular and the most affordable to hunt in today's safari industry.

Cape buffalo inhabit south and east Africa and have inspired fear in the hearts of hunters for eons. Robert Ruark, who famously said that a Cape buffalo bull "looks at you like you owe him money," was so terrified that he would become physically ill when he hunted buffalo.

So why do they hold such an attraction? Hunting dangerous game invokes a much different set of emotions and motivations for those hunters who truly understand what they're doing. This type of hunting accesses the storage banks—deep inside our lizard brains— from a time when men were the hunted as well as the hunters. Sociologists tell us that once we developed the weapons needed to dominate the large predators, it all changed. Our bigger brains and opposable thumbs allowed us to progress until we created art, heart transplants, and the Internet. But something is still locked deep in the recesses of our gray matter that compels a certain type of hunter to test himself against dangerous game.

Many experienced hunters believe that the buffalo, particularly when wounded, is the most dangerous of the African Big 5; it's a debate that will keep the campfires glowing long into the night for generations yet to come. The primary reason the buffalo is so popular with today's hunters is simply affordability.

But don't let its accessibility lull you into underestimating the experience. Cape buffalo, when properly hunted, are perhaps the most exciting and challenging animals on earth—and I'm talking about hunting on foot in the animal's domain. Riding around in a safari truck to shoot a bull is simply cheating yourself of an unforgettable experience.

CHANGING GROUND

With Africa's ever-changing politics, no country is a safe bet year to year. The traditional hunting countries for Cape buffalo have included Botswana, Mozambique, Namibia, South Africa, Tanzania, Zambia, and Zimbabwe.

Botswana and Zambia may be closed for hunting for the foreseeable future. Tanzania has become horribly expensive, and Zimbabwe's corrupt government is having a negative effect on hunting.

Today, hunters tout Mozambique as being productive and affordable. Namibia is limited to northern areas such as the Caprivi Strip, and most of South Africa's buffalo hunting is high fence, put and take.

Dangerous game should never be shot at long range for two reasons. First, the risk of an extremely dangerous, wounded animal is too high. The other reason is it's simply a sin—an insult to the art of hunting dangerous game.

The thrill of buffalo hunting is about getting close, working the thick mopane or jess, anticipating that every step can reveal the buffalo. It's walking miles and miles of bloody Africa while following tracks. It's trying not to be noticed by the multitudes of eyes, ears, and noses as you search for that one trophy bull in the bedded herd. It's sneaking in and creeping so close to a group of grumpy old dugga boys that you can smell their breath.

First light of a typical day might find you at a waterhole checking for tracks. If the buffalo have watered, you wait for the better light, then you follow the tracks.

Often the bulls trail in the back of the herd, so it's best if you catch them still up and feeding. But, just as often, the buffalo have moved into the shade of the thick mopane and bedded for the day. Your task becomes exponentially more difficult now, but also more exciting. You must work the wind and explore the area until you can locate a trophy bull—without all those buffalo noticing you. It will call on just about every hunting skill you possess, and it ends in failure more often than success. But if it were easy, it wouldn't be worth spit.

The soul of buffalo hunting can be found in those moments when you suddenly realize you are breathing again and you can't remember stopping. When you get lost in time, finding yourself so close you can count the ticks on his back as you try to see his brush-hidden horns. If there is any other hunting on earth better, it has escaped my notice.

Buffalo are also hunted by spot and stalk and by waiting at known feeding areas and at waterholes. These can also be exciting ways to hunt, as you must still get in close and sort out the trophy bulls.

Once you find a bull, the shot must be taken with precision so that it will be fatal. The last thing you want to do is follow a wounded bull in the thick jess. When hunting herd bulls, you must also be aware of the background—so the bullet doesn't penetrate the buffalo and hit another behind him. —B.T.

SIZE ISN'T (ALWAYS) EVERYTHING

The "goal" for most buffalo hunters is a 40-inch (100-cm) wide bull. While it's good to have goals, there is a lot more to it than that—and I've seen some 40-inchers that were less than impressive. Look for wide, full bosses, preferably those that have grown solid with little or no soft areas in the middle or on the front edge. Also look for horns that sweep deeply down, as that adds to horn length and aesthetic quality.

In some areas, a bull that size may not exist, so don't burn your safari looking for a lost holy grail. There is nothing wrong with a 35-inch (89-cm) buffalo.

While I understand the quest for size, I don't always agree. Sure, we all want the biggest bull we can find, but the quality of the hunt is a much more enduring trophy.

A breathtaking, life-altering hunt that results in a 37-inch (94-cm) buffalo is a far better trophy than an easily taken, boring hunt for one over the "goal" line. It's the memories that go with us to the grave, not the taxidermy.

BUFFALO ON THE TABLE

While traveling hunters cannot bring home any meat, be sure to ask your camp cook to prepare some of your buffalo. There is nothing quite like sitting around an African campfire enjoying a meal from a bull you hunted fairly and shot truly.

The filet mignon cut is by far the best of the lot. Dust it with spices and cook it over a bed of hardwood coals until the outside is almost charred and the center is bloody red. Oxtail soup is a traditional dish—and for the adventurous, buffalo bull testicles, sliced thin and fried, are also a traditional appetizer. Fortify with an extra Scotch and dig in—you'll be surprised how delicious they are.

RHINOCEROS

ANYBODY WHO BELIEVES dinosaurs are extinct has never seen a rhinoceros up close and personal. These remarkable animals truly are left over from another era—they would be right at home sharing the savanna with a brontosaurus or triceratops. They are huge, with an odd three-toed footprint; they simply look like a critter that time forgot. They are the second largest of the Big 5 animals (only the elephant is bigger), and the rhino is perhaps the rarest trophy of the five in today's world of big-game hunting.

The word *rhinoceros* is derived through Latin from the Ancient Greek and translates roughly into "Nose Horn." Rhinoceroses have tiny brains compared to their body size, which is what makes them dangerous. They are prone to attack first and think later, and with their massive size and yard-long horn, an attack is a serious thing.

Five living species of rhinoceroses exist, but hunters are limited to the two African rhinos: the white and the black.

Legend has it that the name *white* is a mistranslation of the Dutch word *wijd*, which means "wide"—a reference to the width of the rhinoceros's mouth. Early English-speaking settlers in South Africa misinterpreted *wijd* for "white," and the rhino with the wide mouth ended up being called the white rhino, although many texts note that there is no written proof of this—it may just be an often repeated but untrue legend. The other rhinoceros, with the narrow, pointed mouth, was called the black rhinoceros (I suppose because they had to call it something, and basic black always works).

Many texts say the main difference between black and white rhinos is the shape of their mouths. The white rhinos have broad, flat lips for grazing, whereas black rhinos have long, pointed, parrot-like lips for eating foliage and browsing. But the difference doesn't stop there.

The black rhino, *Diceros bicornis*, is the smaller of the two, its weight topping out at about 3,000 pounds (1,360 kg), although some have been reported at more than 6,300 pounds (2,858 kg). The black rhino is much more aggressive than the white rhino—if you bump into a black rhino, the odds are about 50/50 that it will charge you rather than running away.

CHOOSE WISELY

While Hemingway wrote in *The Green Hills of Africa* about shooting a running rhino at 300 yards (or meters) using a .30-06, we lesser humans should pick our guns and our shots more carefully.

A rhino is a big, tough animal with huge bones and a very thick hide. Rifle cartridges should have names that start with a least a four. That means the various .416 magnums through the .458 Magnums. This is a great place to use the big double gun cartridges like the .470 and .500 Nitro Express.

Always pick heavy, solid, non-expanding bullets to insure deep penetration.

When it charges, it will huff and chuff in a sound described like a steam engine getting up to speed. It runs with its tail erect and can hit 30 miles per hour (48 kmh).

It is the black rhino that was traditionally considered a member of the Big 5, due to his disposition and the danger in hunting them, while the white was not considered to be as sporting to hunt. But poaching has devastated both species, the black far more than the white. Today there are only about 5,000 black rhinos left, and any opportunity to hunt them is extremely rare and outrageously expensive. In 2014, a permit to hunt a black rhino was sold at auction for USD $350,000.00, and the price is predicted to hit a million dollars within the next few years.

There was a huge outcry against that sale, but those protesting failed to understand two things. One, this was an old, problem bull that was going to have to be killed anyway in order to protect other rhinos. Two, most of the money goes back into preservation and protection of the black rhino. It might be a paradox, but allowing hunting is the best path to saving these endangered animals.

One interesting fact is that the black rhinoceros has 84 chromosomes while all other rhinoceros species have 82 chromosomes. Do you suppose being different is why he is so mean tempered?

The white rhino, *Ceratotherium simum,* is larger than the black, with big bulls topping out about 8,000 pounds (3,629 kg), making it one of the largest animals on earth. The largest recorded is 9,900 pounds (4,490 kg). On the grand scale, the white rhino is more common than the black, with 17,460 counted in 2007 and 16,255 of that number living in South Africa. They are still very expensive to hunt and opportunities are very limited.

Some hunters elect to dart the rhino with a paralytic drug rather than kill them. This is much less expensive and allows scientific information to be collected from the rhino. The hunter poses with the trophy for photos, then the rhino walks away with nothing more than a hangover. Sort of "catch and release" hunting, I suppose.

WHY THEY DIE

Other than man, the black rhino's worst enemy is itself. Extremely aggressive and not too smart, a black rhino will charge eagerly at any perceived threat, including trucks and even trains. They have even been known to charge tree trunks and termite mounds.

Black rhinos fight each other like drunken sailors. They have the highest rates of mortality due to fighting of any mammal. About 50 percent of males and 30 percent of females die from injuries.

Other enemies are scarce. When you're as big and tough as a rhino, no predators want to mess with the adults. Crocodiles and lions, however, will prey on calves.

Though the white rhino may be more docile than the black, they're by no means well mannered. I was once photographing a female with a calf in Zimbabwe when she charged me. I managed to dive into the truck, and the driver took off in a hurry, outrunning the huge, angry cow. I have a friend who hunted white rhino in South Africa where they targeted an old, solitary, and known to be grumpy bull. The rhino charged as soon as he saw the hunters, well before a shot was fired. It took several shots to stop him.

One reason rhinos are so tough is their armor plating: their thick, protective skin that can be up to 2 inches (5 cm) thick. This armor is formed by layers of collagen fitted into a lattice structure, and the thick hide soaks up a lot of bullet energy.

But then, I suspect that most dinosaurs were hard to kill, too. —B.T.

THE RHINO'S FUTURE

Rhino poaching continues to be rampant in Africa. In fact, 2013 set an all-time high for the number poached in South Africa at 1,004, compared to 6 poached in the year 2000.

This is being driven by two markets: Asia, where they foolishly think that ingesting rhino horn will cure diseases or enhance their sexual performance, and the Middle East, where the horns are used for ceremonial dagger handles.

I was hunting leopard on the Sango Ranch in the Save Valley Conservancy in Zimbabwe in 2009 when poachers killed a nursing mama black rhino. They chopped off her horn and left her calf to die.

When the ranch biologist, Dusty Joubert, was doing a game census a few days later in his airplane, he discovered the poacher's camp. When men approached on the ground, they discovered men armed with heavy rifles and full-auto AK47s. We listened to the resulting, thrilling chase on the radio, and moved our truck into location to try and spot and stop the escaping poachers. Unfortunately, the plane was forced to land in the encroaching darkness, and the poachers escaped across the Save River and into the villages on the other side. The game scouts sent in undercover agents, but these poachers had high-level government connections, and the villagers were too scared of reprisals to talk.

In 2014 I was again in the Save, and despite a new, full-time antipoaching squad dedicated to stopping rhino poaching, it continued at a record pace.

Even so, rhinos are doing pretty well compared to just twenty years ago. If the market for poached rhino horn can be destroyed, they will have a good chance of seeing their populations return to safe levels.

AFRICAN LION

THE AFRICAN LION is the second largest cat in the world and one of the most impressive animals on earth. The old African proverb says that a lion will scare a brave man three times: first, when he sees his track; second, when he hears him roar; and third, when he finally spots the lion. Anybody who has seen a big lion up close in the wild understands that lions carry a certain gravitas—an aura of power and danger that only a fool would ignore.

Perhaps the best story Ernest Hemingway ever wrote was "The Short Happy Life of Francis Macomber," which opens after the protagonist has run from a lion charge and is dealing with the aftermath back at camp. The story explores fear, cowardice, the relationship between men and women, the corruption of money, betrayal, and, in the end, redemption. It is a truly great piece of writing—and it's no accident that Hemingway chose the lion for the role it played.

While the lion may not be the most dangerous of the Big 5 to hunt, it probably inspires the most fear within the hunter's heart. I suspect that's because it's the only true predator that can, will, and does make man a meal. It is the one animal of that elite club that will turn the tables and make the hunters the hunted.

The relationship between lions and man is an old one. Man hunted lions, but lions have always hunted man. That knowledge, buried deep in the recesses of any hunter's brain, rumbles around and through the subconscious, inspiring fear and respect.

The lion (*Panthera leo*) is one of the four big cats in the genus *Panthera* and a member of the family Felidae. With some males exceeding 550 pounds (250 kg) in weight, only the tiger is larger.

About 10,000 years ago, prior to the late Pleistocene era, the lion was the most widespread large land mammal after humans. They were found in most of Africa, across Eurasia from Western Europe to India, and even in the Americas from the Yukon to Peru.

Today, wild lions live in sub-Saharan Africa, with a very few left in the Gir Forest National Park in India.

GO BIG AND GO HOME

The lion is a thin-skinned animal usually weighing less than 500 pounds (227 kg). The conventional wisdom is that a 7mm or .300 Magnum is enough gun, and no doubt a lot of lions have been taken with this class of firearms. But the lion is a very tough animal to kill and can be vindictive if wounded. With dangerous game, it's always better to err on the side of caution.

A better choice would be a .375 H&H or even something like the .416 Rigby or .416 Remington loaded with premium expanding bullets. Be sure your variable-power scope zooms to low magnification so you can shoot fast if you have to deal with a charge.

A pride of lions consists of related females and offspring and a small number of adult males. Groups of female lions typically hunt together, preying mostly on large ungulates. Lions are apex predators, meaning they have no predators feeding on them. They are also keystone predators, which means they have a disproportionately large effect on their environment relative to their abundance. In other words, they truly are the king of the jungle—as well as of the savanna, grasslands, brushy woods, or any other place they live. Other than man, pretty much nothing messes with them.

Back in the days when safaris were two or three months long, the lions were mostly taken as a target of opportunity. But today they are usually the main event in a much shorter safari. Perhaps the most common way to hunt lions is to put up baits using fresh meat. Once a lion has developed a habit of feeding in one place, the hunters will build a blind and wait for the lion to show up.

In some areas, the soil conditions are good for tracking. The tactic is to locate a fresh track, preferably at first light, and then follow it until you find the lion.

Lion hunting in wild country has become very expensive, and booking a hunt usually involves a very long waiting list due to the limited quotas. Some areas of South Africa offer high-fence hunts, which are much more reasonably priced and have more availability. While there is an ethical debate about hunting lions in a high-fence area, this style of hunting could become a much bigger part of lion hunting—especially as opportunities for hunting lions in the wild continue to dwindle. —B.T.

THE MANE EVENT

In the wild, male lions seldom live longer than 10 years, so hunters look for a mature male that is at least 5 years old. The trophy quality is usually judged by the mane. In open country, a male lion can grow a flowing, luxurious mane, but in thorn brush country, the hair is constantly being broken and torn by the brush, so manes are often less impressive.

The record books use skull measurements taken by adding together length and width. The Rowland Ward minimum score to be included in the record book is 24 inches (61 cm), and the all-time record is 28¾ inches (73 cm). The Safari Club International's minimum is 23 inches (58 cm), and their all-time record is 28⁶/₁₆ inches (72 cm).

THE FUTURE OF LION HUNTING

At this time, there is a tremendous amount of pressure from the antihunting groups in the United States and Europe to end all big cat hunting. The lion is still widely available, but areas of opportunity are lost each year. Always do your research before booking any trip to make sure you can legally import your trophy after the hunt.

AFRICAN ELEPHANT

IN TERMS OF "BIG-GAME" HUNTING, this is as big as it gets, the top shelf, the upper limit, the big Kahuna. The African elephant is the largest dangerous game animal left on the planet—in fact, it's the world's largest land-dwelling critter, period. A big male can stand 14 feet (4.3 meters) tall at the shoulder and weigh as much as 15,000 pounds (6,800 kg). The adventure of hunting the largest (and some say the most dangerous) land-based mammal on earth is undeniably exciting—and the difficulty and challenge are part of the allure.

One thing I have noticed about African Professional Hunters is they all respect and fear elephants. That's because they understand the often nasty disposition and propensity to attack humans that so many elephants carry on their shoulders, not so much as a chip, but more like cordwood. These are not the docile creatures the public sees at the circus or the zoo. They are big, strong, intelligent, tough, vindictive, and relentless. Elephants kill people regularly in Africa and a decision to engage them is not to be taken lightly.

Of course, some bulls are taken by waiting at water holes or travel corridors, or by chancing onto them. But traditional trophy elephant hunting is usually done on foot, following tracks.

You check water holes and dusty roads at first light and once a good bull is located, you simply follow his tracks until you can get in close enough to judge the ivory.

You must be able to walk 20 miles of harsh terrain under a blazing sun every day, all day, while carrying a 14-pound rifle. Then get up and do it again the next day and the day after that until you finally connect. You also need to ability to sneak in close without being detected by the extremely sensitive ears and noses of the elephants.

Sometimes just finding the elephant is a challenge. It's amazing to me how easily something the size of a small bus can hide, but elephants can blend into the forest in a way that makes the whitetail look like a neon sign.

It takes a lot of different skills to hunt elephants. But then, hunting an animal as magnificent as the elephant should never be easy. If it were, the value would be lost.

BIG GUNS

Hunting elephant requires a whole new way of thinking about guns, cartridges, and bullets.

While the .375 H&H has taken a lot of elephants, it is a bit small for the job. The .416 cartridges are closer to entry level. The .458 Winchester, .458 Lott, and similar cartridges are better choices in a bolt action rifle. The Lott produces more energy than most of the big bore double rifle "traditional" cartridge like .470 Nitro Express and the .500 Nitro Express.

But no bolt action can match the romance and tradition of hunting with a side-by-side, double barrel big bore rifle with a cartridge big enough to use as a sex toy.

FIRST PERSON: BRYCE TOWSLEY

WHAT HAPPENS AFTER THE ELEPHANT HITS THE GROUND

Consider that in many areas of Africa the natives subsist on *sudza*, a corn porridge that they boil and eat. For the most part, the only protein they get is from the meat hunters provide.

I shot my elephant late in the day. By the time we arrived the next morning, there was a tractor pulling a large flatbed trailer full of native men waiting for us. They cut a road to the elephant and, once we were done with photos, they went to work.

The elephant became like an active ant hill, swarming with men bearing flashing knives, machetes, axes, and meat hooks. A few hours later, all that remained was a wet spot on the ground while the trailer springs were squeezed flat. They took every single part of that elephant.

Nothing is ever wasted in Africa.

WHAT DOES THE FUTURE HOLD FOR THE AFRICAN ELEPHANT?

No other animal had more influence on the exploration and settlement of Africa than the elephant. It was the ivory hunters—those brave souls who were willing to risk everything to penetrate deep into the continent in search of white gold—who paved the way for the rest of us. Say what you want about the ivory trade, it provided an incentive to explore the Dark Continent and to make Africa available to those of us who came along later.

While commercial ivory hunting is banned today, the law is largely ignored; poaching is rampant in places where sport hunting is not allowed. But in places where the hunter's dollars provide funding for antipoaching efforts—and where the value of a single elephant is often higher than that of an entire poached herd—the elephants are doing fine.

At least for now; the future looks a little bleak. Several countries have bowed to antihunting pressure and have shut down hunting entirely. The United States has banned importing ivory from a few more countries where the elephants are doing fine at the moment. It is expected that if this follows the usual path, poachers will move in and completely wipe out the elephants. Unlike hunting, the illegal ivory trade follows no rules; without the money and incentive from sport hunting, there is nobody left to protect the elephants.

There are still a few places that allow elephant hunting, but the pressure to close them is very strong. At this writing, the future of sport hunting elephants and in fact the very survival of African elephants themselves is a bit shaky. They are endangered not due to hunting but rather the politics of emotion.

HIPPOPOTAMUS

DO YOU KNOW WHICH ANIMAL KILLS the most people in Africa? Well, man is first, and the mosquito second. But guess which four-legged critter is the most deadly? Not the lion, buffalo, elephant, or even crocodile. It's the hippopotamus. While Disney may dress them up in tutus to convince ignorant people that the mighty hippos are cute, Africans know the truth of the matter. That truth is that hippos are dangerous, deceptively swift animals with huge teeth and powerful jaws that can bite a man in half with one chomp.

The name hippopotamus (*Hippopotamus amphibius*), or hippo for the spelling challenged, is from the ancient Greek for "river horse." But no horse ever looked like this thing.

The hippo is the third-largest land animal after the elephant and rhinoceros. To some they look like a giant pig, but their closest living relatives are whales. The earliest known hippopotamus fossils, belonging to the genus *Kenyapotamus* in Africa, date to approximately 16 million years ago.

Hippos are found in just about any place in Africa where you also find water. They are yet another dinosaur still walking the earth, at least in appearance. In the book *A Hunter's Wanderings in Africa* by the great African explorer Frederick Courteney Selous, there is a passage in which he describes a place where the trail used by hippos is worn more than 4 inches (10 cm) deep into very hard and solid rock. He noted that in order to achieve this, the time they must have been using the trail "seems almost beyond calculation."

Hippos have hairless, barrel-shaped torsos with stubby legs. They have big heads with giant mouths that open ridiculously wide. They have teeth like fence posts that can be 18 inches (46 cm) long and are always razor sharp.

The ears, nose, and eyes are high up on the head, allowing them to peek out of the water when nearly submerged. The big males can weigh 7,000 pounds (3,175 kg). Don't let all that fool you into thinking them slow moving; hippos can easily outrun most humans and have been clocked at 20 miles per hour (32 kmh).

HUNT IN WATER

The shots are never long when hippo hunting, but precision in bullet placement is important (especially in water). A highly accurate rifle and solid bullets are essential. For hippos in the water, any rifle .375 H&H or larger is a good choice. If you are hunting hippos on land, it's advisable to pick a larger cartridge, like the .416 magnums with 400-grain solids or the .458 magnums with 500-grain solids. Any of the big "heavy rifle" cartridges in traditional double rifles, such as the .470 and .500 Nitro Express, are fine as well.

A high-quality scope is also always a good choice, particularly when hunting in water.

The hippopotamus is semiaquatic, living in rivers, lakes, and swamps. Hippos stay cool by lying in the water or mud—in fact, breeding and birth happen in the water (another reason not to drink it).

Hippos will attack boats and seem to particularly hate dugout canoes, probably because they are shaped like crocodiles, which prey on young hippos. If you are unfortunate enough to be swimming near a hippo, expect to die. And an encounter with a hippo on land is a very dangerous situation, as well.

I was once hunting buffalo in Tanzania along a riverbed that had dried up into a series of pools. We sent a tracker into a bend of the river to make sure there were no buffalo bedded out of sight, but in a pool below a steep bank was a big, nasty male hippo who clearly resented the intrusion. He charged on sight—but had to climb that steep bank, which was about eight feet (2.4 meters) high. I stood with my rifle ready, and as his head came into view, I thought, "We can't stop this thing." The bull slipped in the mud at the top and fell back into the pool with a tremendous splash. He then got up and ran out the back side where it was almost level, looking for all the world like a Volkswagen bus.

We collected all the scattered trackers, including the one who had been chased and was now at the top of a very tall tree, and continued on. Not thirty minutes later we found ourselves between a male hippo and the water. After several tense moments of backing up slowly while keeping our rifles pointed at the belligerent young fella, we managed to put enough space between us that he felt safe proceeding to the water.

Shortly after that, we had to cross yet another pool. At the far end, under the shade of overhanging trees, was yet another old bull soaking in the water. The PH, trackers, and other hunter crossed first while I kept my rifle on the bull—perhaps 30 yards (or meters) away. Then the PH pointed his rifle while I crossed over a set of stones. I'd gone about halfway when the bull let out an ear-shattering bellow and started a charge that threw sheets of water high into the air. (Reports that I screamed like a little girl are not true.) I jumped to the bank and pointed my rifle. He was only about 20 paces away when he stopped.

We decided it was a great time to get the truck

The PH and trackers had to float my hippo down about 300 yards (or meters) of river pool while I stood on the high bank, watching for crocs. One did show up, but a warning shot in front of his nose changed his mind.

We butchered the hippo on a sand bar and loaded it into the safari car, which could not make it up the hill due to the extra weight. So we unloaded the meat onto a tarp, then pushed the safari car out of the river bottom and hooked a winch on the tarp. With the winch and a lot of local help, we dragged the meat to the top of the riverbank and loaded it onto a trailer towed by a tractor brought in for that purpose.

Why all that work? Because hippo meat is treasured by the locals. Our cook made hors d'oeuvres from the tenderloins before dinner that night. I can see why the locals will work so hard. The flavor is outstanding. The meat might be a little coarse and tough, but it's worth the extra work for the taste.

Besides, in Zimbabwe—where people are starving—meat is as precious as gold.

THE ECONOMICS OF HIPPO HUNTING

Hippo hunting provides a less-expensive opportunity to include dangerous game on any safari, as trophy fees are quite low compared to other dangerous game. The Hippopotamus can easily be added to a safari, allowing you to double-dip on the dangerous game.

Remember, too, that when hippos are in the water, they share a trait with zombies: "only brain shots count." High quality optics are important, especially when hunting waterborne hippos.

and hunt buffalo someplace else. But it did whet my appetite for hunting hippos, which I did a few years later in Zimbabwe.

There are two basic methods. If they're in the water, you can sneak in close enough for a shot. When the hippo rises up to breathe, place a shot slightly above and between the eyes, where the "V" shape reaches a peak. The hippo will sink, but within an hour or so the fermenting matter in the stomach will produce gas, causing it to float. Then you send the most disposable member of the hunting party into the croc- and hippo-infested water to attach a rope and tow it to shore. A much more dangerous and exciting way to hunt hippos is on land. The best shot is still a brain shot, but if the bull is broadside, shoot for the off shoulder.

Hippos are an integral part of Africa. On the Selous Reserve in Tanzania, where we hunted from a camp on the Ruaha River, we could see hippos and crocs from our tents, and the roaring of the hippos kept us awake at night. Each morning we would find their tracks where they wandered through the camp under the cover of darkness.

It was wild Africa at its best. —*B.T.*

PLAINS GAME

FOR MOST OF US, African lions and elephants are out of reach, both monetarily and spatially. After all, where are you going to put a full-body mount of a long-maned lion, or the shoulder mount of a jumbo, even if you could afford to shoot it? Instead, most safari hunters opt for plains game, and thanks to the diverse and accessible collection of open-country game, there's no shortage of candidates for wall mounting. There's also no better introduction to Africa's diverse landscape and its tradition of big-game hunting than chasing a mixed bag of plains game.

Plains game hunting brings more hunters to Africa every year than all the Big 5 species combined. The appeal is threefold: affordability (you can hunt multiple animals for less than the price of an outfitted elk hunt in America), abundance (plains game packages routinely include anywhere from 3 to 10 animals, with the opportunity to add more on a trophy-fee basis), and accessibility (most hunts operate out of a comfortable lodge within easy driving distance of an airport).

But those analytical reasons don't get at the real hook of a plains-game safari: This is the chance to see, hunt, and possess those animals that are the very definition of wild Africa: zebras, kudu, impala, wildebeest, and warthog.

The traditional knock-about safari of colonial Africa was a many-weeks trek across the bushveld, hunting a variety of antelope and dangerous game, and camping out of a canvas meru tent. But modern plains game safaris are more commonly operated out of a fixed base—often a modern lodge complete with gourmet meals, housekeeping service, and hot, running water.

Most plains game safaris feature a basic roster of species covered by the price of the hunt, with the chance to add more on an a la carte basis. Impala, either black or blue wildebeest, warthog, blesbok, kudu, and zebra are typically on the menu, and second-tier species lists often include springbok, duiker, and hartebeest.

Regardless of which animals wind up on your lists (or walls), these hunts make for a great introduction to African wildlife—and a great way to see the continent for the first time.

BRING YOUR GUN

Arranging a first safari is a study in dichotomous choices. First, do you bring your own rifle or rent one in-country? Answer: Bring your own.

Second, do you bring your tried-and-true deer rifle, or splurge for a new magnum to air out on plains game? Answer: Bring your old steady. Bullet placement always trumps firepower.

Third, do you hire an expediter to help get through the paperwork, or do you trust your instincts and innate ability to handle bureaucracy? Answer: Hire an expediter. These local experts—I use Gracy Travel—have connections that can guide you through a thicket of rules.

KUDU For most American hunters in Africa, a kudu is the first critter on their wish list. And not just any kudu will do. The Holy Grail of these shadow-dwelling antelope is a spiral-horned 60-incher (152 cm), though there are few hunters who will turn down a 50-inch (127-cm) bull. Native to eastern and southern Africa, the "kude" is a woodland antelope, with a dappled hide that confuses predators as it melts into the thornveld. More are killed in the last 15 minutes of shooting light (when they emerge to feed and water) than the rest of the day combined.

"The kudu is just under your hand, and yet he always manages to escape you." Legendary safari writer Robert Ruark's words were scrolling through my cortex as the sun set on an unsuccessful kudu hunt in South Africa's Eastern Cape Province.

We had seen seven kudu, including two remarkable bulls, file into the cabbage tree grove just after sunup, and my guide Raymond Schenk and I resolved to stay on the ridge overlooking the cleft all day. We sipped water, munched on brown bread slathered in Vegemite, and ate dried figs as we took turns watching the draw. The kudu never appeared during the sweltering afternoon, so we knew killing a big bull was a matter of waiting for him to emerge from the shade before sunset.

We stayed hidden on our ledge until the moon lit up the valley, but the kudu never stepped out of the trees. I'd had 10 days to hunt 10 species of game, and it took half that time kill my first "kude."

They're routinely called the "gray ghost" of Africa, but until I hunted one, I didn't fully appreciate the moniker. They are as elusive as fame and as slippery as deer guts. Their ability to vanish from sight is as impressive as it is frustrating.

Credit their cryptic coloration for part of their Houdini act. Their soft gray coat—like moleskin—is striped with subtle shades of white, slate blue,

and lighter gray that blend into the stabbing shafts of light and shadow that define their woodland cover. Even the white chevron on the bridge of their nose seems to blur them into their surroundings.

And their elegant movement further contributes to their evanescence—more like a slow dissolve than the kinetic punch powered by fast-twitch muscles.

Schenk and I eventually gave up on our fish-barrel kudu— they weren't going anywhere, it seemed—and the next night ended up tagging another great bull, his double-spiraling, ivory-tipped horns measuring just under 55 inches (140 cm).

IMPALA Due to sheer ubiquity, you might think of impala as the walking pantry of Africa. They are often shot for camp meat or leopard bait, and even their tan-on-sand coloration seems to suggest a rifle target just behind their shoulders. But once you hunt a mature male, you'll see that impala can be very game, indeed. And when the rut kicks in and the guttural roar of a ram sunders the bush, you might mistake this prey species for an apex predator.

Judging a trophy can summon all your powers of observation to assess length and mass—often while the horns in question are racing away in a file of lookalike peers—but you can shoot a pretty fair ram without a lot of effort or abstract math, making it very suitable first-game of any safari.

Impala, often called "rooibok," or red deer in South Africa, is a medium-size antelope that has the good manners to herd in the open and graze at midday. That makes them a great way to start a safari; you don't have to wait. Plus, their alarm buffer is about 200 yards (or meters), so they often hover inside the range of most rifles and well within the proficiency of most shooters.

While spotting and even stalking into a herd of impala is no great feat, defining and cutting out a trophy ram is the challenge, because when they are pressured, impala tend to bunch together in tight herds that sift in and out of thornbush.

A better approach is to pattern impala like you might a common whitetail. Watch their daily movements, which almost always center around water, and then get into position.

BLESBOK After impala, the most common plains game trophy is the blesbok, the horse-faced antelope of South Africa's grasslands that can be even harder than the rooibok to judge and hunt.

The blesbok is native to most of South Africa's Eastern and Western Cape provinces and is at home on open, arid grasslands dotted with termite mounds and scattered acacia trees. The antelope gets its name for the white blaze on its face. They're not particularly hardy; a well-placed shot from a .243-class caliber all the way up to the .30 magnums will easily bring one down.

Unlike impala, both male and female blesbok carry ringed horns. Trophy hunters must learn to recognize the heavier, blockier build of a ram, and the longer, base-heavy horns of a trophy—a difficulty compounded by their herding tendencies. When alarmed, as they are when the wind blows, or a zebra brays, or a safari truck passes, blesbok churn into a great, milling herd that makes any subsequent stalk an exercise in futility.

There's a chance you'll encounter a close relative of the blesbok, the bontebok, on South African pasture safaris. The bontebok has more white on his face and legs and tends to herd in sex-specific groups. But beware, as many nations have import restrictions on the relatively rare bontebok. —*A.M.*

WHITETAIL RIFLES FOR AFRICAN GAME

First-time plains game hunters spend more time deciding which rifle to bring than which species to put on their harvest cards. And they frequently make the wrong decision to buy a new gun.

The best advice I ever got prior to my first safari was to bring a rifle I was comfortable shooting for white-tailed deer.

"You want a rifle you know and trust, not only where it shoots over distance, but how it operates without looking down at it," said Limpopo PH Claude Kleynhans. "Shooting can happen fast, and you want to know your rifle—its safety and its balance point, and where it's pointing when it comes to your shoulder."

Generally, any .25 and modestly larger rifle you'd use for back-home deer will work well for plains game ranging in size from the wee duiker to the rangy kudu and even the relatively stocky zebra. It's basically a matter of placing the shot and delivering high-performance bullets to a specific spot.

I'm partial to .280s—especially the flat-shooting .280 Ackley Improved, though either a 7x57mm or a 7mm Rem. Mag. will work fine, and so will a .270 Win. A .25/06 is probably the lightest caliber I'd hunt, but the .30-calibers are great, and you'll probably get approving nods from your PH if you bring out a well-worn and field-tested .30/06.

Equal in importance to your caliber and familiarity with the rifle is your choice of plains-game bullets. You don't want to rely on budget-shelf ammo for an international hunt. Instead, invest in premium bonded or monolithic bullets. You'll want to ensure they shoot accurately in your rifle, of course, but projectiles such as Federal's Trophy Copper, Barnes X Bullets, and Winchester's XP3 are great choices.

WHERE TO AIM: PLAINS GAME

Besides their speed and cryptic coloration, African antelope share another attribute: their pronounced shoulder hump.

That anatomical feature has been responsible for more wounding loss by hunters than all the thornbush branches, trading winds, and misjudged distances combined. Simply put, most hunters aim too high on antelope, and bullets that enter the hump miss the tops of the lungs and other vitals. According to evolutionary biologists, the vacant hump helps prey animals survive neck-wringing attacks by predators.

Most African PHs counsel their clients to pick an aiming point that starts at the line of the belly. "Start at the place where the lower chest meets the front leg, then come up a third of the body depth, and put your bullet in the hollow just behind the front leg," said PH Claude Kleynhans. "You will take out the heart and the bottom of the lungs. If he doesn't go right down, he won't go far."

ZEBRA Pity the poor zebra, because every meat eater in Africa wants to make him a meal. Lions, for example, look at a herd of zebra the way a hungry traveler looks at a Burger King. These striped horses are the symbol of Africa and perhaps the most misunderstood plains game animal. "How could you shoot a zebra?" is the rallying cry of the uninformed. "It's easy," I say, "just aim at the shoulder." The truth is, the zebra is far from a domesticated horse and presents a challenging, elusive, and tough trophy for any hunter.

I have never experienced an easy zebra hunt, and I have hunted them quite a bit. Zebras have incredible senses—they can see, hear, and smell as well as any animal alive. And they travel in packs, so there are a lot of eyes, ears, and noses. Plus, every carnivore in Africa has been eating them for eons, so they have evolved into a very alert and wary species.

Zebras are also extremely tough. Many wear the battle scars from successful fights with lions. That toughness is reflected in their ability to soak up bullets and keep moving. It's always a good idea to bring a big gun to a zebra hunt.

Zebras include several species of African equids (the horse family) united by their distinctive black and white stripes. Their stripes come in many patterns and are unique to each individual. Zebras live in a wide range of habitats, including grasslands, savannas, woodlands, thorny scrublands, mountains, and coastal hills. They are generally social animals that live in small to large herds. Unlike their closest equine relatives, zebras have never been truly domesticated.

There are three species of zebras: the plains zebra, the Grevy's zebra, and the mountain zebra. The plains zebra and the mountain zebra belong to the subgenus *Hippotigris*, and Grevy's zebra is the sole species of subgenus *Dolichohippus*.

GUNS AND LOADS FOR ZEBRA

Zebras are big and tough, so bring enough gun. They can and have been taken with cartridges like the .308 Winchester or .270 Winchester, but a hunter will be far better equipped with a 7mm or .300 Magnum. Even the .338 and .375 Magnums are not out of place when zebra hunting. As always, use heavy, well-constructed bullets.

The Grevy's resembles its close relative the ass, while the former two are more horselike. All three belong to the genus *Equus*, along with other living equids. Most hunting opportunities are for the plains zebra, with some limited opportunities for the mountain zebra. The mountain zebra is prized for its lack of shadow striping and for the yellow stripes on its face. The plains zebra is the smallest of the tree species, but still can weigh 850–900 pounds (386–408 kg) with the average for adult males about 550 pounds (250 kg).

The age old question, "Is the zebra black with white stripes or white with black stripes?" has apparently been settled. It was previously believed that zebras were white animals with black stripes, since some zebras have white underbellies. But embryological evidence shows us that the animal's background color is black and the white stripes and bellies are additions. —*B.T.*

TABLE FARE

Many professional hunters say that zebra is not fit to eat, but others will dispute that. I have eaten zebra backstrap roasted over an open fire and found it quite good. It was slightly tough with a unique flavor that I would describe as close to buffalo—but slightly stronger.

The African natives in Zimbabwe, where I have hunted zebra quite a bit, love the meat and will take any offered.

WATERBUCK Despite his name, the waterbuck doesn't spend a lot of time around water except to drink or to escape predators. The waterbuck has a greasy, smelly coat that was thought to be for waterproofing. But now it's believed that it is for predator protection—the B.O. of a waterbuck is so offensive, and the taste of this grease so rancid, that predators will look for a more palatable meal.

It was a long stalk with very little cover and, the closer we got, the more I realized that this was a very exceptional waterbuck. Expert that I was, this was the first waterbuck I had seen alive. But I had done my homework, and he had a world-class set of horns that would easily make the Rowland Ward record book. Due to the open terrain, the shot was longer than I would have preferred—he was facing us, but the jig was up as soon as he spotted us.

I managed to place the shot perfectly, and he fell in his tracks. After the initial elation, we positioned

him for photos as the trackers brought up the truck. I ran back to the safari car to retrieve my cameras, and, still full of adrenalin, I jumped so my foot landed on the top of the back tire as I grabbed the rail of the platform to vault over into the bed.

The next think I knew, I was flat on my back in the South Africa dust and everyone was laughing. With my brain a bit rattled, I thought they had greased the railing as a joke—but it turns out this was my introduction to the waterbuck. I hadn't noticed that my hands were coated with the grease from his hide. And, yes, it does stink to high heaven!

The waterbuck (*Kobus ellipsiprymnus*) is one of the six species of the genus *Kobus* and belongs to the family Bovidae. The generic name *Kobus* is a New Latin word, originating from an African name, *koba*. The specific name *ellipsiprymnus* refers to the white elliptical ring on the rump. While scientists will go on about 37 different subspecies, hunters

BEST PLAINS GAME BULLETS

Most plains game safaris will include multiple species, so it's always a good idea to choose a cartridge suitable for the largest animal you will be hunting. Excluding eland (which can weigh more than a buffalo), that will usually include zebra, kudu, and waterbuck.

Like most African game the waterbuck can be tough to bring down. He is also a 600-pound (272-kg) animal. Rifle cartridges in the .280–.30-06 category are acceptable, but the various 7mm and .300 magnums are a better choice.

Use bullets that are on the heavy side for caliber and that boast a premium design so they will insure deep penetration.

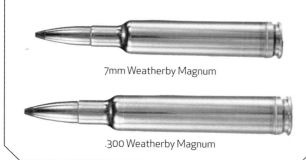

7mm Weatherby Magnum

.300 Weatherby Magnum

TROPHY QUALITY

In most places any bull 25 inches (63.5 cm) or larger is considered a "shooter." Thirty inches (76 cm) is the goal many hold out for—but they're often disappointed. Any horns over 30 inches (72 cm) make for a great trophy.

deal with only the common waterbuck and the defassa waterbuck. Other than location, the primary difference is the white ring on the rump—the common has it; the defassa doesn't.

The waterbuck has a shaggy, reddish brown to gray coat that darkens with age. The hair on the neck is long and manelike. The face has a white muzzle with light eyebrows and inner ears. The cream-colored patch on the throat is called a "bib," and the neck is long while the legs are short, giving a stout appearance. The male has long, spiral-structured (not spiral-shaped like a kudu) horns that sweep back and up. Males top out about 550–600 pounds (250–272 kg). Females are about 25 percent smaller and do not grow horns.

The waterbuck is relatively common throughout sub-Sahara Africa. It is considered a desirable trophy and is on the bucket lists of most hunters.

Just wash your hands before lunch. —B.T.

AFRICA'S UPLAND BIRDS

MY VERY FIRST DAY BIRD HUNTING IN AFRICA, as I pushed through the chest-high grass lining Senegal's Gambia River, I wondered aloud if there happened to be any lions nearby. The game scout, swinging a long stick to flush Swainson's francolin from the thick brush, assured me there were none. "No sir," he said. "No lions. All lions in Niokola," referring to Niokola-Koba National Park, which we had passed just a short way up the road. "Excellent," I replied. "All behind the fence then?" "Oh, no, sir," he said. "No fence."

After such an introduction to African bird hunting, it's easy to understand why I'm now hooked on the endeavor. Thankfully, no lion presented itself that day, but I've since been surprised by everything from warthogs to duiker scooting out of Africa's thorny brush. Such an experience makes the heart drop and reminds us: you're not walking up pheasants in Kansas anymore.

Exciting as the mammalian surprises are, it's really the feathered game that keeps bringing me back to dust my bird-hunting boots in the continent's famous red dirt. Just like its abundant big game, Africa offers varied and virtually unlimited bird-hunting opportunities. From walking up francolin (opposite, bottom left) and guineafowl behind well-trained pointers to waiting around waterholes for sand grouse (opposite, top) to show up at last light, there truly is something for every type of wingshooter.

Africa also delivers what many, myself included, consider the most difficult wingshooting in the world: pass-shooting rock pigeons (opposite, bottom right) in the sunflower fields of South Africa. Dipping and diving at all times, flocks of rock pigeons can accelerate at more than 60 miles per hour (87 kph) at the first sign of a threat, then instantly change direction, humbling even the best wingshots. It's not unheard of for a hunter to burn through a case of shells with only a few feathers to show for it, but the challenge is addictive—and finally connecting after a long dry streak is a well-earned reward.

If you can overlook the bounding impala and menacing crocodiles, wingshooting in Africa is not all that different from what you might already know in terms of tactics.

HELMETED GUINEAFOWL

Prehistoric in appearance and a challenge to bring down, the helmeted guineafowl ranks high on the list of reasons to take the long flight to Africa. A study in contrast, its beautiful, speckled plumage is capped by an ugly, unfeathered head with a bony topknot. The birds' tendency to run ahead may be familiar to pheasant hunters, but when it flushes, the experience is like none other. Picture a volleyball-size burst of feathers blowing up from the scantest patch of grass, a short burst of wingbeats followed by a long glide out of range before the guinea alights on the savanna, legs running full speed before it even hits the ground.

Each species demands its own unique strategy, and where walk-up hunting might be the ticket one day, a driven shoot may be in order the next. But of all the varied and exciting opportunities Africa offers, I crave hunting sand grouse the most.

Sand grouse hunting takes part during the two most beautiful parts of the day. At sunrise and sunset, the buff-colored grouse descend onto small waterholes in large flocks, dipping quickly out of the gray light to get what may be their only drink of the day. For the hunter, the only thing curbing the anticipation of the grouse's arrival is the awe-inspiring display of Africa's famous red sun meeting the horizon.

That reverie is soon interrupted as birds dart like teal into the landscape. The shooter's challenge is to pick a bird from the darkness, track it speeding through the shadows, and pull the trigger before it disappears. Often, the bird hunter will find himself kneeling, twisting, or bending at the waist in a futile attempt to highlight a darting grouse above the horizon line—the reward being the never-to-be-forgotten image of a burst of feathers silhouetted in the fading golden light. —*D.D.*

GEAR UP

THE BENELLI ETHOS

An African PH once admitted to me that he rarely sees semiautomatics, his mostly European clients preferring double-barreled shotguns. Call me uncultured, but particularly on high-volume shoots for rock pigeons, doves, and driven guineafowl, a repeating shotgun seems more in order. Of course, it should be one that functions flawlessly, as Africa's famous heat and fine, red dust can quickly ruin the hunt you traveled around the world to get to.

For a week in South Africa, I relied on the Benelli Ethos, and although I was impressed with the improved inertia-driven system to cycle rounds quickly, the feature I appreciated most was its incredible recoil-reduction system.

I would never have fired that many 12-gauge shells without the use of a shoulder pad, but I did it in Africa, trusting Benelli's engineers, who claimed that it wouldn't hurt a bit. They were right, and I never bruised or developed a flinch. The Italian-made Ethos also has the pedigree and styling that left even my normally stern PH impressed.

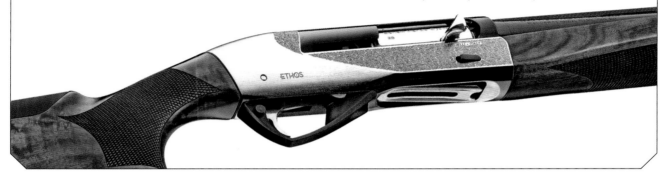

RIDE THE ROVOS RAIL

Imagine traveling through the Kalahari Desert via your own private rail car, a Colonial steam engine chugging ahead of you, enjoying the view of passing Africa with a refreshing sundowner in your hand. The only distractions are memories of a day spent gunning flighted birds pushed toward you by the chants and drums of a line of beaters 100-strong.

Of the few opportunities still available for hunters to experience the Golden Age of Africa, hunting via a luxury train is the most capital-I Imperial. Legendary among well-heeled wingshooters, the 20-carriage Rovos Rail departs from Pretoria, South Africa, and takes hunters on a circular journey like no other, with five days of extraordinary driven shooting for Africa's diverse array of both upland birds and waterfowl. Of course, double guns are required, as is appropriate dress for the Victorian-era dining car, where dinner is a coat-and-tie white-linen affair.

AFRICAN WATERFOWL

IN THE PREDAWN LIGHT, it might be easy to imagine you're sitting along the shores of any nondescript Dakota waterhole. That is, until a lion's roar rolls out of the darkness or the spiral-horned silhouette of a kudu snaps you out of your comfort zone, and you're reminded: this is waterfowling in Africa. Soon, too, the birds prove you're far from home, with the arrival of fantastical flocks of Egyptian and spur-wing geese, white-faced whistling ducks and red-billed teal, all settling into the shallow, muddy pan surrounded by vast stretches of arid desert.

From reed-covered blinds expertly built the night before to permanent pits dug into the hard, dry soil, hunting ducks and geese in Africa does feel a lot like home. The same comparison can be made between stalking pronghorn in the western United States and glassing large herds of antelope in the veld. Still, the differences are stark, and the shooting hot enough that more and more hunters from around the world travel to Africa exclusively for bird hunting. The appeal isn't just sensory; liberal bag limits, the ability to shoot just about any variety of shotshell projectile, and the gentlemanly nature of hunting in Africa make water fowling here a study in both variety and comfort.

If the actual act of hunting is similar, the species vary widely, and in some cases Africa is the only place in the world where certain types are found. Probably the most coveted by hunters are a pair of geese: the gaudy Egyptian (affectionately known to hunters as gypos, opposite top), and the aggressive spur-winged (so named for the pronounced spur located at the joint of their wing bones, which is used to battle rivals during breeding). The spur-wing is the world's largest species of goose, with large males nearing 20 pounds (9 kg).

Waterfowlers looking to round out their life list will also find several types of ducks during hunts across sub-Saharan Africa. Similar in appearance, both the red-billed (opposite, bottom left) and Hottentot teal feature distinctive plumage with a dark brown cap of head feathers. Only the latter's blue bill marks a difference between the two. Other ducks an African waterfowler can expect to encounter are yellow- and knob-billed ducks, white-faced whistling ducks (opposite, bottom right), and Cape shelducks. —D.D.

PASS SHOOTING

Pass shooting waterfowl is a grand tradition in Africa, where the continent's first European settlers supplemented their larders pulling birds from the massive flocks of ducks and geese circling the savannas in search of water. Today, such shoots are social affairs, set up by hunting clubs to take advantage of predictable flight patterns. A shooting line is put in place between ponds or lakes and agricultural fields, each station manned by a shotgunning sportsman. If it sounds easy, you might be surprised—the giant spur-winged geese are flying faster than you think. Plan on missing more than a few until you establish your lead.

AFRICA'S LARGEST ANTELOPE

AFRICA'S LARGEST ANTELOPE—the elands, sables, kudus, and oryx—are the very face of wild Africa. Their masked features look like those of haughty Maasai warriors, and their horns—curved, curled, spiraled, and ringed—have a shape and appeal for any trophy hunter. Hunting these largest antelope in the bush, forest, and savanna is always challenging, and bringing them down routinely takes the right combination of a well-placed shot and a tough bullet. They are abundant and (mostly) affordable and should be part of any plains game bag.

Africa is home to some 80 species of splay-toed ruminants—you know them as antelope—ranging from the shy and dainty to the ponderous and immense. About all this family has in common, besides their descendants, is that they are all hard of horn and fleet of feet.

The largest antelope concern us here, just as they are generally first-order trophies for most hunters traveling to sub-Saharan Africa. Here, in arbitrary order of preference (kudu are my second favorite), are the outsize antelope of the continent.

SABLE The royalty of African antelope, this majestic specimen (opposite) is known for its gleaming black coat (females are a rich chestnut brown) and long, backward-sweeping horns. Sable are savanna animals of the eastern highlands and are precious enough that they command the highest trophy fees of Africa's antelope. Most of us budget hunters watch these aristocrats prance over the horizon, as unattainable as the governor's daughter at the high school prom.

ELAND You could mistake a common eland, or its cousin the giant (or Lord Derby) eland, for a Brahman bull. Same ponderous stature, same shoulder hump, same fleshy dewlap, and same lordly posture and gait. But to see a herd of sand-colored eland sift in and out of acacia groves like whitetails through cornstalks removes any comparison to lumbering, dull-eyed cattle. The Lord Derby eland is the largest of all antelope, and while big bulls weigh well over a ton and can have girths of nearly three feet (1 meter), they move like gymnasts.

A VARIETY OF GUNS

Given the widely variable size of antelope, it's hard to recommend a single caliber that can handle both steenbok and eland. The closest I've come to bringing a single rifle to a plains game hunt was a three-barreled CVA single-shot. I brought barrels chambered in .243, .300 Win. Mag, and .50. The latter was a muzzleloader.

A .30-caliber rifle is considered minimum firepower for larger antelope, and a .300 WSM or .300 Win. Mag. is a good choice. A .338 Win. Mag. is about right for eland. The fact is, buffalo hunters who pursue any of these larger antelope with their .375s rarely feel overgunned.

Their mass becomes a factor when shooting eland (top left), though. They can absorb bullets like sandbags, so heavy .30 magnums should be considered minimum rigs, and .375-class or larger calibers are not out of place.

NYALA Extravagantly beautiful, the cautious nyala (top right) looks like a cross between a spiral-horned kudu, a dagger-horned bushbuck, and a runway model, and indeed, the woodland antelope behaves like each of its cousins. Like a bushbuck, it tends to live in thickets and groves, its striped coat perplexing its many predators. Like a kudu, it craves the grass, and hunters often surprise bulls as they step out of the shade to graze in glades. And like a model, it elicits audible gasps from any hunter who sees one.

ROAN Widely distributed across the shrubland of central and southern Africa, the roan (bottom right) is one of the so-called horse antelopes,

rangy and large-boned. In fact, the roan is the largest antelope next to the eland. It's a sort of in-between antelope—the black mask of a roan looks like an oryx (in Afrikaans, the roan is called the "bastergemsbok") and its ringed horns like those of a stunted sable. But the milquetoast appearance of a roan is deceiving; they are extremely territorial and frequently charge hunters, making hunts for roan a little like a poor man's buffalo hunt.

LECHWE The red lechwe (opposite page, top left) is almost always found near water, and the more pressured this modest-sized antelope feels, the closer it moves to the swamps and bogs of its homeland. One Namibian PH once told me that to hunt a lechwe is to "get your feet wet," and we knew we were closing in on a herd in dense reeds when we heard the splashing of their hooves. Lechwe look like a cross between an impala and a waterbuck, its horns flaring like those of an impala, but they're not as heavy as those of a waterbuck.

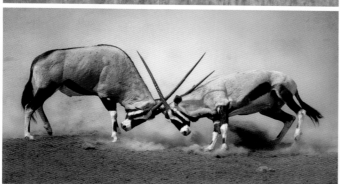

Be prepared for longish shots at red lechwe, as the nervous, herding animal rarely lets a hunter get within 300 yards (or meters). And expect your retrieve to be from a boat, as wounded lechwe nearly always head to the closest water.

GEMSBOK The very face of Africa, the gemsbok (also called the giant oryx or, simply, oryx) is one of the gamest antelope of Africa. Native to the harsh Kalahari Desert, the southern gemsbok (bottom left) has spread across South Africa thanks to the game farm industry. Hunting a free-ranging, javelin-horned bull in the dry, open wasteland of Namibia is to experience the essence of ancient Africa. The oryx is one of the few antelope that PHs fear, for a wounded bull will often turn on his persecutors and make a last, valiant stand. Northern varieties of oryx are far less populous than the Kalahari gemsbok. In fact some, like the Arabian oryx and the scimitar oryx, have been eradicated from their native range in the Sahara Desert and Arabian Peninsula and are now found only on game ranches in Texas, where they were introduced. A free-ranging herd of gemsbok exists on New Mexico's White Sands Missile Range.

HARTEBEEST "God made the hartebeest at 5:30 on a Friday afternoon," says South African PH Hans "Scruffy" Vermaak, citing the assembled-from-spare-parts look of this savanna dweller. To me, the hartebeest (top right) looks something like Picasso's version of an antelope: a Cubists' angular face, bug eyes, oversized shoulders and gut, gangly neck, knobby knees, and screwing horns that are neither wide nor tall. But don't let its homely appearance fool you—hartebeest are savvy escape artists. When they spook—which they will do when they notice the ostriches that they graze with getting edgy—they run in a zigging pattern that makes for delightfully challenging shooting, and their hair-trigger instincts make followup stalks almost impossible.

OBSCURE ANTELOPE

Collecting antelope is a little like collecting old coins. Even within the same species, or denomination, there's plenty of variety. And a true accumulator cannot stop until their collection is complete. For antelope hunters, that means finding obscure regional variations and color phases even within the same species. Waterbuck, for instance, have no fewer than 13 subspecies, distributed from Somalia to South Africa. Here are the antelope that will help you complete your African collection:

PUKU Picture the marsh-loving puku (top left) as a grown-up impala or a petite waterbuck. Most hunts take place during the wet season, when flooding pushes puku into uplands, where they are easier to find and hunt.

SITATUNGA Sometimes called the marshbuck, the water-loving sitatunga (top right) is closely related to both the bushbuck and the nyala. It shares their ivory-tipped, twisting horns and their dappled, cryptic pelage. Like most African antelope, it has a number of subspecies, including a cousin that lives in the forests of the central highlands.

KOB Built like a stocky impala, the kob (second from top) is one of the most widely distributed antelope in central Africa. Hunters often intercept huge herds on their daily trek to water.

ADDAX Another Saharan antelope, the screwhorn addax (second from bottom, left) is rarely found in the deep desert. Instead, you're more likely to hunt it on a game farm.

TOPI/TSESSEBE With a hartebeest's funky profile and the ringed horns of a roan, the topi (second from bottom, right) is found in areas of northern South Africa into Botswana. It often climbs termite mounts to scan for danger.

SCIMITAR-HORNED ORYX This native of the Sahara Desert is extinct in its original range, but one of the curious benefits of game farming is that you can hunt this oryx (bottom) behind high fences at several Texas ranches.

NAMIBIAN ELAND

If I can't kill an animal with a single shot, I feel like I've let both of us down. It's unfair to the animal, but it's also evidence that I've let my concentration slip or I've had a mechanical problem.

So when I found myself reloading after pumping four 180-grain bullets into a Namibian eland, it was all I could do to keep my emotions in check.

We had seen the herd of eland moving along a line of leadwood trees in the last light of day, and my PH Johnny Hogobeb and I had sprinted across a grassy pasture to get the wind right. When they emerged from the cover, Johnny said, I should have a 150-yard (150-meter) shot.

Right on cue, the herd fingered out of the brush, and I got on the best bull of the bunch. When his mates stepped clear, I made a solid behind-the-shoulder shot. Then another. And then, as the bull ran to join his herd, I connected again. By the time I could put another bullet into him, he was slowing down and headed for cover. I reloaded quickly and aimed for the point of the shoulder. That brought him down, but I'm amazed—and ashamed—to say it took another five bullets to kill the bull.

When we skinned him, we found eight entrance wounds, all in the vitals. Only one of the bullets had exited. The bull's horns are on my wall, testament to one of the grand antelope of Africa, and to the amazing toughness of the species.

TAXIDERMY CHOICES

Mere moments after your game is grounded and you've posed with photos of your trophy, you will be asked a question that you probably aren't prepared to hear: "How shall we skin him, then?"

Your PH is asking whether you will have your trophy shoulder mounted or if you'll just take the horns with a skull (or European) mount. Your answer determines how the animal will be skinned in the field.

The next decision you must make is whether you will have your trophies mounted in Africa or whether you'll have the cured skins and skulls shipped to your taxidermist back home. Here are the pros and cons of each:

IN-COUNTRY TAXIDERMY Until recently, this was almost always a bad idea, since indigenous taxidermists had a stilted idea of how a mounted animal should look. But that's changing as a new generation of taxidermists has replaced the old assembly lines. Ensure that your in-country taxidermist is up to snuff and have your trophies mounted in Africa. It will be slightly more expensive than shipping the constituent parts, but it's less trouble later.

DIP-AND-PACK This is the term for trophy parts that are prepared for shipment to a taxidermist out of the country. It's slightly cheaper than having your complete mounts shipped overseas. But be aware that dip-and-pack skulls are not bleached white and that skins are sometimes so stiff with solvent that they can be hard to make supple again.

AFRICA'S SMALLEST ANTELOPE

THE CAT-SIZED ANTELOPE of Africa have probably made fools of more safari hunters than all the spiral-horned kudu and homicidal buffalo combined. These furtive, shade-loving pygmies—with their finger-long horns and the uncanny ability to vanish before your eyes—are even more cryptic and elusive when you're trying for a trophy specimen. Little wonder, then, that the most common plains species left uncollected at the end of a safari is a duiker or steenbok, let alone the dozens of more obscure midget antelope.

At some point in nearly every safari, as dust-numb hunters settle into a sundowner and consider the blanks on their trophy list, someone curses the wee duiker.

"I coulda had one if the driver had stopped sooner." Or, "If I had my rifle loaded, I could have shot 10 of those puny things." Or, "I was on him, but my PH wouldn't let me shoot into the bush."

Some camp hang-about will then suggest hunting "under the midnight sun"—code for firing up the spotlight and heading back to collect all the animals that were too elusive in the daylight. If you are a participant in this conversation, you should resist the invitation. Yes, it is effective, and it's one of the most efficient ways to kill duiker, steenbok (opposite), dik-diks, klipspringer, and suni—all antelope that are not much larger than a common jackrabbit of the American West, and which come out of their obscuring cover at night. You'll probably also see jackal, hyena, bushpig, caracal, and genet cats in the high beam of your midnight sun.

But that's cheating. You *can* bag Africa's smallest antelope, but not by hunting them as you would impala or wildebeest. Instead, hunt them as you might a cottontail or a fox—glassing likely habitat, waiting for them to emerge from cover, and even flushing them from the tightest holds. This is the essence of hunting in Africa: it's actually hunting, and it puts a premium on your field skills, including detecting subtle differences between shady leaf and shadowed ear and then threading a shot through thornbush limbs and other bullet-deflecting cover. Simply put, there is no plains game that will test your hunting abilities more acutely than these diminutive antelope.

GO SMALL

Almost every duiker-sized antelope is shot with a rifle that's better suited to kudu. That makes for gaping holes in the dainty animals.

Instead, bring a rifle sized to the diminutive stature of these antelope. For steenbok and suni, that might mean a .22 Magnum or a .222—or even a .17 HMR. The upper end of rifle calibers is a .243. Any of these rifles should be scoped with optics powerful enough to reach out for distant shots but with lower ends for close-in work.

It's also a good idea to bring a shotgun if you target these heavy-cover antelope. A fast-shooting semiauto is great for walking up rabbit-sized animals.

THICKET-PICKING Africa's most common small antelope, the various species of duiker (top) and steenbok, are almost always in plain sight. You simply have to know where to look: on the shady side of pockets of isolated brush and stunted trees, in the rank weeds of overgrown roadside ditches, and on the edges of fields and fence lines.

If you approach these areas quietly, walking instead of driving a safari Jeep, there's a good chance you'll catch a pint-sized antelope in the open. In that case, you'll have the rare opportunity to size them up, determine if it's a male or a female, and make a solid shot.

That's in direct contrast to the typical encounter with a duiker: a random spot in transit to another area, a hurried evaluation of trophy quality, followed by a rushed shot.

The best argument for hunting these antelope is that they are ignored by most trophy hunters. That isn't to say that they're not game animals—they surely are—but only that they haven't been coveted and managed to death. Considering Africa's trend toward fenced safaris, these are some of the only game species that haven't been commercialized. That means every duiker and dik-dik you see—and all that you don't—is truly wild.

THE TINY 10

Writer Peter Flack defined South Africa's "Tiny 10," arguably the most frequently encountered of the 30+ pygmy species:

DAMARA DIK-DIK Named for its alarm call, the shrubland dik-dik (below) has a dark gland at the inner corner of each eye.

BLUE DUIKER The smallest member of the antelope family, this duiker is a forest-dweller, rarely encountered by hunters.

COMMON DUIKER This abundant antelope (also called the gray or bush duiker) is found south of the Sahara. Three-inch (7.6-cm) horns are good; 4-inchers (10-cm) are rare trophies.

RED FOREST DUIKER This hunched-up, roan-coated antelope stands 16 inches (41 cm) tall and eats fallen fruit of forests.

CAPE GRYSBOK Native to the Southern Cape Province, this yellowish antelope lives in shrub and overgrown orchards.

SHARP'S GRYSBOK Also called the northern grysbok, this widely distributed runt has a tawny coat flecked with white.

KLIPSPRINGER This rabbit-sized antelope means "rock-hopper," and it is found in boulder-strewn mountains throughout eastern Africa. Here's something you didn't know: all four of its dainty hooves can fit in a circle the size of a Canadian Loonie.

ORIBI With a shoulder height of up to 26 inches (66 cm), this is the giant of the midget antelope. It is largely white and prefers sparsely-treed plains.

STEENBOK You'll know this antelope by the black veins in its pale ears. That, and when you flush one, it runs in a zig-zagging course that's nearly impossible to track with a rifle.

SUNI This tiny, 10-pound (4.5-kg) antelope lays still in cover, then whistles in alarm as it bounds into even denser brush.

WARTHOG

PITY THE LOWLY WARTHOG. More commonly depicted as a bulb-eyed, slow-witted buffoon than a game animal, its intellect is questioned as often as its athleticism. But the ground-burrowing warthog is one of the most elusive, savvy, and nimble animals of Africa. Hunters who hold out for a trophy boar will spend days flushing and accessing scores of pigs, watching their held-high tails flag through the grass and trying to get a glimpse of their slashing tusks. These hunters will curse the warthogs' ability to melt into the brush and the clay-gray soil of Africa.

Distributed across sub-Saharan Africa, warthogs are part of almost every plains game hunt. They are abundant, ubiquitous, and frankly a blast to hunt. Most antelope hunters take their bonus warthog by busting a family group somewhere on the savanna and then either getting the largest member of the sounder or ambushing the lead hog.

More deliberate hunters wait for warthogs at water holes, where they have more time to size up the trophy quality and place a killing shot. While warthogs' vision is limited, they have remarkably keen senses of smell and hearing. You can also hunt warthogs by patterning them as you might a whitetail or a black bear. They don't roam far from their subterranean dens and always return to the sanctuary after a day of foraging the plains and pans of the neighborhood.

But neither of those hunting styles access the kinetic gift of warthogs, which is that you can never anticipate when you'll encounter one. You'd think that the low-slung, blocky animals would give you plenty of time to grab your rifle, track the individual you want, and take your shot. In reality, warthog hunting is more like flushing quail. The sounder scatters, you scramble for your gun, and by the time you cycle a cartridge and get on the stock, the quick-trotting squealers have dissolved in the leopardgrass and curly leaf.

When you do finally kill a warthog, you'll generally be as surprised as your victim. Make sure you're staying in camp long enough for the kitchen to roast a young suckling or spit an older specimen, for there are few finer entrées in the bush (or anywhere) than a freshly seared and salted warthog. And there are few more durable trophies than a bead-eyed boar of the open savanna.

SPOT A BUSHPIG

How can you tell a bushpig from a warthog? That's one of the churlish questions a particularly aggressive African PH may throw your way.

Warthogs run with their tails held high. Bushpigs run with their tails down. There. Now you can show up the piker.

There are more differences. Bushpigs are primarily nocturnal, and they tend to gravitate to agricultural operations, where they are notorious pests.

Bushpig run in sounders of a dozen or more, and you'll also know them by their longish manes of coarse hair and their barely noticeable tusks.

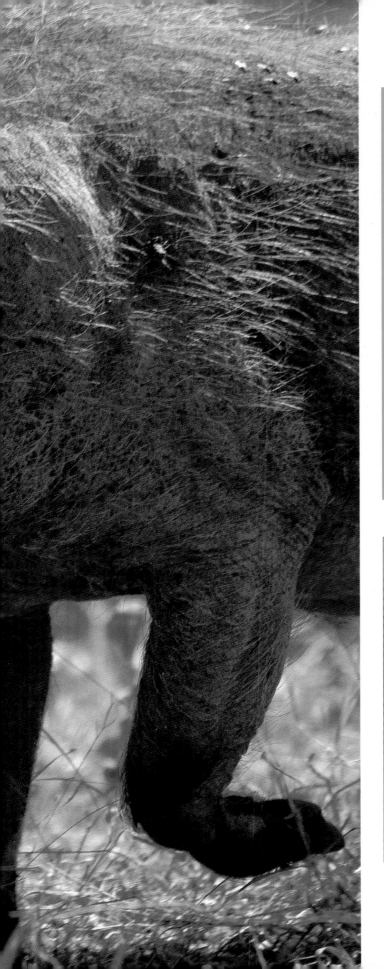

SNAP-JUDGE A WARTHOG

Because both sows and boars have tusks, simply sighting ivory isn't enough to compel you to pull the trigger on a warthog. If you are hunting the oldest boars, look for some of the following secondary cues:

PRONOUNCED WARTS Mature boars will have four large, fairly obvious warts, two on the sides of the face just below the eyes, and another pair above the upper tusks along their muzzle. Sows typically have just the upper warts.

HEAVY TUSKS A warthog with long, heart-shaped tusks that seem to meet over the bridge of the muzzle is probably a sow. Trophy boars have heavy, blunt tusks that jut out but don't necessarily curl upward.

NONSYMMETRICAL TUSKS Older boars almost always prefer one tusk to the other as a digging tool and weapon. The dominant tusk may be as much as half the length of the off-side tusk. The oldest boars often have tusks that are nearly completely broken off.

WARTHOG GUNS AND LOADS

More important than delivering a specific payload, the best warthog rifle is one that you can swing easily and quickly. Warthog hunting happens in close quarters and within short order—so heavy, ponderous rifles aren't particularly useful. Instead, think about a driven-game rifle; a Blaser R8, a Sauer 101, or a similarly quick-pointing rifle is a good choice.

Moderate calibers will handle warthogs. I shot my best boar with a .243, but most safari hunters will want to employ their lighter .270s, .30/06s, and .308s. Shoot a good-quality bullet, as warthogs are dense, low-slung animals that can easily duck into the undergrowth when wounded.

AFRICA'S DESERT ANTELOPE

THE GREAT KAROO IS THE DRIEST, coldest, most desolate piece of southern Africa, and to early settlers, the only thing "great" about the arid shrubveld was the hardship they experienced there. This empty scabland that stretches across the southwestern quarter of South Africa is the homeland of springbok, the national symbol of the country, and one of the most unique and hard-won trophies of the continent. North, in the even more serious desert of the Kalahari, the same can be said of the native gemsbok, or oryx.

It's called "pronging," the crazy, pneumatic leaping of a springbok (opposite)—a repeated, stiff-legged vault as high as 10 feet (3 meters) straight up. Apparently rams use pronging as a breeding display, but I've only seen it when they were spooked. An entire field of pronging springbok looks like popcorn popping in a skillet, and while it's dead serious to the tan- and cream-colored antelope, it's side-splittingly comical to me. And it's hard to aim a rifle when you're laughing.

Luckily, in springbok country, there's no shortage of rams that will stand still if you've made a quiet, stealthy, and sober sneak.

There are four varieties of springbok—common, black, copper, and white—and they are a sort of missing link between the savanna antelope and the Thompson's gazelle. Trophy rams have ringed horns that nearly meet at their tips.

If you shoot one, don't waste time getting to your trophy; if you dawdle, you'll miss one of the oddest death displays I've ever seen. A springbok's final physical act is to stand all the hollow hair on its back upright, then lay them down again as it expires. In its way, it's a sad sort of surrender. And there's something else to be detected in the acquiescent act: the smell of Wyoming.

While springbok and pronghorn antelope of the American West are not evolutionarily linked, their deathbed emanation smells exactly the same—the sweet, dusty, caramel-like scent of dried cornhusks. It's a wonderful, evocative smell, and it links the loneliest landscapes of two very different continents: the brittle-dry karoo of Africa with the high plains of North America.

CALIBERS FOR OPEN-COUNTRY ANTELOPE

It's hard to recommend one rifle for animals ranging in size from the 100-pound (45-kg) springbok to the 600-pound (272-kg) gemsbok. But what they all have in common is habitat and flight instincts that make long shots the norm. Here are three classic desert calibers:

6.5MM CREEDMOOR This .264-class caliber generates a flat trajectory comparable to the venerable .300 Win. Mag. without all the nasty recoil.

7MM REM. MAG A bit much for springbok, you can bring 140-grain bullets for smallish antelope and bone-crushing 175-grain bullets for oryx and larger antelope.

.257 WBY. MAG This flat-shooting magnum pushes 80-grain Barnes TSX bullets at nearly 4,000 feet (1,200 meters) per second.

KALAHARI ORYX Go north into Namibia, and you'll experience Africa's second-greatest desert after the Sahara: the Kalahari. This is the homeland of one of Africa's most distinctive species, the hardy oryx, also known as the gemsbok.

Like most African antelope, the gemsbok is divided into subspecies. There are four, but the one that concerns most hunters is the Kalahari gemsbok, which is well distributed across South Africa, Namibia, Botswana, and parts of Zimbabwe.

Because it evolved in the desert, gemsbok can go for days without water; they're often found in the most open, sparsely vegetated landscape. The best trophies come from their native Namibia; most of South Africa's oryx are in high-fence game ranches, and they don't get as big on a diet of acacia leaves.

FIRST PERSON: ANDREW MCKEAN

NAMIBIAN GEMSBOK

My first gemsbok was a long-horned female, shot in a verdant river bottom of South Africa's Eastern Cape. It was a fair stalk and hunt, but I never celebrated my trophy—it seemed to me like that animal didn't belong in the bushveld.

So when I had a chance to hunt Namibia's Kalahari Desert, my sole focus was on a native trophy gemsbok. It took a long day, but finally my PH, Johnny Hogobeb, spotted a herd, and we moved in for a closer look.

These Kalahari oryx are spooky as spies. When they get nervous—when the wind blows, or the sun shines, or they spot a stalking predator—they herd in the open, then sift through the thornbrush, their silver-and-gray hides vanishing in the vertical confusion of trunk and limb ,like quail disappearing through corn stalks.

We were tracking a herd with a very good bull, but Hogobeb wanted to wait to finish the approach. We crouched behind a snarl of brush until the antelope—their polished black horns impossibly long, sharp, and glinting in the sun—stopped to feed. Then Hogobeb grabbed my shirt and pulled me into him. "We move as one," he hissed. And we did, spidering from one patch of shade to another, freezing when the oryx looked up, creeping when they returned to feeding.

I knew it was time to deploy my Thompson/Center rifle when Hogobeb slowly opened his shooting sticks and planted them in the sand on the shady side of a leadwood bush. And there he was.

THE ETHICS OF CHEETAH HUNTING

I received harsh looks when I told some friends that I was interested in hunting cheetah in Namibia. "It's illegal," was the collective response. But it's not illegal to hunt them; it's illegal to import their hides into the United States. The import restriction is designed to discourage illegal killing, but it isn't working. Many hundreds are killed by Namibian ranchers, and, because they have no value to the trophy-hunting market, the bodies are left to rot. It's a shame, as cheetahs are one of the great challenges of an African safari.

Unlike leopards, which feed on bait, cheetahs only eat fresh meat. So most hunting is the "encounter" method—opportunistically, in the course of other hunts. Their speed, cryptic coloration, and the difficulty of tracking them make pursuing cheetah a classic, thrilling challenge.

EYE ON TOMMIES

Of all the members of the gazelle family, hunters will surely encounter the small, nervous Thompson's gazelle, almost always referred to as a "Tommie," which is shot for leopard bait and camp meat across eastern Africa.

These 70-pound (32-kg) rams look and behave like South African springbok, but their horns are longer and thicker, and herds are often associated with wildebeest and plains zebra. These animals graze down the taller grass, leaving the preferred shorter grass for the grazing gazelles.

Tommies are the most abundant of a family of antelope that ranges across eastern and northern Africa, into the Arabian Peninsula, Turkey, and as far north as Mongolia.

Wherever they are not protected as endangered species, gazelles are considered a favorite game animal. Regardless of subspecies, gazelles occupy similar habitat: open plains, rocky wastelands, and dry wadis, or the wide plains of seasonal rivers.

GAZELLES OF THE WORLD

DORCAS GAZELLE (North Africa, bottom left)

GOITERED GAZELLE (Iran, Iraq, and Azerbaijan)

CHINKARA GAZELLE (India, Pakistan, and Iran, top left)

MONGALLA GAZELLE (Sudan)

RED-FRONTED GAZELLE (Africa) Very closely related to, if not indistinct from, the Thompson's gazelle

GRANT'S GAZELLE (Eastern Africa, top right) Very similar to the Thompson's, the horns of this antelope are lyre-shaped, similar to those of the impala

GERENUK (Horn of Africa and African Great Lakes region, bottom right) The long-necked gerenuk is notorious for grazing on its long hind legs to browse on acacia trees and taller brush

AFRICA'S FOREST AND MOUNTAIN ANTELOPE

AFRICAN PROFESSIONAL HUNTERS ARE, as a rule, unafraid. They stalk wounded game, dispatch poisonous snakes, and address clients' unrealistic expectations with courage and tact. But they are universally respectful of the bushbuck, a shy, brown-dappled antelope of Africa's shady places—forests and brushy ravines. When wounded or cornered, the bushbuck will charge, trying to impale hunters on its sharp, corkscrewing horns. "Their eyes burn green just before the charge," one PH told me, revealing a deep wound in his thigh from a cornered bushbuck.

It's fair to call these antelope of the high grassy slopes and deep forests second-tier trophies for African hunters. It's not that they're somehow less fun or challenging to hunt. Quite the opposite is true. It's simply that the reedbuck, bushbuck (opposite), and klipspringer are harder to manage and market than impala, kudu, and wildebeest.

In other words, these species don't easily fit into a game-ranching model, in which breeding stock is bought at auction and trucked to a fenced ranch. The unfortunate reality of modern plains game hunts, mainly in South Africa, is that the first-tier trophies—think kudu, nyala, sable, wildebeest, waterbuck, and even impala—are managed in a manner similar to livestock.

Not so the secondary trophies. These more obscure and solitary animals are generally available for a trophy fee, and few outfitters will guarantee success or trophy-class animals, simply because few really know the number or size of the critters on their properties. To me, that makes them truly wild—and makes them first-tier trophies.

The tradeoff, of course, is that you might hunt for days without seeing one, and when you do, it might not be a Rowland Ward-qualifying specimen. If you're presented with this gamble—a sure-thing trophy or an elusive unmanaged antelope-take the risk. You'll cover more ground than in a safari truck, and the more ground covered, the more surprising the encounters. You'll see baboons, bushpigs, and maybe a black-backed jackal or a flowing-quilled porcupine. This is the essence of Africa, the surprise of the bush. And who knows? The more you stab into the interior of game farms, the more you'll find those trophy-class kudu bulls and impala rams.

THE TREE OF LIFE

Called whistling thorns, thorntrees, or wattle, the acacia tree is the most abundant and recognizable plant of Africa. And it's the most critical habitat component for the continent's browsing animals.

The umbrella shape of the tree's foliage should clue you in to its popularity among long-necked antelope. What you see is the browse line, or the extent that local kudu, nyala, and even giraffes can nibble the lower, succulent leaves.

To say that you'll kill a kudu or an impala in sight of an acacia tree is a little like saying you'll kill a pronghorn antelope near sagebrush. They just go together.

FOREST ANTELOPE

BUSHBUCK One of the most widespread antelope of southern Africa, bushbuck are nearly always found in the shade. They're most active at night but can be found in the daytime by setting up on a height of land and spending hours glassing the brush. When you spot a good ram, take your time stalking within shooting range, and make sure your shot is true. No one wants to push the brush after a wounded animal.

NYALA We've discussed this large, lovely antelope in another section, but include it here as well because it, too, is a shade lover. It is also anathema to bushbuck—you'll rarely find both in one area.

BONGO One of Africa's most coveted trophies if the bongo (top left)—partly because it's so rare, and partly because it is so elusive that finding one, let alone taking a mature ram, is a weeks-long odyssey in the tangled, muggy forests.

MOUNTAIN ANTELOPE

REEDBUCKS Southern Africa is home to three species of reedbucks (top right), all of which sound the same shrill whistle when alarmed, and all of which are solitary and elusive. The southern reedbuck prefers lower-elevation savannas where it hides in towering reed hummocks. The bohor reedbuck is mainly confined to big river valleys. The mountain reedbuck is an antelope of grassy boulder fields and switchgrass highlands.

VAAL REHBOK The high-country animal that gave the Reebok brand its name, vaal rehbok (bottom left) lives at the very top of southern Africa's rugged mountains. Its thick gray coat insulates it from the harsh weather of Lesotho and Swaziland's highlands as well as the Drakensberg Mountains of northeastern South Africa. Much of this hunting is done with optics. Set up on a height of land, spot a ram, and then work in before making a shot.

A DRAKENSBURG REEDBUCK

My best African trophy is a tiny mountain reedbuck with 6-inch (15-cm) horns. It just misses the Rowland Ward record book, but it's how I hunted the little ram that makes him a trophy.

I spent half of a 10-day safari in South Africa's Limpopo province hunting reedbucks on unfenced land on the shoulders of the Drakensberg Mountains, and while I heard the reedbucks whistle daily, I couldn't see the animals in the tall grass of the steep slopes. At last, on my final day, I spotted a ram with two ewes, but they saw me first and scrambled up rocks the size of Volkswagens.

I steadied my rifle, and when the ram stopped, I dropped him with a shot from my .243 Win. He tumbled for maybe 100 yards (or meters) before hanging up on a tree growing horizontally from the rock face. It took me an hour to climb to him, but every painful step is remembered fondly when I look at his head on my trophy-room wall.

HUNTING GIRAFFE

No discussion of forest hunting is complete without mention of the giraffe. Easy to spot, and fairly easy to stalk because of their tendency to herd together and watch a hunter's approach, the trick to hunting giraffe is making a good first shot.

Most PHs advise hunters to aim for the heart, which is located very high up in the chest. A frontal shot is recommended, partly because they tend to turn to face danger, partly because you can avoid bullet-blunting bones. If you only have a broadside shot, then shooting high on the shoulder will work, but only with premium bullets out of a larger-caliber rifle. A giraffe's tough skin and heavy bones are no joke.

Hold out for a mature bull, with his recognizable dark, tobacco-brown coloration and immense size.

WILDEBEEST

NEARLY EVERY PLAINS GAME OUTFITTER will give you an option of wildebeest as part of your basic bag. Your main decision across sub-Saharan Africa is whether to hunt a blue or a black specimen—that's how ubiquitous these cattlelike antelope are. You're more likely to encounter the blue wildebeest—also known as the "brindled gnu," for its distinctive striping. A trophy black wildebeest, also known as the "white-tailed gnu," is the more difficult to identify and to hunt. Black or blue? When it comes to wildebeest, there is no wrong answer.

"Wildebeest are concrete," whispered my South African professional hunter, Raymond Schenk. I nodded, figuring he meant their cement-gray color, streaked with charcoal, that looked like an industrial conglomerate. We were studying a herd of maybe two dozen blue wildebeest, and in the acacia shade their blue-gray bodies overlapped like slate shingles. I waited behind my propped rifle for a good bull to separate from his mates, and when he did I sent 180 grains of Winchester XP3 through his shoulder. He ran—and kept running.

"See what I mean?" Raymond snapped over his shoulder to me. "Like concrete. Tough to shoot through."

When we finally caught up to the wounded bull, hours later, he was holed up in a cockspur thicket, waiting on us, back to safety and horns toward danger, like a hamstrung Cape buffalo might face a lion.

That was my introduction to wildebeest, sometimes called "poor man's buffalo" for their surprising gameness and toughness. It would be easy to dismiss wildebeest as cattle, not only for their bovine profile but also for their bugging eyes, phlegmatic snorting, and tendency to herd in the open. But once they know they're being hunted, wildebeest become cagey as kudu, weaving into the thornbush and circling up, stationing calves in the middle and sharp eyes around the perimeter.

Of the two species, blue wildebeest are more commonly associated with the bushveld of southern Africa. In eastern Africa and especially the Serengeti, they are famous for their annual rainy-season migrations in herds numbering in the hundreds of thousands. But where they are hunted, blues are never far from shading acacia trees.

THE AFRICAN CHAIN OF ALARM

It usually starts with an ostrich. The big birds have the best eyes on the continent, the suspicion of an auditor, and a trip-wire flight instinct. They are the first to spot danger, and you know they're alarmed when you see their heads bob up and down.

Every other animal watches the ostrich. The zebras get prancy first and start to mill nervously. Then it's the red hartebeest, which tend to gather into milling herds, then the wildebeest, and lastly the impala are on the run, away from danger.

So remember, while stalking your next trophy head: don't startle the ostriches!

MAKE YOUR OWN BILTONG

The favorite snack food of Africa—paired with a cold beverage on your evening return from the bush—is a dried meat that Americans might call jerky. Just like jerky, there are infinite variations on the theme, but biltong has a few constants. The first constant is the presence of coriander seeds in its seasoning. Second, the best biltong is made from game meat, especially wildebeest. Other classic ingredients include rock salt, brown sugar, bicarbonate of soda, black pepper, and vinegar. Many home cures also call for Worcestershire sauce.

Black wildebeest, on the other hand, prefer the interior's open pans and short-grass karoo. You'll rarely see a black bull in the thornbush, so hunters who can slink on their bellies and shoot far and well have an advantage over their truck-riding fellows who rarely see a bull that's not on the run.

A name is just about all these wildebeest cousins share. The blue is larger, and its horns protrude from the side of the head, curve down, and then hook up and in. The horns of a black wildebeest erupt from heavy bosses atop the skull, and they curve forward before hooking upward.

BLACK WILDEBEEST AT THE "SHOOTING BOX"

It may be the most historic property in southern Africa, a 140,000-acre (56,650-hectare) ranch once owned by Cecil Rhodes—diamond-mining magnate, father of Rhodesia (now known as South Africa), and creator of the Rhodes Scholarship. The ranch, called Rooipoort, is located in the Northern Cape Province west of Kimberly, and has a rich history as an elite hunting destination. In its center is a white frame house called the "Shooting Box," which has hosted prime ministers and industrialists across two centuries. I was interested in hunting black wildebeest here, in a series of shallow pans (or dried lakes) where the species evolved.

My PH, Coenraad "Scruffy" Vermaak, had spotted a good bull, but he was 500 yards (or meters) out in the pan. We'd have to crawl to a closer tuft of grass. As I crawled, I kept finding other hunter's cast-off cartridges: a modern .308 Win., the brass still shiny; an ancient 7x57mm pressed into the brick-red soil; a .30/06, the crumbled remains of an unidentified cartridge; and finally, before I settled to make a killing shot, a burnished old 9.3x74mm that was ejected here, I'd like to think, by a Gilded Age hunter, aiming for an ancestor of the bull I had in my scope.

AFRICA'S OBSCURE GAME

AFRICA BECOMES A DIFFERENT PLACE after dark. In the daylight, it's a menagerie of antelope melting in and out of the thornbush. But in the darkness, the continent comes alive with scavengers, furtive predators, and cryptic animals built to ambush and slink rather than stand and display. The best way to see these nocturnal creatures is either by driving rural roads or by setting up with a spotlight. While it's not especially sporting to hunt under the lamp, it's a great way to see all the obscure animals that daylight conceals.

Oceans of ink have been spilled writing about the grand and glorious animals of Africa: the elephants, rhinos, buffalo, and kudu. But precious little is written about the dozens of other animals that are just as fun to hunt, even if they don't have spiraling horns or fan clubs. I'm talking about the ubiquitous vermin and varmints of Africa, few of which are seen, some of which are difficult to classify, but nearly all of which can be added to a hunter's bag with a little negotiation with your PH. Here are Africa's least appreciated critters, ranging from the most to the least common:

BABOONS While hardly obscure—you'll see troops of baboons crossing rural highways—reviled baboons are generally taken incidental to hunting other species. Hold out for an older male and have his skull bleached for a remarkable, somewhat spooky trophy.

HYENAS The striped and spotted hyena is among the most thoroughly loathed animals of Africa. Slinking scavengers, they are also prodigious hunters, and hyenas have been known to take down game as large as blesbok and will even prey on humans. Most hyenas are killed incidentally, but some outfitters call them with prey-in-distress calls. You may also see a relatively rare brown hyena.

BLACK-BACKED JACKALS Think of these canines as Africa's coyotes. They are ubiquitous, elusive, and a hard-won trophy. They are most often taken in the course of hunting other game, though they can be called, and are frequently seen in the spotlight's beam.

NIGHT HUNTING IN AFRICA

If you have an evening to spare in Africa, grab a few friends, a high-beam light with a red lens filter, and an electronic predator call, and see how many species you can call out of hiding.

If you're in the right spot, you can call in half a dozen species within 30 minutes—commonly serval cat, bat-eared fox, and black-backed jackal. Shooting is a challenge, as few completely emerge, and their shining eyes make it tough to judge distance or body orientation. Plus, most ethical hunters want to identify their target, and under the spotlight it can be hard to tell who's looking back at you.

PORCUPINES The barred quills of both the Cape and crested porcupine (top left) are classic Africa, sold in gift shops and given as presents. So when you stumble across a porcupine in the bush, you might be tempted to collect your own. Whether you pot the lumbering vegetarians is your business.

GOLDEN JACKALS Native to northern Africa, you can find this jackal (bottom left) as far east as India and as far north as Romania. In Africa, the strongest numbers are on the fringes of the Sahara.

AARDWOLVES The curious, insect-eating, almost entirely nocturnal aardwolf (top right) is related to the hyena but is much more bashful. Spotlighting hunters often see them but shooting is discouraged, as the aardwolf is a useful predator of termites.

BAT-EARED FOX Another insect-eater, the bat-eared fox (bottom right) is often found scampering across open savannas at last light. They are frequently called into range by the high-pitched sounds of a bird in distress.

CARACALS One of the most common felines of Africa, the tawny caracal (opposite page, top left) looks like a rangy lynx, with tufted ears and large paws. An ambush predator, a caracal might often

be spotted watching from underbrush or stalking after birds—or even after springbok.

CIVET CATS Another critter that's rarely seen in the daytime, the civet cat (bottom right) is often seen in vehicle headlights, darting across rural roads. It looks a little like a raccoon, but with larger back quarters and a distinct crest along its back. Killing them is discouraged, however, because civets prey heavily on poisonous snakes.

GENET CATS You may see the genet cat (middle left) in a tree or slinking through underbrush. It's more active in the daylight than other cats but is still considered a great and rare trophy.

SERVAL CATS Long-legged and striped like a jaguar, the bobcat-sized serval cat (top right) hunts mostly at night and preys almost entirely on rodents and birds. While you can often call these cats at night with predator calls, in practice many escape because in spotlights it can be hard to distinguish a large serval from a juvenile leopard. Just as with bobcats, most serval cats will sneak into range of a predator call by using cover for their approach. So study the brush for flicks of movement.

HARES Africa has two main species of hares: the scrub (bottom left) and savanna hares. Both are often seen at night under the spotlight.

PERFECT PREDATOR GEAR FOR AFRICA

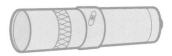

FOXPRO FUSION A good-quality electronic caller loaded with a variety of distressed rabbit, bird, and fawn bleats.

FEATHER DECOY Pick up a feather in the bush and tie it to a 4-foot (1.2-m) length of fishing line with a barrel swivel-tied near the quill. You can tie the feather to a branch to swing in the breeze and add a visual to your calling set-up.

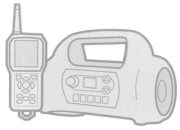

WINCHESTER'S .17WSM This new, hot rimfire is perfect for Africa. Bring the 25-grain load and reach out to 200 yards (or meters) with a flat-shooting rig that's capable of handling every varmint in Africa up to and including hyena.

COYOTE LIGHT This rifle-mounted spotlight ensures that your crosshairs are always aligned with your light. The red beam focuses out to 300 yards (or meters).

ARGENTINIAN DOVES

LIMITLESS. That's the best single word to describe a South American dove shoot—I won't call it a hunt, quite. Seemingly infinite birds, all the shells you care to pay for, and always a fresh gun handed to you by a youngster whose only other job is to keep track of your hits and misses. Wingshooters are a species so accustomed to restrictions—on the sex and number of the birds to shoot or shotshell numbers and types—that the freedom created by almost limitless birds here is refreshing—even if it's also a little unsettling.

I've never known a hunter to mount an Argentine eared dove. It's not that the quick-flitting birds are not lovely—they are, but it's a matter of perspective. After seeing millions of doves, and killing thousands, how do you pick out just one to celebrate?

Until you experience a dove shoot in the best of the Cordoban fields, or in a cattle feedlot on the Buenos Aires plains, you simply can't comprehend the numbers of birds here. On my first trip to Argentina, I stood and watched, dumbfounded, as wave after wave of clay-drab doves poured over the thorn trees and into my stand. If I hadn't shaken myself awake and started swinging it, I'm fairly certain a dove would have landed on my shotgun barrel. Within an hour, I had a pile of gray-feathered birds on the ground in front of me that would give an ornithologist nightmares.

A South American dove hunt is the last of the world's big-bag shoots. In a week of heavy gunning, it's possible to rack up a five-figure tally, and while your bag will contain mostly eared dove, you'll also shoot hundreds of Day-Glo parakeets and dusky pigeons. The abundance of birds here—some might describe the swarm as evidence of ecological imbalance—stems from the proliferation of small-grain production over the last half-century.

Argentina, mainly, but also Bolivia, Paraguay, and Uruguay, are converting rural landscape into production agriculture, and the shift away from pasturing has benefited grain-eating birds, namely the eared dove, South America's equivalent of the mourning dove. Argentina alone has an estimated 30 million eared doves, and on the best days, it seems like every one of them is dropping into your stand.

A MIXED-BAG WINGSHOOT

Doves get the headlines—and most of the lead pellets—in Argentina, but they are hardly the only game to be bagged here. On a four-day hunt with Roberto Zovich's Majan Safaris we started with eared doves on Day 1, then decoyed pigeons in harvested wheat fields on the morning of Day 2, before returning to doves during the afternoon. On the third day, we rode shaggy Andean horses across the marshlands of the Salado River to hunt Argentine teal, rosy-billed pochard, and huge, high-flying pampas ducks.

The final day was spent hunting perdiz in hay fields and rank grass.

There is no shortage of competent outfitters, especially in Argentina's Cordoba region. But here are a few considerations when booking your first high-volume South American bird hunt:

BORROWING GUNS Rather than bringing your own shotgun, it's wise to borrow one from your outfitter's rack. Their guns are up to the volume of shooting you'll experience, and their bird boys are familiar with their operation and daily cleaning.

BUYING SHELLS Just about the only constraint on shooting here in South America is the price and availability of shotshells. Make sure to inquire about ammunition prices and limits before you send your deposit.

BRANCHING OUT Argentina's Cordoba region has the most established bird shooting, but it's by no means the only option. Look at areas across the Pampas, and north to Santiago del Estero.

SOUTH AMERICAN WATERFOWL

While doves and (to a lesser degree) pigeons get the attention, the waterfowl hunting across South America has all the variety of Northern Hemisphere duck and goose hunting. The main difference is the time of year—seasons run from April to July—and the fact that most species migrate north as the season progresses.

Bag limits and seasons differ by region, but the daily bag is commonly 50 birds. Like in the Northern Hemisphere, waterfowl species vary, but you can expect to see Chiloe widgeon, rosy-billed pochard, white-faced and fulvous tree ducks, yellow-billed (bottom right) and white-cheeked pintail, and cinnamon teal (top), Brazilian teal, and red shovelers (bottom left).

Hunting styles differ, but in the marshes and estuaries of larger rivers, small spreads of decoys are arranged around moving-wing decoys. In the harvested fields of Argentina's Pampas, big spreads of shell decoys are used to lure in pochard and geese ranging from the ashy-headed goose to the huge Magellan goose.

North American wildfowlers will recognize some plumage and behavior as Southern Hemisphere equivalents of their familiar fowl. In fact, the main difference between waterfowling on the two continents is ballistic: in most of South America, lead shot remains both legal and highly effective.

THREE GREAT DOVE GUNS

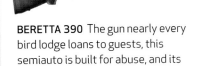

BERETTA 390 The gun nearly every bird lodge loans to guests, this semiauto is built for abuse, and its cast-neutral stock fits most gunners.

REMINGTON 1100 Well-balanced and easy to clean, this may not be the fanciest gun in the lodge, but it will be one of the most reliable.

BENELLI CORDOBA This lively inertia-driven semiauto is built for the dove fields. Its design is modern, with great balance and weight.

HIGH-VOLUME DOVE GUNS

Conventional wisdom for dove hunters who measure their bag by the thousands is that you need a lightweight semiauto 12 gauge with longish barrels to sustain your swing. But I beg to differ. My perfect gun is indeed a semiauto, but I would go for a heavy-ish 20 gauge with a 28-inch (71-cm) barrel, chambered for 3-inch (7.6-cm) shells. The heavier gun—7 pounds (3 kg) is about right—dampens recoil and remains comfortable to shoot after your 12-gauge companions have returned to the lodge to nurse sore shoulders and cheeks. The barrel length lets you hit distant crossers and keep up with flitting, juking incoming birds. Even shooting light 2¾-inch (7-cm) shells loaded to ⅞ ounce, you'll have plenty of range for almost every dove stand.

AUSTRALIAN SPECIES

THAT AUSTRALIA IS AN ISLAND is a fact lost on most visitors to its metropolitan areas, but Down Under hunters are constantly reminded of the limitations and freedoms of its geography. There are precious few native game animals (saltwater crocodiles and kangaroos lead the list), but abundant and guilt-free opportunities to cull the rest—all the introduced, nonnative fauna that thrive without natural predators. At nearly 3 million square miles (4.8 million square km), bring plenty of gas and ammo—and an open mind—to hunt this remarkable island.

You'll need to keep your mind open to fully appreciate all the bonus opportunities you will encounter on an Australian safari. You might be targeting Asiatic water buffalo, but few native Aussies will turn down the opportunity to drop the bonus burro, dingo, feral hog, or feral horse. Or feral camel. Or kangaroo (opposite, top left). The list of shootable species here reads a little like the combination of an ASPCA adoption roster and Dr. Doolittle's menagerie. But these feral animals have neither an owner nor a name.

By far the most abundant hunting opportunities in Australia are for nuisance populations of feral animals. These range from cottontail rabbits, which number in the millions, all descended from two dozen brought here as a gift to a native Englishman—to red foxes, wild boar and many others.

Most such hunting takes place on the aboriginal land of interior Australia. Hunters make arrangements with aboriginal councils, which define the parameters. Besides a prohibition on alcohol, there are few rules, and hunters are often welcome in rural areas because their firepower is one of the few tools aboriginal cultures have to control the ecologically damaging feral mammals.

If you hear anything about Australia's hunting, it's for the big, cane-break buffalo of the northern coast. Cape buffalo have nothing on these ill-tempered bovines. Native to Indonesia, they were introduced here as beasts of burden and beef for outposts. As is so often the case with invasive species—think wild hogs of the American South—the escaped buff have grown wild, big, and savvy on their own and are now the dominant mammal of the northern coast.

LEARN THE LINGO

You've heard the usuals: "Mate" for friend, "barbie" for grill or barbecue, and "shark biscuit" for surfer (well, that one may be new to you), but Down Under hunting has its own vocabulary. Learn these before you join your mates for an Outback hunting expedition:

PROJIE — Projectile
DONK — Feral donkey, burro (top)
SOAK — Water hole
DINGO — An ugly woman
YAKKA — Hard work
BRUMBY — Feral horse
SHOTTIE — Shotgun
BILLABONG — Stagnant water/bog
SALTIE — Saltwater crocodile

Australia has at least three huntable bovines:

WATER BUFFALO With impressively massive, sickle-shaped horns and a surly disposition, these bulls tend to charge when pressured or wounded. The most exciting hunt is during the wet season, when vegetation becomes dense and hunters can silently stalk within 20 yards (or meters).

BANTENG Endangered across much of their native Indonesia, banteng (page 302, top right) are the stout, wild cattle scattered across the rainforests and swamps of the Northern Territory. Hunts are usually at close range in dense cover, tracking bachelor herds of bulls.

WILD CATTLE Descendants of Brahman cattle that escaped from agricultural operations, feral bulls roam much of the interior Northern Territory. Stalk in swampy timber or catch them on open pastures.

The other destination species of the Outback is the saltwater crocodile, the world's largest reptile, which can stretch 20 feet (6 meters) and weigh two tons. These voracious predators live in brackish river mouths and estuaries.

Hunting is carefully regulated; if you want to collect an Aussie croc, check the rule book. Many of the outfitted hunts only allow you to observe as someone with a depredation permit does the killing. You can then buy the hide and skull.

FIREPOWER FOR A CULLING JUNKET

What do you bring on a hunt that might include everything from feral house cats up to water buffalo?

No one caliber will cover the gamut, so Aussie hunters are accustomed to bringing a huge arsenal on these multiday journeys into aboriginal lands to cull feral animals. The light side generally includes a .17 HMR or a center-fire .22. Standard medium caliber—.270, 7x57mm, .30/06, and .308s are all popular here—sufficient for kangaroo-sized game, which includes feral hogs and burros. But most hunters also bring a larger-bore rifle for encounters with water buffalo, camels, and larger horses and wild cattle.

One Aussie I know says he always brings a brace of "pill-poppers" (his term for these large-bore rifles)—a .416 Remington Magnum and his father's old .458 Lott.

NEW ZEALAND SPECIES

IT'S HARD TO IMAGINE that the ancestor of every towering-antlered stag, alpine chamois, and trophy fallow deer hunted in New Zealand arrived here on a boat. This South Pacific island nation, now synonymous with trophy big game, was devoid of mammals of any kind until only a few hundred years ago. It's a testament to both the energy and enthusiasm of big-game hunters and to the richness of the Kiwi habitat: species that evolved oceans away have thrived in the generous and diverse landscapes of the two main islands.

Many of New Zealand's game species arrived gift-wrapped, so to speak. They were presents from benefactors: American elk from President Teddy Roosevelt, red stag from a British lord, fallow deer (opposite, top right) from Europe, and chamois (opposite, bottom) from Austrian Emperor Franz Joseph. Even moose were introduced, though it's debatable whether any of the ungulates remain.

For decades, all these antlered game were considered novelties. But as both populations and dimensions increased, New Zealand started to become a destination for big-game hunters. These days, if you're serious about hunting a gold-medal stag, you should look to New Zealand's North Island even before you consider its native range in central Europe. Same with Himalayan tur, the wild goats on the highest ridges of central Asia—the largest and most accessible tur are found in New Zealand's Southern Alps. Plus, getting here without a visa is much easier and hassle-free than hunting (and toting a rifle into) nations with dubious, ever-changing visitation rules.

New Zealand's abundant foothills habitat offers sufficient forage and cover to sustain good numbers of stag, and outfitters who control access allow red deer (opposite, top left) to grow old. It helps, too, that a number have red deer herds under fence, enabling them to manage populations and age structure just as they might a domesticated herd. Mind, you'll pay a small fortune for the largest of these trophy specimens.

As you think about hunting this South Seas paradise, consider: do you want to hunt a game farm or free-ranging animals? The former is more accessible, the latter more risky—and more rewarding.

GOING IT ALONE

New Zealand is full of expensive, outfitted hunts. But it is possible to hunt on your own here.

Inquiries into freelance hunting should begin with the Department of Conservation (doc.govt.nz). The agency has all the details on which areas are open, permits, and restrictions. For instance, you need a special meat-recovery permit to bring your trophy off public land, and another if you intend to hunt small game or birds. But obtaining a basic open-area permit is one of the best ways to see the landscape, and you can hunt pigs, goats, deer, wallabies, chamois, and even tahr entirely on your own.

DESTINATION TROPHIES

While New Zealand's stag get most of the attention, Kiwis have plenty of other trophies:

CHAMOIS Mainly hunted well above timberline, chamois—a European alpine goat—thrives on the South Island's Franz Joseph Glacier and the surrounding cirques.

FALLOW DEER Both islands host large numbers of fallow deer, which are mainly hunted in lower foothills and forest fringe.

HIMALAYAN TAHR (BOTTOM RIGHT) Nearly all tahr hunting takes place in the South Island's "Southern Alps," with helicopters often used to ferry hunters up to the remote, wind-blasted ridges where these long-maned goats graze.

ELK Also known locally as "wapiti," these Rocky Mountain elk were introduced to New Zealand early in the last century. All elk hunting is done on estates, under high fence.

RUSA, SAMBAR (TOP RIGHT), AND SIKA DEER All three of these Asian deer species exist in varying densities. Most are bonus opportunities for outfitted stag and chamois hunters.

WILD BOAR (BOTTOM LEFT) Called "Captain Cookers" by some locals, many of today's feral pigs in New Zealand are descendants of hogs released by early explorers. They can be hunted year-round and can be found across much of the nation's lower-elevation habitats.

FIELD-JUDGE A GOLD-MEDAL STAG

When it comes to antler assessment, beauty and measurement are subjective—even among officials. The Safari Club International (SCI) system counts all points, symmetrical or not. The Douglas Score System rewards symmetry and balance. The CIC (International Council for Game and Wildlife Conservation) awards "beauty points" for weight and mass.

Whichever you choose, consider a few universal attributes as you size up a mature stag:

MAIN BEAM [A] The main beam is the long, heavy antler that all the secondary points erupt from. If it's big at the base and sustains that mass well along its length, it will score well. Gold-medal stags typically have main beams that swell into massive palms, similar to moose.

CROWN POINTS [B] Red stag tend to have numbers of points at the upper end of the main beam. Called "crown points," these often form paddle-shaped palms. The more numerous and heavier, the higher the score.

FRONT POINTS [C] If the stag has long and heavy "dagger" points that parallel his nose, he will score well.

SYMMETRY [D] A high, wide, and long-tined antler whose symmetry is reflected by its matching antler will score well.

ABOUT THE WRITERS

ANDREW MCKEAN The editor-in-chief of *Outdoor Life*, McKean has hunted around the world and the calendar. The pursuit of game has taken him to the peaks of the Pyrenees, the foothills of the Andes, the banana-leaf forests of Southeast Asia, across southern Africa, and to nearly every game-rich corner of North America. He's not done getting his passport stamped, but his favorite hunting range is around his home in rural northeastern Montana, where he—along with his friends and his three children—hunts mule deer, elk, pronghorn antelope, wild turkeys, prairie grouse, and predators. McKean is the former editor of *Fishing & Hunting News*, has worked for Montana's Fish, Wildlife & Parks Department, and remains *Outdoor Life*'s Hunting Editor. You can read his regular contributions in *Outdoor Life* magazine and online at outdoorlife.com.

DAVID DRAPER An avid hunter and accomplished writer, Draper has traveled the globe in search of the story, whatever it may be. His passions for travel and the outdoors have taken him from the shores of the Gambia River to Alaska's Brooks Range, yet his roots remain firmly planted on the Great Plains. Draper is a Contributing Editor for *Field & Stream* magazine, the primary writer of the Wild Chef blog on fieldandstream.com, and a frequent contributor to *Outdoor Life*.

JEFF JOHNSTON Although Johnston hasn't hunted all the world's game animals, he's not done dreaming. As you read this, he's likely in an Oklahoma deer stand or duck blind—recalling past adventures or plotting fresh ones. His most exotic game to date: a Kenyan wingshooting safari. Eight thousand miles is a long way to go for a few birds, but it says everything about his bird-hunter's passion for just one more flush.

BRYCE M. TOWSLEY An award-winning writer and photographer, Towsley's work covers a wide diversity of subjects, but none more than the field of hunting and firearms. A field editor for NRA's *American Rifleman, American Hunter,* and *Shooting Illustrated* magazines, Towsley is a gun buff and an avid hunter with almost 50 years of experience, taking his first whitetail in Vermont in 1966 at the age of 11. Since then, he has hunted extensively throughout the United States and Canada, as well as across Mexico, Africa, Argentina, Russia, and Europe. Towsley lives in Vermont with his wife, Robin, and a bunch of dogs.

KYLE WINTERSTEEN A freelance outdoor writer specializing in bird dogs, waterfowl, and upland game, Wintersteen has written for numerous nationwide publications, including *Outdoor Life, American Hunter,* and *Wildfowl*. When he isn't hunting, Wintersteen competes in English springer spaniel field trials; he's owned two field champions and one National High Point Champion. He lives in Bellefonte, Pennsylvania, with his wife, Amanda, his son, Jackson, and two spoiled gundogs.

CREDITS

PHOTOGRAPHY: *Andyandersonphoto.com:* cover (upper right), 125 (lower right); *Charles Alsheimer:* 70; *Bettmann / CORBIS:* 113 (historical); *Chuck & Grace Bartlett:* 78, 84; *Troy Batzler / Windigo Images:* 240; *Benelli:* 259 (upper); 300 (córdoba); *Beretta:* 300 (model 390); *Browning Firearms:* 29 (BLR); *Burris Optics:* 208 (scope); *Denver Bryan / Images on the Wild Side:* 10, 40 (lower), 48, 80, 96, 144, 147 (upper, lower left), 181, 184, 194 (upper right), 224, 245 (upper right), 253 (upper), 254 (left), 264 (left), 284 (upper left), 294; *Becky Blankenship / Images on the Wild Side:* 117 (upper); *Bill Buckley Photography:* 44, 124; *TimChristiePhoto.com:* 98, 101; *Connecticut Valley Arms:* 76 (CVA Apex); *Kevin Cooley / Redux:* 62; *Dustin Coppedge / Images on the Wild Side:* 100; *Chris Crisman:* 164 (left), 165 (inset), 172, 173 (all); *DPMS Panther Arms:* 208 (AR); *David Draper:* 258; *Peter Eades / Images on the Wild Side:* 142; *John Eriksson / Images on the Wild Side:* Cover (lower left), 26, 72, 77; *Federal Premium:* 29 (shotshell), 83 (ammunition), 163; *Tim Flach / Stone / Getty Images:* 204; *Timothy C. Flanigan / www.NatureExposure.com:* 58, back cover (upper left); *Russell A. Graves / Windigo Images:* 146, 188, 206, back cover (lower right); *Brian Grossenbacher:* Cover (lower right), 93 (lower left); *John Hafner / Windigo Images:* 228, 229 (upper); *Andrew Hetherington:* 131; *Tim Irwin / Images on the Wild Side:* 33, 116; *Donaldmjones.com:* 6, 16 (bottom), 20, 22, 46, 50, 57, 64, 66–67, 69, 73, 90, 94, 180, back cover (upper middle, lower left); *Spencer Jones:* 37, 223, 255 (both bullets); *Mark Johnson / Images on the Wild Side:* 24; *John F. Kennedy Presidential Library:* 231; *Heidi & Hans Jurgen-Koch / Minden Pictures:* 186; *Lee Thomas Kjos / www.TheRawSpirit.com:* 45, 61; *Knight & Hale:* 189; *Bill Konway / Images on the Wild Side:* 166; *Karl Krieger Photography:* 41; *Lance Krueger:* 62, 74; *Jonathan Larsen / Diadem Images / Alamy:* 112; *Paolo Marchesi:* back cover (upper right); *Tom Martineau / www.TheRawSpirit.com:* 30, 42, 75 (hunter); *Luke McComb:* 68; *Andrew McKean:* 9, 23, 87, 145, 151 (lower), 152 (upper), 167 (inset), 191 (lower left), 237 (lower), 247, 249 (all), 269, 279, 289, 298, 300 (large image); *Ralph Minnitte:* 177; *Neal & MJ Mishler:* 88; *Matt Nager:* 164 (upper right); *T. Edward Nickens:* 93 (dog); *Pete Oxford / Minden Pictures:* 296; *Carol Polich / Images on the Wildside:* 264 (upper right), 268, 274; *Dean Powell:* 31; *PSE Archery:* 76 (X Force); *www.TheRawSpirit.com:* 92 (hunter); *Remington Arms:* 29 (700 XCR), 76 (model 700), 275 (model 770), 300 (model 1100); *Royalty Free Arctos Photos / Alamy:* 36, cover (upper middle); *Dan Saelinger:* Cover (upper left), 162; *Savage Arms:* 29 (model 212), 76 (model 220F); *Vic Schendel:* 102; *Shutterstock:* all photos not otherwise noted; *John Snow:* 254 (lower right); *Stryker Crossbows:* 76 (Strykezone 380); *Sturm, Ruger, & Co.:* 83 (American rifle); *Bryce Towsley / The Outside Connection:* 32 (upper & lower right), 34, 229 (lower); *Christopher Vernon-Parry / Alamy:* 170; *Wikimedia Commons:* 121 (right), 235; *Wikimedia Commons / GregTheBusker:* 63 (upper); *Wikimedia Commons / Jan Frode Haugseth:* 16 (ptarmigan); *WindigoImages.com:* 251; *Windigo Images / Joe Byers:* 191 (upper); *Windigo Images / Lon Lauber:* 19, 28 (hunter), 114; *Windigo Images / Mitch Kezar:* 132, 161, 178; *Windigo Images / Mark Palas:* 52; *Windigo Images / Micke Schoby:* 228; *Lucas Zarebinski:* 92 (shotshells); *Leonard Zhukovsky / Shutterstock.com:* 259

ILLUSTRATION *Conor Buckley:* 23, 25, 27, 49, 57, 95, 127, 193, 225, 251, 311; *Lauren Towner:* 19, 39, 52, 73, 140, 182, 195, 295

ABOUT *OUTDOOR LIFE*

Ever since it was founded in 1898, *Outdoor Life* magazine has provided survival tips, wilderness skills, gear reports, and other essential information for hands-on outdoor enthusiasts. Each issue of the magazine delivers the best advice in sportsmanship, as well as thrilling true-life tales, detailed gear reviews, insider hunting, shooting, and fishing hints, and much more to nearly 1 million readers.

A NOTE FROM THE EDITOR

A book of this scope requires broad expertise, and while I have hunted many animals and time zones around the globe, I called on friends to help me with my blind spots. I had invaluable help from a number of outdoor-writer friends. Bryce Towsley contributed perspectives on Africa's Big 5 and some of North America's most ferocious predators. Kyle Wintersteen pitched in with birds, mainly waterfowl. David Draper covered some upland species, and Jeff Johnston helped me handle deer, hogs, and exotic (to most North Americans) species.

I also had the unflagging assistance of my editor, Mariah Bear at Weldon Owen, whose patience and good nature both were tested during this process. The art and design are the work of Will Mack and his crew at Weldon Owen, and I had help from my editors at *Outdoor Life*, including John Taranto and John Snow. And lastly, I had the forgiveness of my family, from whom I took months of relaxed weekends, summer evenings, and leisurely dinners as I immersed myself in the wide world of hunting.

weldon**owen**

President, CEO Terry Newell
VP, Publisher Roger Shaw
Director of Finance Philip Paulick
Associate Publisher Mariah Bear
Editor Bridget Fitzgerald
Editorial Assistant Ian Cannon
Creative Director Kelly Booth
Art Director William Mack
Designer Allister Fein
Illustration Coordinator Conor Buckley
Production Director Chris Hemesath
Associate Production Director Michelle Duggan
Senior Production Designer Rachel Lopez Metzger

Weldon Owen would also like to thank Jan Hughes, Amy
Bauman, and Bill Schuch for editorial and production
assistance and Larry D. Sweazy for the index.

© 2014 Weldon Owen Inc.
1045 Sansome Street, Suite 100
San Francisco, CA 94111
www.weldonowen.com

BONNIER

Library of Congress Control Number
on file with the publisher
ISBN 978-161628-816-7
10 9 8 7 6 5 4 3 2 1
2014 2015 2016 2017
Printed in China by RR Donnelley

OUTDOOR LIFE

Executive Vice President Eric Zinczenko
Publisher Gregory D. Gatto
Editorial Director Anthony Licata
Editor-in-Chief Andrew McKean
Executive Editor John Taranto
Managing Editor Jean McKenna
Senior Deputy Editor John B. Snow
Deputy Editor Gerry Bethge
Assistant Managing Editor Margaret M. Nussey
Assistant Editor Natalie Krebs
Senior Administrative Assistant Maribel Martin
Design Director Sean Johnston
Deputy Art Director Pete Sucheski
Senior Associate Art Director Russ Smith
Associate Art Director James A. Walsh
Photography Director John Toolan
Photo Editor Justin Appenzeller
Production Manager Judith Weber
Digital Director Nate Matthews
Online Content Editor Alex Robinson
Online Producer Kurt Schulitz

2 Park Avenue
New York, NY 10016
www.outdoorlife.com